Aspiring

Also by Kieran Kelly

*Hard Country Hard Men – In the footsteps of Gregory
Tanami – On foot across Australia's desert heart*

Aspiring
Kieran Kelly

MACMILLAN
Pan Macmillan Australia

First published 2008 in Macmillan by Pan Macmillan Australia Pty Limited
1 Market Street, Sydney

National Library of Australia
Cataloguing-in-Publication data:

Kelly, Kieran, 1952– .
Aspiring: mountain climbing is no cure for middle age.

ISBN 978 1 4050 3862 1.

1. Acrophobia – Biography. 2. Mountaineering – New
Zealand – Aspiring, Mount. 3. Middle-aged men –
Australia – Biography. I. Title

616.852250092

Cartographic art by Laurie Whiddon, Map Illustrations

Typeset by Midland Typsetters, Australia
Printed in Australia by McPherson's Printing Group

Papers used by Pan Macmillan Australia Pty Ltd are natural, recyclable products
made from wood grown in sustainable forests. The manufacturing processes
conform to the environmental regulations of the country of origin.

Dedicated to the lives of
Marc Freedman (1982–2005)

Susan Fear (1963–2006)

And to the lives of all our children: May their road be not too steep, may a warm wind be always at their backs, and may God hold them in the palm of His hand.

Contents

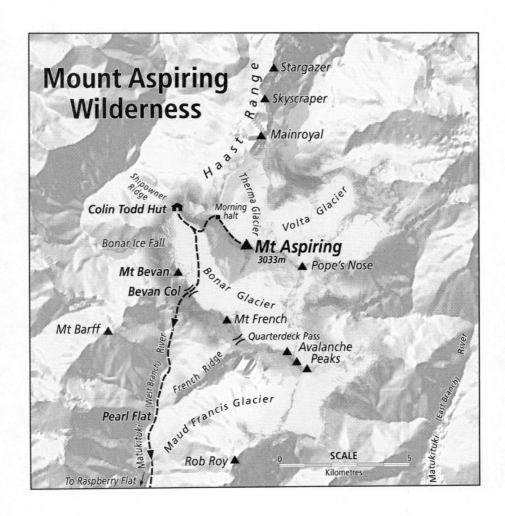

Mount Aspiring Wilderness

Haast Range

▲ Stargazer

▲ Skyscraper

▲ Mainroyal

Shipowner Ridge

Therma Glacier

Volta Glacier

Colin Todd Hut 🏠

Morning halt

Bonar Ice Fall

▲ **Mt Aspiring**
3033m

▲ Pope's Nose

Mt Bevan ▲

Bevan Col

Bonar Glacier

▲ Mt Barff

▲ Mt French

Quarterdeck Pass

▲ Avalanche Peaks

Matukituki (West Branch) River

French Ridge

Pearl Flat

Maud Francis Glacier

Rob Roy ▲

Matukituki (East Branch) River

To Raspberry Flat

SCALE
0   5
Kilometres

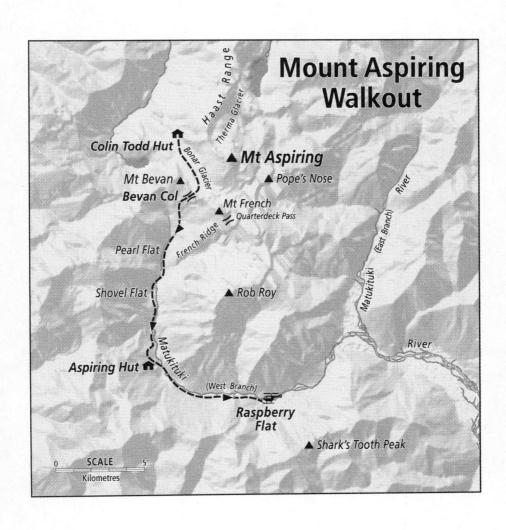

Mount Aspiring
Walkout

Haast Range

Therma Glacier

Colin Todd Hut

Bonar Glacier

▲ **Mt Aspiring**

Mt Bevan ▲

▲ Pope's Nose

Bevan Col

Mt French

Quarterdeck Pass

French Ridge

Pearl Flat

Matukituki (East Branch) River

Shovel Flat

▲ Rob Roy

Matukituki

River

Aspiring Hut 🏠

(West Branch)

▲ **Raspberry
Flat**

▲ Shark's Tooth Peak

SCALE

0 _____ 5

Kilometres

Introduction: I can do this

You gain strength, courage and confidence by every experience in which you really stop to look fear in the face. You must do the thing which you think you cannot do.

ELEANOR ROOSEVELT

The rope snaked up into the darkness. Through the pre-dawn shadows, Anton climbed like a spider on the sheer wall of the ramp.

'You call out "five metres" when there's about five metres of rope left. I'll call "safe – begin climbing" when I've got the anchor in, then you come up. Don't come up until you hear me,' he'd said as he prepared to head up into the gloom. I'd nodded.

He'd prodded the narrow ice bridge with his axe one last time and, deciding it was safe, stepped towards the gaping blackness of the crevasse. His left foot landed solidly on the far lip of snow. He kicked a toe hole with the front points of his left crampon, lightly stepped over the gap and was gone.

I waited in the dark, my boots wedged into the stance he'd cut earlier. Fear, excitement and a sense of anticipation surged through me, but my breathing was steady and regular.

Soon I'll have to step over that gap, I thought. I could just see Anton's boot-print on the other side of the bergschrund, the gaping fracture at my feet, and the start of his tracks up the ramp.

Somewhere below me was the Bonar Glacier. There was no sound except the *thud, thud* of Anton's ice tools and the *kick, kick* of his boots growing fainter as he made his way up the wall. I couldn't see him now. Small showers of snow cascaded down on my face, then a small chunk of ice bounced off my helmet and disappeared onto the glacier below. The rope flaked on the snow in front of me made a whizzing sound as it slowly unwound and followed Anton up into the gloom. I concentrated, determined to get my call exactly right. Five metres on a coil of rope is hard to judge for a first-time climber in the semi-darkness.

The long handle of my ice axe was driven deep into the snow just below the crevasse lip. With my right hand I gripped the heavy head of the axe where it protruded from the snow. The pick of the ice hammer in my left hand was embedded about 60 centimetres to the left of the axe. The toes on my crampons dug deep into the ledge Anton had cut. My boots and the two tools gave me four points of contact with the wall, a good stance.

Behind and below was blackness, the Bonar Glacier a silver river in the moonlight; in front was the Mount Aspiring bergs-chrund. Above me rose the infamous ice ramp, the killer of at least a dozen mountaineers in the past two decades, the most recent an expert young Australian climber in the prime of his life. I waited, looking up, my hands gripping my tools. It was quiet and very still.

The moon was setting to the northwest. Orion was visible next to it – low in the cloudless sky. This was a sight I'd seen many times in the Australian desert and it gave me great comfort; I knew exactly where I was. The Shipowner Ridge running off to my left was touched a golden colour.

What a beautiful morning, I thought. My watch was buried under my jacket and gloves and I'd lost all track of time. I guessed it was about 6 am and focused on the slowly uncoiling pile of rope.

'Five metres!' I yelled into the dark. The rope stopped moving, and I waited. From far above, I heard a dull *whack, whack, whack* as Anton cut himself a stance. Next he would cut a box out of the snow-covered wall and wind in an ice screw as an anchor. After he screwed in the anchor, he would secure himself to its cable by connecting the rope to a karabiner attached to his harness. He would then secure the rope that ran down to me, also using a karabiner attached to the screw.

He'll probably use an Italian hitch, I thought. I'd read about these knots and practised them in the gym. A type of clove hitch, it's used to secure the climber coming up. It allows the lead climber both to haul in the rope as the second one climbs, and to immediately lock a fall. Well, that was the theory. This was real, and like many novices I was beset with doubts.

From the ice screw I pictured the rope running down the cliff, across the bergschrund, then on to my harness, where it was secured with a figure eight knot. It was my 50-metre lifeline. My life was now in Anton's hands. The rope remained motionless at my feet.

I waited. The thudding stopped. There was a rattle as Anton took the ice screw and karabiner off his harness. I peered upwards but could see nothing. The rope started to move again as Anton wound in the slack. It stopped with a gentle tug on my harness.

'That's me,' I called.

'Safe – begin climbing,' his voice drifted down.

This is it, I thought. I checked my harness one last time and made sure the leashes on my wrists for the ice axe and hammer were cinched tight.

'Climbing,' I called back.

With my heart in my mouth, I stepped up to the lip of the bergschrund. It was less than a metre wide but seemed a terrifying moat of darkness. I looked at Anton's boot-print on the far lip, then launched myself across. The crampons on my left boot bit into the snow, and I immediately hit the mountain with my axe and hammer and followed with my right foot. I was across. I paused to collect myself, to try to control my nervous heartbeat, and looked up. Still the dark clung to the slope. It was probably fortunate that I couldn't see anything. I began the process of lifting myself up to where Anton waited. My first pitch of climbing began.

That I was on one of New Zealand's premier alpine climbs, two days after my 54th birthday, with no climbing experience whatsoever, should have crossed my mind. It didn't. I was too scared, and had too many other things to think about.

The stars have begun to fade; it'll be light soon, I thought. Gentle spindrifts of snow fell on my face from above. *No wind, and not as cold as I thought it'd be.* I noticed that the first faint stirrings of dawn were dusting the slopes of Mount Aspiring. But I looked in vain up the slope where I knew Anton would be squatting next to his belay point, slowly winding in the rope as I tried to match his rhythmic climbing cadence.

From the moment I crossed the bergschrund, I tried to establish a rhythm. *One, two* with the hand tools, breathe; *three, four* with crampons, breathe. I punched the spiked toes of my boots into the indents made by Anton. Breathe. I had gone less than twenty metres on the first pitch, only halfway up to Anton's stance, when I hit my first snag. Anton had used a 'dagger' technique. Holding the head of each of his tools near its handle, he'd rammed the spikes of the axe and hammer straight into the ice at about chest height. This gave him a secure hold, with two tools

4

embedded in the wall supported by front crampon points also punched in.

The technique proved difficult for me. I'm partially paralysed in my left hand and I never felt that I had the hammer all the way into the ice. My hand just wasn't strong enough. I felt exposed and unbalanced, convinced I would topple backwards into the dark.

Improvise, I said to myself. My left *hand* might not have been strong enough, but my left *arm* was. I shifted my grip on both tools to the bottom of their handles, right at the extremity of the wrist leashes, and pounded the points into the snow above my head. It was a bit like standing on top of a ladder and driving a nail into a wall as high up as you could get. *One, two*, pound the tools; breathe, *three, four*, thud, thud with the boots – following Anton's holes all the way. This was the Chouinard technique, named after the famous American blacksmith and rock climber. I'd only seen photos of it in books and I'm sure I executed it badly, but it made me feel more secure and confident, so I planned to stick with it.

It was getting lighter by the minute, the long slope emerging grey from the darkness. Anton's hunched figure was now only twenty metres above me, then fifteen, then ten. I dared not look down as I painstakingly edged upwards. *Whack, whack*. I drove my tools into the snow and ice, sinking their heads as deep as I could.

With five metres to go I could see Anton peering intently down at me, winding in the rope as I climbed. The rope that had run down all the way to me at the bergschrund was now flaked neatly at his feet. As I'd expected, the rope hooked him securely onto the ice screw, but he'd set up a much more complicated belaying device than a simple Italian hitch. He was using a karabiner as an extra braking device on the anchor.

This bloke knows his stuff, I thought. Two metres and suddenly a volley of instructions came down to me.

'When you get here, step into this space and clip on.'

His axe handle pointed to a broad step he had cut into the snow. He watched with intense concentration as I stepped onto the ledge and whacked my long-handled ice axe into the snow. I extracted a karabiner and sling from one of the gear loops on my harness. The sling was already tied onto the front part of my harness. It would ensure that I didn't tumble backwards down the slope while I stood waiting for the next pitch.

'Good,' he said as I clipped on. 'Now this's what's going to happen. I'm going to unclip and climb up the next rope length. When there's five metres of rope left, you sing out again. I'll set up and then call out "safe". Clean out the gear here before you come up – unwind the screw and clip it on here,' he said, pointing to a spare gear loop on the harness. 'Bring it all up with you and I'll take it at the next pitch,' he said.

'Got that?'

I nodded. My mouth was dry. Mountaineering is unlike any other sport in that it is counterintuitive. As you start to climb and the risk increases, you become more frightened. The usual human response in such a situation would be to remove yourself from the source of danger. But not with climbing. To go higher, a climber has to expose himself or herself to more danger, while becoming more frightened and still having to keep functioning. It's as much a test of mental discipline as anything.

'Don't unclip until I sing out "safe",' Anton reminded me.

With that he was gone. If I'd hoped for some encouragement, maybe a 'Well done', or 'How'd you enjoy your first pitch?', I wasn't getting any. I was learning that this Kiwi guide was a deadly serious climber engaged in a deadly serious business. He had a client with no climbing experience to look after. He wasn't in the compliments business.

It was getting lighter now, and as Anton took off on the second pitch I saw what real climbing is. He almost danced upwards in a rhythmic routine, his kicking-in perfectly coordinated with the movement of his hand tools. He was all rhythm and economy – no wasted movement, no wasted energy and no chances taken. I waited for the rising sun to chase away my fears of the night, waited for the rope to stop running out, waited to start on the second pitch. *I can do this*, I told myself over and over, and I looked forward to the second stanza.

I realised then that Anton hadn't shown me how to clean out an ice screw. I looked at the anchor, then up the slope. I was alone, clipped to the screw anchor by a short tether. Anton had disappeared.

Bugger!

I knew from the books I'd read that mountains are ruthless exploiters of hubris. New Zealand mountains wouldn't be any different. As I prepared to follow Anton, I might have guessed that I would soon make a series of mistakes that could have killed us. What I couldn't have known was that what I was about to endure would bring back searing memories of a childhood I'd tried hard to forget. I couldn't have known that Anton's anger and sharp tongue would strip me of my self-esteem as efficiently as my stepfather had always done.

I was undertaking this climb to fulfil a long-held ambition – and as a rebellion against encroaching middle age. But in a savage irony, my long-anticipated adventure would plunge me back into memories of some of the saddest formative events of my life.

The scab was about to be ripped off wounds inflicted long ago. I would bleed on this climb, and for a long time after.

I would be a different person when next we crossed the bergschrund on the way back to the hut, but that all lay ahead. For now, my concentration was focused on cleaning out an anchor screwed deep into the mountainside. Unbeknown to me, the mountain, my guide and my own personality had already begun to conspire against me.

This is a very dangerous way to prove that you're a worthwhile person, a small voice whispered to me.

Chapter 1

Annapurna Dreamtime

*There is always one moment in childhood when the door opens
and lets the future in.*
GRAHAM GREENE, *THE POWER AND THE GLORY*

I'm getting ahead of myself. Stories should start at the beginning,
not near the end. This story really began in July 1999 in the
snows of Australia's Perisher Valley. It involved a number of seemingly inconsequential decisions that over time had large unforeseen
consequences.

It was a bitter winter's day in the Southern Alps; the last day of
our annual family skiing holiday.

'I'm not going out in that,' Prue, my wife, said, after pulling
back the dining-room curtains. Outside the snug confines of our
lodge, the snow gums bent away from the gale, which was driving
the snow and sleet like bullets into the large windows. It was a
miserable day.

'Come on, you're getting soft. You used to go out in anything,'
I said, pulling on my parka as I stood up from the table.

'Not anymore. I'm going to curl up on the lounge with a book and spend the day in front of the fire,' she said, moving to a shelf of reading material above the fireplace.

I headed out into the storm. Many hours later, soaking wet and half frozen, I clumped back into the lodge. After shedding my gear and exercising my frozen fingers, I found my wife where I'd left her that morning – in repose and absorbed in a book. She didn't move or look up as I entered. I noticed she was already halfway through the book, which was unusual as she's often a slow and methodical reader.

'Have a good ski?' she asked cheerfully, continuing to read.

'Not bad. A bit bloody cold and wet. Typical Perisher day. Good book?'

'Yes. You should read it when I'm finished.'

'What's it about?'

'Mountain climbing. All these people get killed on Mount Everest.' She held up the cover for me to see. I peered down and read, *Into Thin Air: A personal account of the Everest disaster*, by Jon Krakauer. A surprising choice; not something my wife would normally read.

'It's very exciting. I can't put it down,' she said.

'I read a lot of mountaineering books when I was young,' I said.

'Really?' But she wasn't listening, her focus turned back to the book.

'Yeah, I even dreamed I'd be a mountaineer one day. Even before I'd seen any snow or any real mountains.'

It might have ended there, but it didn't. If it hadn't been such a bitter day in Perisher, what follows in this book may never have happened. If my wife had picked up a different book, I may never have been propelled down the dark corridors of childhood memory and had to face the rigours of self-examination and dangers that awaited.

About a week later, I came home from work and I found a hard-cover copy of *Into Thin Air* on the kitchen table. 'What's this? You still going with this? You *must* be enjoying it.' My wife had a habit of starting many books and dropping them halfway through.

'I didn't finish it down at Perisher so I got a copy from Manly Library. I want to see what happened to everyone. Cup of tea?' she said.

I sat at the kitchen table and picked up the book. I turned to the photos. One photo was of a climber whose bandaged hands were crossed over his chest; his nose and cheeks were black from frostbite, and his face was a mass of dead skin. The only thing that seemed alive about him were his eyes. It was a confronting image and immediately pricked my interest. There was another photo of the same climber, Beck Weathers, being loaded into a helicopter, his feet swathed in bandages.

I began to read.

Straddling the top of the world, one foot in China and the other in Nepal, I cleared the ice from my oxygen mask, hunched a shoulder against the wind and stared absently down at the vastness of Tibet.

I was hooked, gone and toasted. I didn't know it, but the gears in my life shifted that afternoon and a story began to move forward.

Into Thin Air is an account of attempts by five separate expeditions to summit Mount Everest on 9 May 1996. Eight climbers died, while others lost noses, hands and feet to frostbite. It remains Everest's worst tragedy on a mountain defined by tragedy. It was a tale of egos gone mad, of selfishness and sacrifice, courage and cowardice, and of climbers – both clueless and accomplished – perishing together in the death zone above 7925 metres (26,000 feet). Two who died that day were the climbing guides, Rob Hall from New Zealand and the American Scott Fischer, among the best-known mountaineers of the time.

'Can I have my book back, please? I want to finish it,' Prue said, handing me a cup of tea.

'Just give us a minute . . .' I read on, sitting at the kitchen table.

Some time passed. 'Can you turn the light off now? It's after midnight,' Prue, lying beside me in our bed, half-groaned and half-pleaded.

'In a minute. I'm nearly finished,' I said. I was propped up on a pillow, the page illuminated by an overhead reading light. It was the early hours of the morning. I finally finished the book at around 2 am, but when I switched off the light and fell back on my pillow, sleep wouldn't come.

I stared up into the darkness. The book had touched something in me, had awoken memories from my childhood, some of them painful and disturbing. That's the point. This story really started a long, long time ago in a place far removed from either my kitchen table at home in Seaforth or the bitter winds of Mount Perisher. It started in a place where snow *never* fell. It started over 40 years ago, in 1963, on a small farm in western New South Wales where I grew up. I was eleven years old.

The country that nurtured me was blindingly hot in summer and frostbitten in winter. In the flat-bottomed Wuuluman Valley, generations of hard-scrabble farmers had fought to make a living from the backs of sheep that should never have been there, and from wheat that wouldn't grow there, in an environment where the rain never fell when you wanted it to. About the only things we could be certain of were that banks would always be predatory, and that when we needed a period of dry weather it would bucket down. The first settlers in this valley had been hard-case Irish gold-miners who, from the 1850s onwards, drove out the blacks and worked the seams. Eventually, when the ore played out they converted the mining leases to pastoral leases. My stepfather's family had been there ever since.

Towering above the valley were huge, impenetrable mountains. Or so I thought when I was young. A tall 'mountain' rose right at our front door. It was, I would later discover, part of the Dickerton Ridge. From the back door I could see the dying rays of the sun on the steep, scrub-covered peak of Black Mountain. These were among my earliest landscape impressions – the 'mountains' of my childhood. Mountains in my mind.

My lasting impression of my childhood spent on that small farm is of loneliness. Before and after school was spent travelling on dusty buses to and from the closest town, Wellington. Other boys my age learned to play cricket, tennis and football after school, or to swim in the town pool. Not for me the socialising process that is imperative in the development of young males.

Weekends were spent on my own, amusing myself. Initially, I wandered up and down the creeks in the flat country; then, and as I grew, I started to penetrate into the mountains. When I acquired a horse, I was able to range further, discovering the old miners' camps and the remains of ore-stamping batteries buried deep in the scrub, as well as the shell middens and artefacts left behind by earlier inhabitants.

It was exciting, it was interesting. It was profoundly lonely.

In my primary school years I had also to endure that crushing rite of passage of being selected in youthful sporting teams. The two biggest boys in the class lined up everyone against a schoolyard wall and took it in turns to pick teams. Once they had enough members for each team everyone not picked was left to amuse themselves. These were called the 'left overs' or the 'please themselves'. Slow of foot and never having the opportunity to practise ball sports, I was always among the 'please themselves' group.

The combination of an isolated rural upbringing and a

weakness at sports led to my being socially awkward and shy, and lacking in self-esteem. If, growing up in the 1950s and 1960s, you were no good at sport, you were a nobody.

It's no surprise that I retreated into the world of books. I spent a fair part of my young life daydreaming and reading. My parents had little money, but lots of books. My mother, a voracious reader, had cupboards full of them, borrowed from the town library or culled from the town's secondhand bookstore. I was forever pulling likely-looking titles from out of a newly arrived box. My mother was of her time and selected Agatha Christie whodunits or literary fiction by authors such as John Steinbeck, but my tastes were different. The books I was drawn to were always about heroes and adventure, about struggling and winning under horrendous conditions. I lived a life through books that I could never live in the real world. They chased away the loneliness.

One day, into this emotional stew of a pre-pubescent country boy, dropped a book that would change my life. From one of Mum's dusty piles of books, I pulled a book I had never heard of, the name of which I couldn't pronounce.

'Mum, what's that word? Is it an Aboriginal word?' I pointed at the cover.

'No, it's the name of a mountain. It's a French word, I think. Maurice Herzog . . . The author's certainly French.'

'Is it like our mountain out the back?' I asked.

She laughed. 'Well, sort of. It's a lot higher than our mountain and it's covered in snow.'

Baking-hot summer days in our part of the world made even the idea of snow seem impossible.

'Have you ever seen snow?'

Mum paused and looked reflective. 'Yes, just once, when I was at school at Bathurst a long time ago.'

'Do you think I'd like this?' I turned the book over in my

14

hands, looking again at the photo on the back that had drawn my attention. 'It's got a map on the inside of the cover.'

'I think so. It's a very exciting story, but it's got a lot of strange words in it and a lot of technical terms and I didn't understand all of it.'

To her credit, Mum never tried to talk me out of reading anything and never restricted me to children's literature.

'How do you say it?' I asked, pointing to the name.

'I think you say it, just as it's spelled: *Ann-a-purn-a*. That's how you pronounce it, I think.'

I grabbed the lantern and took the book and wandered off to bed, where my mother read to me nightly.

So began one of the great literary journeys of my life. *Annapurna*. The name would crop up again and again and shine a light into another world. I still have the book with its battered cover and scuffed dustjacket. It has travelled to many different places with me. By the light of a hissing hurricane lantern, with the heat and smells of a high Australian summer pouring in through a window open for air, my mother would sit on the edge of my bed and, over successive nights, read to me the story of the French assault on the Himalayan peak of Annapurna. I was captivated from the first page by the tale of sacrifice, courage, struggle and friendship set against the impossibly unknowable backdrop of the Himalayan mountain range in a far-away country called Nepal.

On 3 June 1950, Frenchman Maurice Herzog became the first person to climb an 8000-metre mountain when he and Louis Lachenal, a guide from Chamonix, France, finally stood on the summit of Annapurna. At 8091 metres (26,545 feet) it's only the tenth-highest mountain in the world but is the cruellest, having killed countless climbers since the Herzog/Lachenal ascent. Along with K2, on the border of Pakistan and China, it's the hardest mountain to climb, far surpassing Everest in difficulty. I knew none of this at the time. The book, originally published in French, was written for adults but conveys in simple language the excitement and trauma of an attempt to explore and climb, within one season, this pitiless Asian peak. The achievement had been even more remarkable as the ascent was made without bottled oxygen.

The retreat from the summit was as hair-raising as the climb. Lachenal fell and had to be rescued by his friend and fellow guide, Lionel Terray. Terray spent all night in a tent, just beneath the summit, massaging Lachenal's feet in an attempt to ward off the inevitable frostbite, while a blizzard threatened to blow them to oblivion. At daybreak, Terray couldn't get Lachenal's boots onto the now delirious climber's swollen feet and was faced with the grim prospect of leaving his friend to a miserable death. Courageously, he squeezed his own, larger boots onto his friend's feet and was left contemplating a descent in freezing conditions wearing only woollen socks.

Improvising, Terray cut open Lachenal's smaller leather boots, squashed his feet into them and then, risking a climbing guide's most valuable asset – his feet – half-carried and half-dragged his friend to safety off the most treacherous mountain on earth. Terray not only risked his life, but also gave up his own shot at the summit. He wouldn't get another chance.

The story had me wriggling down in bed and pulling up the covers in fright, but if asked who I wanted to be when I grew up I would have said an explorer or climber like Lionel Terray.

Both Herzog and Lachenal lost all their toes, and Herzog most of his fingers. The account of amputations without anaesthetics on the floor of a packed Indian train was one of the most searing things read to me as a child. It remains vivid in my mind. The story of the raw courage and achievement of these men electrified a world struggling to recover from the Second World War, and eleven million copies of the book were sold. It caused a sensation.

It would be another 48 years before a mountaineering book, Krakauer's *Into Thin Air*, broke through and captured the public's imagination to anything like the same extent.

In Australia, which felt very much part of the British Empire, even though it wasn't, we heard only about the New Zealander Edmund Hillary and the sherpa Tenzing Norgay, who had conquered Everest the year after I was born and three years after Herzog and Lachenal claimed Annapurna.

At its core, *Annapurna* is a book about people helping each other to achieve a goal. It's about sacrifice and teamwork, and people looking after each other; about an elite team of athletes using their combined talents to get to the top of a dangerous mountain. The account of Lachenal and Herzog being carried for miles and being cared for by their friends had a profound impact on me. In the loneliness of my childhood, I realised that I wanted to be part of a team. The comradeship among the men shone through the pages of the book.

Mum would read to me until my eyes grew heavy. The deal between us was that she would keep reading so long as I could keep one eye open, so I would alternately keep one eye open and rest the other. Sometimes she would nod off and I'd shake her awake. Off she would go again. Finally, admitting defeat, she would lay the book on the beside table, tuck me in, kiss me goodnight and then turn off the lantern by closing the kerosene valve. The lantern would die with a sigh as the mantle turned from white to a dull red before a slow fade to black. I would wait until the door closed, then would sprint out of bed. Unbeknown to my mother, if I was quick enough and got to the lantern while the mantle was still hot I could open the kerosene valve, pump like mad, and *pop*, the mantle would ignite again, flooding the room with light. I could then read long into the night. I was at an age when no country child was ever trusted with matches, and so couldn't relight the lantern myself. I would often read until the lantern ran out of kero and the mantle dimmed and went out. Mum was forever wondering why that particular lantern used so much kerosene and continually checked it for leaks.

I've never humbugged anyone as much as I humbugged my mother about that book. As she read, I interrupted her with a fusillade of questions: 'What's a *couloir*?' (A steep gully on a mountainside.) 'What's a *gendarme*?'

'That's a French word for a policeman, like Peter Sellers' Inspector Clouseau.' Mum loved Peter Sellers.

'What does the list say?'

Mum would continually turn to the glossary at the back of the book, as I hammered away with my questions.

She laughed. 'Oh, no. It's not a policeman. It's a French word for a rock tower or tooth on a ridge,' she said.

'What does that mean?' I asked, still stumped.

'I don't really know. It must be a large rock that's hard to climb, I suppose.'

These words often beat us, and we both pored over the book while she tried to work out the context. There was one we couldn't even pronounce, but sure enough there it was in a 1960 edition of the *Concise Oxford Dictionary*, a gift from my grandmother to help encourage my reading. She had been illiterate as a child and was taught to read and write by my mother. 'How do you say that?'

'Bergschrund. *Bark'shrŏŏnt.*' She read it out in parts following the dictionary's phonetic guide. 'It's a German word; it means a crack or crevice on a glacier, separating it from the mountain.' We looked at each other, neither of us any the wiser.

Annapurna was the first book with a glossary ever read to me, and I became acquainted with a new language. I saw words such as *piton*, *sérac* and *arête* for the first time. They seemed to me to be part of a secret code of a brotherhood that had its own language.

The book ends with the oft-quoted line, 'There are other Annapurnas in the lives of men.' This was the first murmur I'd heard that you could achieve anything if you were determined enough.

I have no idea how a book on French mountaineering found its way to our isolated home, but I'm forever grateful that it did.

Annapurna and *Into Thin Air* were like bookends in my life – one read while I was very young, the other while I was in middle age. One told of the heroic, noble endeavour of mountain climbing; the other was a tale of a sport sullied by egos and greed for the summit – now known as 'summit fever'. Attaining the summit and exercising the bragging rights that went with it was all that mattered, not the manner in which the mountain was climbed. Mountaineers even set goals such as climbing the tallest mountain on each of the seven continents, known as doing the 'seven summits'. Or they tried to climb all fourteen peaks in the world higher than 8000 metres. While a very entertaining read, Krakauer's book also disturbed me. Could things have changed that much since Herzog's time?

The early climbers had treated the mountains with respect, almost reverence. Modern climbers, on the other hand, had an almost atheistic attitude, as if no spirit inhabited these massive ice-bound structures. They were impassive, dead things that were climbed as quickly as possible, descended in haste and then bragged about. The separate nature and spirit of each peak seemed to be unimportant. Possibly this was because many of the current climbers were novices. The early heroes – Terray, Tenzing and Hillary – were superb technicians and athletes. Many had gained years of experience on dangerous rock climbs before they even set foot on an alpine or Himalayan peak.

Krakauer's book showed that with expert guides performing

route finding, and Nepalese sherpas preparing the climb in advance with tents, fixed lines, and portage of food and bottled oxygen, climbers arriving on the mountain often had the hard work already done for them. Often the sherpas even carried the climber's personal gear. Complete novices could now climb Mount Everest. Sandy Hill Pittman, a journalist and socialite, joined Scott Fischer's 1996 team for no other reason than the bragging rights that a successful summit would give her in fashionable New York salons. I believed little of this. With a naivety that surprisingly had persisted into middle age, it never occurred to me that Krakauer's book may have been closer to today's mountaineering truth than Herzog's. It was a lesson that I would shortly have to learn.

These two books may have provided no more than a bit of ambient noise to my life. Plenty of people have read both *Annapurna* and *Into Thin Air* without choosing to emulate any of the activities therein. The catalyst for me in all that followed was tripping over an important milestone in my life.

In November 2004, my eldest daughter, Amelia (then aged 21), finished her studies at University of Technology Sydney and flew out of Australia for her twelve-month 'Grand Tour' overseas. This left me feeling a little queasy, with an odd sense of loss. I would wake each morning with a peculiar feeling that I'd misplaced something but couldn't quite think what it was. I would then recall that I'd misplaced my eldest daughter. The empty chair at the dining-room table tormented me.

Two months later my middle daughter, Hilary (nineteen) also flew the coop. I had promised her that if she worked hard at school and applied herself in her first year at university, she could move into a residential college for the last two years of her commerce degree. Punching well above her weight and showing fierce determination in her school and early academic studies, she called my bet at the end of 2004. When Sydney University's first semester began in late February 2005, Hilary Kelly took up residence at the stately Women's College at the Camperdown campus.

I had mixed emotions. I knew my mother would have been immensely proud to have a granddaughter at Women's – something she couldn't have even dreamed of for herself or her daughter. But it came at a cost for me. I would come home to a house seemingly much emptier of noise, laughter and tumult. In the space of twelve weeks, our Seaforth home had gone from having three resident children to just one. My youngest daughter Catherine tried hard to keep up the level of noise and aggravation, but even she felt over-whelmed and lonely without her sisters' presence.

'Having two older sisters is like having two extra parents. But gee, I really miss them,' she told me one day. I knew our family life would be profoundly changed by the children growing up, but I was unsure of exactly how it would change. I moped along in 2005 with a sense of life winding down, of the intense experience of childrearing coming to an end.

It hit me hard for the first time only a month after we lost Hilary to Women's College, at the schoolgirls' Head of the River rowing finals at Penrith Regatta Centre in western Sydney. This event marks the end of the schoolgirl rowing calendar, and Catherine had competed in the first senior quad sculls for her high school. As we headed out of the regatta centre, I said to Prue: 'You know, we'll never drive through these gates again. We'll never see another one of our children row again. It's over.' (Catherine had already told us she wouldn't be competing again, that the demands of Year 12 and the HSC meant she couldn't handle sport plus her academic commitments.)

'Everything has to end sometime,' my wife replied.

'Yeah, but what're we going to replace it with?'

'We'll find something,' Prue said matter-of-factly.

'Yeah, but what?'

'We'll see. We still have to get Catherine through the HSC. That'll be enough to keep us both busy.'

I turned into the traffic on the busy M4 Motorway lost in thought. Rowing had been a passion for my family. Swimming had swept up our eldest daughter Amelia, while rowing had engaged the younger two, and Prue and I were inevitably embroiled in this high-parental input activity. We had never missed a regatta, and I had served on the school's rowing committee for over five years.

The end arrived with the shock of a mugger jumping out of a dark alley and smashing me over the head with a baseball bat. I slid into a morass of quiet and loneliness at home and a panicked search for purpose in my life post-children. Soon there would be no more sidelines to stand on. I wouldn't be needed anymore. With my career winding down and my children leaving home at a rapid rate, I found myself in a situation that is experienced by many men my age. However, knowing I wasn't the only one didn't help. I became determined to do something about it. In mid-2005, the first glimmer of an idea came to me, like the weave in a rug slowly being loomed into a pattern. I decided I wouldn't slide away into irrelevance. I began a series of discussions with my wife that would go on for another eighteen months.

'Do you ever wonder what we're going to do when Catherine leaves home?' I asked over dinner one night.

'I'll worry about it when it happens,' Prue replied. 'She hasn't even finished school yet.'

'Yeah, but that's only about twelve months away. I think we should be making some plans now. This thing with Amelia and Hilary has caught me a bit unawares.'

'*Omigod*, Dad, leave Mum alone. You worry too much,' Catherine chimed in, ending the conversation. She didn't seem at all concerned for the future. My wife and I, both products of the baby boom, were sidling up to a problem that has probably never confronted parents before. My parents were the centre of my universe. Products of the Depression, they had nothing but a lifetime of misery and desperate struggle trying to raise a family, educate them to a basic level and keep three meals a day on the table.

The lives of my sister, my brothers and me revolved around our parents, and as they trudged along through life they dragged us with them, we revolved around them. My generation continued to orbit when we matured and had our own families but it is our children around whom our lives now revolved. Their every need is met no matter what the cost; their every nuance analysed and dissected.

So what happens to the orbiting parents when the bright suns of their children's lives leave the universe? Nothing much, it seemed to me. There was just a black hole.

'We've spent our lives managing these kids, going to parent/teacher nights, music concerts, standing on the sidelines for every sporting contest they've ever been in,' I said to Prue one day later that year.

'Well, yes, that's what parents do. What's your point?'

'Well, what happens after? Our main shared interest is our kids. What're we gunna do when they're not around anymore?'

'We'll find something to do.'

'What? It'll have to be something we both enjoy.'

'I don't know, but we'll find something.'

'Yeah, but I'm worried . . .'

'Shut up, Dad,' Catherine said. 'Have you taken your medication? Get his tablets, Mum. He's lost them again.' End of discussion.

I was getting nowhere, so I decided to change tack.

'Catherine, would you be interested in doing a rock climbing course with me?'

She gave me that look of intense boredom that will be so familiar to any father of a seventeen-year-old girl.

'I've already done one at school. I don't need to do another one.'

'Well, you're not rowing this summer and it might be fun. We could both do it and it'd be a bit of a break from study. How about it?'

'Wonder if there'd be any boys doing it?'

'Heaps! There'd be heaps of them doing it in the lead-up to the HSC as a break from study,' I lied.

After some cajoling and bribing, she reluctantly agreed to give it a try, and I booked a course at Climb Fit gym in St Leonards, a nearby suburb. As we drove to our first lesson on a late spring evening in November, she asked, 'Dad, why are we doing this? You're frightened of heights and you've only got one good hand. How're you going to rock climb?'

'Mmm. Yeah, I know. But I think that sometimes you have to try to confront your fears. If you don't, they just own you. I've been able to face most of my fears, except this one. I reckon it's time to have a go. Also, I'm thinking of giving your mother a surprise present for when you leave school, so there's a few reasons for doing it.'

Silence. She turned to look at me. 'What sort of present?'

'A *nice* present.'

'What *sort* of present, Dad?'

'I'm going to take her on a mountain climb.'

'*What?*'

'A mountain climb. It'll be great, something neither of us has ever done. We can learn it together. It'll give us something to do after you leave school.'

Catherine shook her head. 'She'll never go for it. You're wasting your time.'

'Yeah, she will. She read Jon Krakauer's book and really loved it. I'll learn a bit about it, see how it's done, then talk her into doing some small peaks, maybe in New Zealand, not very challenging. Then we could have a go at something bigger. I know she'll like it if I can just talk her into having a go.'

'Whatever. I think you're only doing it because *you* want to do it.'

'No, it'll be great. She's a good athlete, your mother. She'll love it if she just has a go.' She rolled her eyes.

'Our little secret. OK, Caps?'

The rope shook slightly; a voice came up from below.

'Ah, Dad. There's something we've got to discuss.'

Again, the rope shook slightly. I looked down. Twenty metres below, on the floor of the gym, Catherine was belaying me through a stitch or friction plate attached to her harness.

'Not now, Caps. I've got my hands full right now.'

Beside her stood our climbing instructor, Kevin Melville. The rope shook again.

'Will you stop doing that?' I asked.

'Well, can we talk about my allowance? I think 50 bucks a week would be nice.'

My fingers were gripping two climbing holds on the wall of the gym and were becoming slippery with sweat. I was standing on tiptoes on two small wall dimples, having reached the ceiling for the first time after numerous attempts. 'Not now. And $20 is my top offer.'

We had been negotiating her allowance for several weeks – what I would pay her so that she wouldn't have to work during her final school year.

'One hundred and twenty-five a month, or I won't let the rope go.' *Shake, shake.* I needed her to pay out more rope so that I could get down.

'Oh, for Christ's sake, alright. Now can you let the rope out so I can get down?'

I started to clamber down the wall.

'*Yes*. Awesome!' drifted up from below. There was a great deal of laughter when I finally reached the floor.

'Well done, Kieran. But an important part of climbing is never to negotiate with one of your kids about their allowance while they're belaying you up a wall. You haven't got much to bargain with.'

'Thanks. Kevin. I'll remember that.'

Kevin Melville had proved to be an excellent instructor who seemed completely unfazed by my clumsiness and Catherine's impertinence. She gave him cheek all the time while making smart comments to all the boys in the gym.

I took away from this course – which moved outside out onto a small rock face in Lindfield, on Sydney's North Shore – the importance of belaying. This technique, fundamental to rock and mountain climbing, enables the first climber up, the leader, always to be protected by the second climber. The second gradually feeds out a rope attached to the stitch plate on his or her harness, which then passes through an anchor – often a piton driven into the rock near the second's feet.

The combination of belayer, anchor and a secure rope is known as a 'stance'. The leader climbs, putting in protection as he or she ascends – usually pitons or ice screws through which the rope runs. When the length of rope is completely run out (a 'pitch'), the leader hammers in a final piton and ties the rope to it, creating a new anchor. The second then climbs this rope, pulling out the pitons on the way up. This is known as 'cleaning'. Often the second keeps on going when he or she reaches the leader's stance and puts in protection during the climb up the next pitch. In this way, the second and lead roles alternate and both climbers are never left exposed without an anchor.

Catherine picked it up immediately. I couldn't match her for speed or agility, but I enjoyed it immensely.

Chapter 2

It's My Turn

Children begin by loving their parents; as they grow older they judge them; sometimes they forgive them.

OSCAR WILDE, *THE PICTURE OF DORIAN GRAY*

With my initial training completed, it was time to decide which mountain Prue and I would climb. Argentina's Aconcagua (6962 metres), the highest mountain in South America, and Tanzania's Mount Kilimanjaro (5895 metres), Africa's highest peak, were possibilities. However, after considerable research on the internet, I rejected them both. While they are high enough to cause altitude sickness and hypoxia (oxygen deprivation), they can be climbed without ropes or crampons, or any specialist technical knowledge, and they have only minimal objective dangers such as crevasses, avalanches or big walls. A high level of physical fitness, a stout back and strong legs are critical, but these mountains are climbed by thousands of people each year. My wife would scoot up either of these peaks.

A second possibility was to tackle one of the 'technical' peaks, such as Alaska's Mount McKinley (6194 metres) or Mount Cook

(3764 metres) in New Zealand, which require mountaineering gear and specialist knowledge. While the smaller of the technical peaks don't have the problems of extreme altitude, they do threaten other objective dangers such as steep walls, extreme weather, cold and avalanche risk. Mount Cook would offer sufficient challenge to both of us to make it interesting, without exposing us to extreme danger due to our lack of experience. Or so I thought, as I sat in my study in Seaforth looking at images of the mountain on the internet.

I waited for an opportunity to break the news.

It came just before Christmas, about a fortnight after Catherine and I finished our rock climbing course. Seated around the dinner table, Catherine, Prue and I had been chatting about what university courses Catherine might take after she finished school the following year. Catherine was still unsure of where her interest lay.

'Well, at least I've worked out what you and I are going to do when Caps leaves school,' I said, turning to Prue.

'Oh, no!' Catherine put her hands to her face, trying unsuccessfully to stifle a guffaw. Prue looked at her, then at me, as if to say, 'What's the joke?'

'Yep, I've worked it out. We're going mountain climbing,' I said proudly. I looked at my wife, expecting some shock and then 'Tell me more.' Instead, there was stunned silence. She had a look of initial disbelief and horror on her face. Catherine had her forehead on the dining-room table and was shaking with silent laughter.

'What?' Prue said finally.

'Yeah, climbing. It'll be great. We'll go and do a course together, then go and climb a small peak – something like Mount Cook in New Zealand.' There was more silence.

'You're not serious?' Prue said, her voice sounding strained. I pushed my carefully prepared folder full of information towards her. 'It'll be great. We'll start off on a couple of small peaks and set ourselves a goal like climbing Pumori in Nepal before we're 60. Nothing too big. Pumori's only 7000 metres,' I said.

Again there was silence. My wife's jaw was gradually dropping.

'What do you think? It'll be *fun*.'

There was another moment's silence before she replied.

'I think you're out of your mind.'

Catherine looked up, saw the look of complete disbelief on her mother's face, and burst into hysterical laughter, slapping her hand on the table.

I looked at her. 'Caps, stop laughing. Help me out here,' I pleaded.

'I know what would help you out, Dad. If you stopped smoking all that crack.'

'No, seriously, Caps. It's a good idea,' I said.

'No, seriously, Dad. I think it'd be a good idea if Mum took your crack pipe away and hid it. It's starting to affect your brain.'

She was breathless from laughter and continued slapping the table in mirth.

'*No one* touches the crack pipe! OK, Caps?'

I started to laugh, too. Catherine always cracked me up. Prue seemed to take our laughter as a sign that I hadn't been serious. She relaxed and began to collect the dishes.

'I'm not climbing anything, up there in the freezing cold with ropes and things. Forget it. I hate the cold, and it'd be incredibly dangerous.'

'But you'd do it easily. You're a much better athlete than me, and I'd like to have a go.'

'Kieran, we don't know *anything* about mountain climbing!'

'No, *we* don't know anything about it. That's the point. Doesn't mean *we* can't learn. Look, we can do this thing called the

Technical Mountaineering Course in New Zealand. It's 'specially for people who've never climbed before,' I said, quoting from a brochure downloaded from the internet for a course run by Alpine Guides (Aoraki). The company, based near Mount Cook, seemed experienced and very well organised. Prue dismissed the brochure with hardly a glance.

'Forget it. Besides, I get altitude sickness down at *Perisher*.'

She got up from the table, taking the dishes with her. Catherine, still laughing, patted me on the arm. 'There, there, Dad. Told you she wouldn't go for it. You'll have to try something else.'

She headed upstairs to study, still chortling to herself, 'My dad, the crack addict.'

I was left alone at the table with my pile of brochures. I was surprised by Prue's reaction. When I first met her in 1980 I noticed that she walked on the balls of her feet. She *looked* like an athlete and it was no surprise to learn that she was a champion tennis player, a good swimmer and a keen snow skier. In later life, while still playing badge standard tennis in Sydney, she took up rowing and within two years moved from the bow seat to stroke in a Senior Women's Eight. She was poised and fit and, despite being in her mid-fifties would, I thought, make a great climber. For all this she was also stubborn, so I knew I had a job in front of me.

I picked up the information and filed it away in my office. I had lost the first battle, but maybe not the war.

As 2006 got under way I continued researching and occasionally dropped into conversations with friends, as if it were a *fait accompli*, our planned climbing adventure together. This was always met with a torrent of denial from Prue. Catherine went back for her final year of school, and I kept pushing and planning.

From my explorations on the internet I was surprised to learn that Mount Cook had claimed the lives of 214 people since it was first climbed in 1894. I lowered my sights. Mount Tasman, though smaller, was arguably more difficult and also had produced numerous fatalities. The third-tallest New Zealand peak, Mount Aspiring in western Otago, was a mountain I'd not heard of, but it turned out to be the only possibility for a guided climb for novices. The guiding companies wouldn't take anyone of our inexperience on either Cook or Tasman. That settled it. With a sense of capitulation I showed Prue the information on Mount Aspiring, conceding that we would be climbing a much easier peak for starters. Same result: no interest.

'Look, you don't even need climbing experience for this. You just have to be fit. Won't you even consider it?' I said, exasperated.

'No!'

Despite the rebuffs, I continued my research and read all I could find on the mountain – its history, weather conditions, climbing difficulties and fatalities. But it was academic, as there was no interest at home. As 2006 developed, I gradually became absorbed, as every parent of an HSC student does, in the rhythms and routines of my youngest daughter. Catherine's routines governed how our home functioned.

Then, unexpectedly, fate intervened.

On a beautiful, late winter's day in August, Catherine was playing in the senior hockey finals against another girls' high school from south of the harbour. It would be her last game of school hockey and the last time I would stand on the sidelines at one of my children's winter sporting events. I was fully aware that an era was ending.

Our girls were down 1–nil for most of the game and were getting clobbered but fought back with a late goal to level just before full time, forcing the contest into extra time. They were out on their feet when Catherine suddenly set up a goal to take the final 2–1 and lift the trophy. She was later awarded the 'best and fairest' trophy for her efforts.

I felt proud, wrung-out, euphoric – and sad. I wandered down the sideline where groups of parents were congratulating their children, wishing each other well, and talking about the next season. This ritual had seemed part of my life forever. Most of these parents had younger children at school. They'd be back next year. It was just another day for them.

A hearty slap on the back broke into my thoughts.

'Well, Kieran, you've gone to your last game of hockey. It's all over, mate.'

Gary Green, a champion bloke and another sporting tragic, had stood on the sidelines for years in the mud and sunshine watching his daughter Sophie. He had younger children, so he would be carrying on. Not me.

'What'll you be doing on Saturdays now?'

I laughed, but a big black hole of despair opened up beneath me and I went in feet first.

'Dunno, Gary,' was all I could think to say. I felt lost, but between the end of the hockey pitch and the sportsground carpark I made a decision – time, place and method. *I'd be climbing Mount Aspiring a fortnight after Catherine's HSC finished, and I'd do it with the Alpine Guides company, with Prue if she'd come, but by myself if necessary.* For better or for worse, Gary Green had helped me make a decision – it was my turn now.

I broke the news to Prue that night at the place where most of our discussions were held – around the kitchen table. For some reason, I felt the need to justify my decision. 'We've worked hard all these years and done everything for the girls. They've been our whole life, but that's finishing now. Soon we'll be just two old codgers rattling around in an empty house. We've got about five or six years left to do things before we're too old. I've got lots of dreams I've had since I was a kid, and climbing mountains is right up near the top of the list. This is my last chance.'

She wouldn't budge. 'I won't stop you going, if it's that import-ant to you. But *I'm* not coming. We still have these children. Imagine if we were both killed. That's not responsible. They still need parents.'

'I'm not planning on getting killed. That's why I picked a smaller mountain. The children can't call on us forever. We have to have our own lives sometime. It's our turn now. But if you won't come, I'll go on my own.'

There was no acrimony. We were simply two people who had known each other a long time and refused to budge.

'I just wish I understood your real reasons for wanting to do something so dangerous,' were my wife's last words on the subject. We didn't discuss it again. While Prue's reasons for staying at home were clear, the underlying forces that were pushing me towards Mount Aspiring would often perplex and torment me in the coming months.

I achieved a lot in the weeks following the hockey final. I filled out an application form and gave my credit card details and sent it off to Alpine Guides. I dispensed with the Technical Mountaineering Course run by the company. Prue asked me why and I replied, 'They don't demand it for Aspiring, so I'm not doing it. I want to get stuck straight into it so I'll learn on the job.' I would later realise this decision was foolish and regret it.

The section of the application form asking for previous climbing experience was easy to complete – nil. I selected a time, the first week in December, organised my airfares and accom-modation, and booked a refresher Alpine Ropes course at Climb

Fit gym. I began training immediately. I had just three months to prepare myself.

The training was a killer, and I had precious little time to start slowly and build up. I loaded bricks into my backpack and, after work, began doing a twelve-kilometre circuit from Balmoral Beach Club on Sydney Harbour to Taronga Zoo and back along the harbour foreshore. I set a goal of completing it in less than two hours before I went to New Zealand. This became a routine twice during the week and religiously every Saturday and Sunday. I started with twelve kilograms of bricks and spare driveway pavers in my pack, then fourteen, then twenty, finally topping out at 25 kilograms.

Round and round that circuit I went, combining walking with step-ups onto a park table next to the beach club, stepping up twenty times with each leg, then 40, then 80, then 100. As I got fitter I would throw my pack off on the verandah of the club after one circuit, catch my breath, get a drink of water, then set off and do it all over again. I grew fitter and fitter, but I noticed that my legs tired more easily. Only four years earlier, these same legs had carried me for 750 kilometres across central Australia's Tanami Desert in 35 days of non-stop walking. Now something seemed different. The leg drive I'd always prided myself on seemed to be fading. I registered the feeling, then forgot about it. The 25 kilos was much lighter than weights I'd carried in the past, but now seemed a wearisome burden.

I was probably in a state of denial. No man aged over 50 wants to acknowledge the ravages of time. *I* certainly didn't. I kept reminding myself that I didn't smoke, hardly drank and swam six days out of seven. I felt I shouldn't have been any less fit than I'd been at 30, but my legs were sending me a different message, which I ignored. Even though my 60th birthday was closer than my 30th, I wouldn't accept – couldn't accept – the physical decline that accompanies encroaching middle age. It was a thought too horrible to contemplate. Round and round I went, the warnings from my legs going unheeded. 'It's *my* turn now,' was the only message I listened to. It blotted out everything else. But I would soon be reminded of the importance of fit legs in surrounds infinitely more dire than Mosman's Middle Harbour.

Because time was so short, I had to squeeze training in between running a business, deciding on and buying climbing gear, and attending school functions for Catherine as she wound down her final year. It was hectic and stressful. I trained as hard as I could. I combined the walking and step-ups with daily swims to build my aerobic fitness. I didn't want to get near the summit and be beaten back by lack of breath.

By late October I had accepted that my wife wouldn't be climbing with me in New Zealand. By then the debate between us had become a debate about marriage and family life. One Sunday afternoon I arrived home soaked in sweat after an all-day training session. I dumped my pack and trekking poles in the family room and threw the empty Platypus drinking bladder from my pack in the kitchen sink.

'You look exhausted,' Prue said.

'I'm absolutely stuffed. Jesus, it was hot.' I'd swum a three-and-a-half-kilometre race at Balmoral Beach Club in the morning, then had gone trekking on the scrub trails through Frenchs Forest with my friend Jon Attwater. We'd walked from 10.30 am until about 5 pm and I'd lugged my pack full of bricks and pavers the whole way. Jon, in his 68th year, was a veteran and tireless walker and was an inspiration to me.

I splashed water out of the sink over my face.

'I can't believe you're really going to do this,' Prue said, as I sprawled into a chair at the kitchen table.

'Well, I am. And *you* should be, too. I'm not going to sit around and let life pass me by. I can't believe you won't come with me – at least have a go.'

'Well, I would, except what you do is so extreme. Why can't we do a nice walk in Tasmania, something that's not so hard, or the Cinque Terre. Everyone seems to love that.' She was right. Italy's famous five lands walk sounds civilised and sophisticated and might've been perfect for us, except I didn't want to do it.

'Cinque *bloody* Terre. Everyone's done it. It's not exciting. I'll do that when I get old,' I snorted.

'I've got just six years left before I hang up the boots. While I can still bust a gut, I'm going to wring every last little bit out of it that I can. Anyway, by definition, if *I'm* doing something, it's not extreme. I don't have the skills.'

'But you're not going to die when you're 60,' Prue said. 'There's still a lot of things to do. We've still got grandchildren to look forward to.'

'Rubbish. We can't just sit around waiting for grandchildren to arrive. Our girls might never get married, might never *have* kids, and might not even end up living in Australia. They might be on the other side of the world. I'm not sitting around waiting for grandchildren to arrive. We can't have another vicarious family through our kids. It's *our* turn now.'

We would often lapse into silence after such exchanges. My thoughts would then sometimes return to my unhappy and lonely childhood. My self-esteem had always been low and I feared that I would die still believing I was a worthless person. I had first noticed this anxiety when in my late forties and it seemed to be worsening. From the time I was a child, mountaineering and mountaineers embodied everything I admired in people. Someone who had the skills and courage to climb to the top of a mountain peak would have no reason to doubt their worth. I hadn't achieved that sense of self-worth through my life to date or my career, or even from raising a family, but I was certain that mountaineering would do it for me. In all the discussions I had with my wife and my children I gave all sorts of reasons for why I was going to New Zealand and defended them vigorously. But they were surface justifications for my attempt to heal a very old and very deep wound.

Sometimes in my attempts to avoid the real issues, the conversations with my wife would wander onto very sensitive ground, into areas where I'd never really ventured before. We hadn't had the time or felt the need in the past, but I felt somehow that this climb would be a watershed for us both and it was time for some frank discussions.

'You know when I first met you we used to do everything together?' I said.

'We used to go to the beach every day for a swim, go for a run or play tennis. Now you never want to do anything with me. I end up doing all this stuff on my own, and it's lonely.'

My wife's life had changed when our children came along. She stopped working and the children became her focus, her *raison d'être*. They were, and are, her joy. If I came home from work and asked her what sort of day she'd had, she would tell me what sort of day the children had had. If they were happy, she was euphoric; if they were sad, she was devastated.

'I would do more things with you if you just did some things I like,' she replied.

'Yeah, but the problem is if it involves carrying a pack, sleeping outside, or getting mud or leeches on you, you just won't do it.'

'Mud and leeches! No woman my age is interested in that, and I'm not either. And I'm too old to be lugging a pack around. I want a hot shower at night, a decent meal and somewhere dry to sleep. That's not too much to ask, is it?'

'Yeah, but we can do all that when we get old,' I said. That was where it always seemed to end for me – 'We'll do it when we get old.'

The New Zealand trip exposed a widening gulf between me and my wife. Children were the cement that had held us together – they were our great shared interest, our consummate joint endeavour. We had grown into a partnership for raising children, but now they were leaving. The mortar was leaching out from between the bricks of our relationship and it was now shaky. I wondered if the structure would just fall over.

'Well, I'll never stop you doing anything. You'd just ignore me, anyway,' she said.

Catherine, who had wandered into the end of this conversation said: 'Yes, Dad. Don't criticise Mum. Find something that she would like doing, too.'

'OK, Caps.' I always lost the arguments at our house, especially when Catherine was involved. I found it very hard to disagree with her, but then we were talking about different things. While I was saying that the reason for my climb was it was my turn now, there were *many* reasons why I wanted to go to Mount Aspiring, some of which had been buried for decades deep in my subconscious and I kept these deeper motivations to myself. I wasn't telling my family a lie; I just wasn't telling them the whole truth. I was running out of time to prove something to myself, and you can't explain that to a seventeen-year-old.

In the first week of November I was back in the gym for my second Alpine Ropes course. David Lucas, a young English rock climber, arrived to find me looking at his photograph and climbing CV on the wall. He had climbed rocks all over the world. We shook hands.

'So, you're the chap who wants to climb Mount Aspiring, is that right?' He spoke with a broad Midlands accent.

'Yeah, mate. I've done a preliminary course here, but I just want to brush up on the rope work and revise the crevasse techniques.

But I warn you, I haven't done any climbing. Presume I know nothing, 'cause I don't.'

'No worries,' he replied cheerfully. We sat down while he explained, in a methodical way, exactly what he was going to teach me over the next month. Some of it – ropes, knots and abseiling technique – I'd done before with Kevin Melville, but David also wanted to instruct me on roping up for glacier travel, how to carry a coiled rope, and various ways of tying off to a harness. I bought my own harness the week before at Paddy Pallin, the outdoor equipment specialist. I was taking no chances with this vital piece of equipment. It was a top-of-the-line Black Diamond Blizzard harness, and when I walked out of the shop I couldn't believe I finally owned one. Underlining the importance of this critical bit of gear, the staff warned me that once I took it out of the shop it couldn't be returned *under any circumstances*. I had to test it for fit there in the shop, hanging from a rope attached to the ceiling.

Dave checked it and pronounced it ideal for the job.

'Before we start the course, there's someone I want you to meet,' he said. We walked to the counter, where a fit-looking, grey-haired bloke who seemed to be running the show was bent over some paperwork.

'This is Jim Josephson. He climbed Aspiring a couple of years ago to celebrate his 60th birthday.'

Josephson looked up, looked me up and down, and said, 'You're going to Aspiring, eh? Done any climbing?'

I shook my head.

'Well, you look fit enough. At least you're not overweight. If you were, you wouldn't make it.'

'It's that difficult, eh?'

'The ramp's tough. You have to get up it, and then you have to get down it, but the rest of the climb's pretty straightforward.

From the top of the ramp, up the northwest ridge to the summit, you shouldn't have too much trouble. The real killer's the walkout. The walkout's what I'll always remember about Aspiring,' Josephson said.

This was news to me. I hadn't even considered how climbers got out of the place. 'Why's that?'

'It's so rough. We had to get down French Ridge, down cliffs, over boulders, down gullies, down wet rock walls, and we were stumbling over these big tree roots. I was with an extreme athlete and he was nearly dead at the end of it. Yeah, I found the walkout the toughest part of that climb.'

To my surprise, on the gym wall was a postcard of Mount Aspiring which he had sent to his staff when he did the climb. He pointed out the different stages of the climb and where I would be climbing. He showed me the extremely steep parts and I commented that they looked difficult.

'Well, don't worry. You'll be short-roped up there. The guide'll have you under his control.'

'Won't we be belaying off anchors on those slopes? Won't he belay me up, and then I hold him as he climbs up the next pitch?' I asked. This is how it was done in the books.

'No, that'll never happen,' Dave Lucas chimed in.

'The guides are never belayed by the clients. They'd never allow a client to control a rope they were climbing on, not unless the client was really experienced and they were confident he could hold a fall.'

'That's surprising. So, what you're saying is the guides would rather have no belay than a bad belay from a client.'

'That's right,' Dave said.

Doesn't seem much like teamwork, I thought.

Over the next three weeks, Dave Lucas packed as much as he could into refining my techniques for abseiling and rope handling.

I learned how to coil rope, how to tie it off to my harness, how to extricate myself from the rope in the event of a fall into a crevasse. I abseiled off the gym roof again and again and again, until I could do it automatically. I learned to tie prusik knots – knots tied with a thin piece of cord which can slide up, but not down, a rope – and slings into a rope, vital for getting out of crevasses.

Carrying a heavy pack, I climbed a long rope suspended from the gym ceiling using the prusik slings as footholds. My right hand slid the prusik knots up easily, but I struggled with the other hand and it took me much longer than it should have to get from the floor to the gym roof. It was also exhausting, as I would end up jammed on the rope swinging back and forth trying to free myself.

'You seem to have a problem with your left hand,' Dave said, after I struggled down off the rope.

Explaining this was always the hardest part. 'Yeah, I'm partly paralysed in the left hand. I'm finding it hard to undo the prusik with that hand.' I haven't any fine motor skills in the index finger and thumb on my left hand, and the fourth and fifth fingers are completely paralysed. I found the tiny prusik knot almost impossible to operate with it. It would be worse with climbing gloves. This was a real setback.

'Show me,' he said. I held out my hand and demonstrated the lack of mobility. I thought for a horrible moment that my nascent climbing career was about to end.

'We'll have to come up with something different.' He showed me how to tie the slightly larger klemheist variation of a prusik knot, and up the rope I went again. It was easier to use and I went up and down the rope a bit faster.

'Better, but you don't want to be stuck in the dark in a crevasse fumbling around with one hand trying to set up slings. We'll try some tiblocs,' Dave said.

Tiblocs are small metal grips that attach to a rope and slide up but not down, enabling the climber to ladder himself gradually up a rope. They perform the same function as a prusik or klemheist. Dave set up a tibloc sling on my harness which would take my left boot and could be used with my left hand, while still manipulating the traditional klemheist sling with my right hand. It was fantastic and I shinnied up and down the rope over and over again with comparative ease.

It was a great relief to think I wouldn't be stuck on the end of a rope deep inside a crevasse and not be able to get out.

During the frequent pauses when I was catching my breath between shinnies up the rope, I plied Dave with questions about climbing.

'So, this idea that the client never belays the guide means there's an assumption that the guide's never going to fall, is that right?'

'Absolutely correct. Guides don't fall.'

'Well, sometimes they do. I've read of plenty of instances where guides fell.'

'Yes, but that's only through an accident. A big avalanche or a piece of rock falls and knocks them out. No professional guide would ever take a client on a slope where the guide felt there was some chance of him peeling off; that will just never happen. The guide won't fall, all other things being equal.'

Dave Lucas is a patient and thorough coach. He seemed not at all annoyed by my complete lack of experience and my incessant questions. He was happy to go through the knots and techniques over and over again. On the last night of my training, he turned up with a complete tibloc system with foot slings attached that could be carried on my harness and simply clipped on to the rope if I went into a crevasse.

'Well, there's one last thing I've got to ask,' I said as we packed up after my final lesson. 'Crampons! How do you walk in crampons?'

'I haven't got a set here, and I'm sure your guide'll show you once you get on the mountain, but you do it like this.' He set off across the gym floor walking with bent knees, taking small steps with his toes pointed outward in a duck-footed style. 'That looks awkward,' I said.

'Well, that's how it's done. The boots are heavy and all the crampon points have to hit the deck at the same time. You have to get all those points in. You've got to learn to walk all over again in crampons; it's critical to survival in the mountains. You've got to be especially careful that you don't clip yourself.' He explained that the teeth, or sharp points, on the crampons protrude slightly, and that it's easy to snag them in your gaiters as you walk.

'You've really got to concentrate on walking with your feet further apart than you normally would. Most importantly, for God's sake don't stand on the rope,' he laughed.

'Crampons are really sharp, and if you walk on the rope you'll probably cut it. Guides get very annoyed with clients who walk on climbing ropes and it's very easy to do, so always be aware of where the rope is. Another thing: don't hit the rope with your ice tools. They're sharp, too, and again you don't want to cut the rope. Anyway, the guide'll show you all this.'

We shook hands. He had been a great teacher and I thanked him for all his help.

'Don't underestimate how dangerous mountaineering is,' he said.

'But you've climbed rocks all over the world; you must've been in some tight spots as well.'

'No, rock climbing bears no comparison to climbing mountains. Rock climbing is fairly safe, that's why I prefer it – there are fewer things out of your control. There are no avalanches, no crevasses. And most of the time it's not freezing cold, as it's usually done at lower altitudes. Also, the gear is much harder to handle on snow and ice than it is on rock. If I drive a piton into a rock and I hear it ring – that's the noise it makes when you pound the spike into good rock – I know that it'll hold me in a fall. When I've put screws into ice, I've never been really certain that if I peel off and the rope hits that screw, it won't tear out of the ice. There's this continual uncertainty in mountain climbing which I find unnerving. So, good luck, take care, and make sure you let me know how you get on.'

The last week went by in a blur. One outstanding thing on my 'to do' list that I had to tick off was a fitness test to see if I could do the climb, or if I was likely to conk out. The assessment report from the gym at North Sydney Olympic Pool was surprising. My resting pulse rate was only 42 beats per minute, one of the lowest they'd seen in someone who'd just walked in off the street for a test. More importantly, my oxygen uptake, at 5.4 litres per minute, was in the top ten per cent of the population. The VO_2 max score is a measure of aerobic fitness – the capacities of heart and lungs to process oxygen – and would be important in the thinner air around Mount Aspiring's summit. I was quietly chuffed that all the swimming and training had paid off. I felt great, and apart from a torn Achilles tendon in my right leg, courtesy of too many trips up and down Mosman's Awaba Street carrying my brick-filled backpack, training had gone without a hitch.

Unfortunately, I would learn later that I had asked for the wrong tests, and, unbeknown to me, my imagination was making an appointment that my body would find hard to meet.

November 30, 2006 – my 54th birthday and my last day in Sydney. My eldest daughter Amelia rang from the Gold Coast to say goodbye. Amelia is the family worrier, as many eldest children are, but she still surprised me.

'Dad, I just want you to explain to me what your *real* goal is in doing this trip,' she demanded after initial pleasantries had been exchanged. I immediately switched to my pat answers.

'I want to learn mountain climbing. You and Hilary have left home, Caps has left school. I'm free now. I've wanted to have a go at this all my life. It's my turn.'

'No, but what's your *real* goal?' she persisted.

'That's it, to climb a mountain and learn something new. Something I could do with your mother, a bit of renewal, but she wouldn't be in it, so I'm going anyway.'

There was a moment's silence on the end of the phone. The real conversation hung out there, lurking.

'I don't think that's really why you're doing it at all. I think you're trying to get respect from people. I think you want to be admired and recognised.'

'Hey, Dr Freud, do I have to pay for the consulting session?'

'No, be serious. I don't think you got any recognition from your father and you've craved it ever since. You want to feel good about yourself. You won't be happy even if you do get to the top of this mountain. You'll plan something more dangerous to do. You'll never be satisfied because you'll never get the recognition you want. You're just going to end up killing yourself.'

Her words came as a real shock. It was the first time any of my children had spoken to me as an adult and voiced an opinion about me, and she had touched on some deeply buried fears. I thought about what she'd said. She knew me pretty well and of all my children was most like my mother.

I was chilled to my marrow that a child could see through me, could sense emotions kept long hidden and could render me so transparent. Nevertheless, I tried to brush it aside and kept running my conventional defence.

'Wow, we're deep today, Amelia.'

'No, *seriously*, Dad. No one's going to respect you more or admire you for going mountain climbing. This is Australia. No one *cares* about mountain climbing. People will just think you're odd.'

How did I answer that? How did I tell her that what she'd said was correct, but that what I felt about myself was also important?

'Well, that's not how I see it and someone my age sees life very differently from someone who's 22. I'm just going through what a lot of blokes go through at my age, Amelia, thinking the best part of life's over. It's worse for me. I came down from the bush with a head full of dreams about things I was going to achieve in Sydney and didn't. Goals I set myself in business and didn't achieve. There were lots of those. Things I hoped to become and didn't. But I'm not giving up on life. I've still got five or six years left, and if old age wants me it's got to come and get me. I'm not going to let it walk in the front door and escort me out. Can you understand that?'

'Yes, I can, but I don't think that's the whole reason. It's not the main reason you're doing this. And what about us? What'll we do if something happens to you? What about Mum? We want you around when we have kids.' She was now verging on tears.

'Amelia, if I got killed you'd never have to work again.' Another standard defence.

'Stop it. Don't say that. You *always* say that. Anyway, you should involve Mum and at least do some things she wants to do.'

'I try, but her default setting is to say "no" to everything I suggest, and she's a more capable athlete than me.'

We went round and round, with no resolution, as Amelia sought to put her fears into words and I tried to parry her intrusion into areas of my life that she knew nothing about, that existed behind bolted doors and had never been revealed to my family. She finally wished me luck and a safe return.

Chapter 3

Abandonment

What's gone and what's past help
Should be past grief.
WILLIAM SHAKESPEARE, *THE WINTER'S TALE, ACT 3, SCENE 2*

The long-suppressed story that was driving me towards Mount Aspiring and which I'd never discussed with my wife and children is a tale as old as time.

In 1952 a 34-year-old, unmarried nursing sister at Wellington Base Hospital, probably thinking that love had passed her by, had a casual fling with a friend while visiting Sydney and became pregnant. Unbeknown to her, he was married and simply walked away, washing his hands of her. The shy, bookish nurse, a devout Catholic, had only three choices: have an abortion, a back-room job in those days; give birth then have the child adopted, a gut-wrenching choice for a new mother; or face the difficult prospect of raising a bastard child in a small country town. For several weeks, two lives hung in the balance as her nurturing, maternal instinct battled with the knowledge that her life would be ruined if she raised the child. With no family money to fall back on, an extra mouth to feed would condemn her to a life of struggle and hardship. She knew that to have the child and continue to live in the small country town that had been her home all her life would likely spell the end of any hopes she might have of marrying and raising a family. It is a wrestle between conscience and emotions with few good outcomes. The Catholic Church, ruthless and authoritarian, and seeing life only from a man's point of view, would be merciless.

In a decision that speaks of bottomless courage, she saw the pregnancy through but couldn't have her child in her home town and returned to Sydney. She came home months later bearing her baby son and a burden of guilt and shame that never left her. She moved in with her mother and went back to work. Like many single mothers since, she worked day and night to support her baby while her mother tended to mother and son.

The hard-working nurse in question was my mother Alma Muss, and the baby boy was me. It wasn't much fun growing up an illegitimate child in a country town in Australia in the 1950s, but my grandmother, Mary Maude Muss, was a tower of strength and a rock during the early years of my life. The whole town knew every detail of our lives. Adults often used the word 'bastard' around me. I soon learned that I wasn't welcome in some of the homes of kids my age, many of whom also weren't allowed to come to my grandmother's house to play with me.

These thoughts came rushing back as I packed my climbing harness and carefully folded thermals into my black travelling bag. The super-fine, ultra-light garments were made of merino wool, but felt like silk. I marvelled at their texture. Waves of sad memories washed over me as I continued to pack for my journey.

My mother was treated like a leper by many people in Wellington. My birthdays were often lonely occasions, as many of my friends weren't allowed to celebrate them with me. I didn't understand why, sheltered as I was by my mum and grandmother, who had an inventive list of excuses. I knew I didn't have a father like other boys, and this gave me an outsider's view of life. I knew that I was somehow different, but like a typical only child I was doted on by my mother and grandmother, who wrapped me in a protective cocoon. They were my whole life and I trusted them unconditionally.

Then my private little world suddenly fractured. As I approached my sixth birthday my mother was courted by – and then married – a local farmer, Alec Kelly, who in his own way must have been quite courageous to take my mother and me on board – a fallen woman and her bastard child. I think Mum's weight of guilt was temporarily lifted, as she finally had a home for us and a father for me. We packed up and left my grandmother's house in town and moved to a small farm. I found this a big wrench. My grandma had been at the centre of my life to that point, and her home was the only one I'd known. But I also had confidence in my mother and believed that she would always do the right thing for both of us. The months sped by as I struggled to adjust to life on a farm with a new father and travelling long miles to school every day on a dusty bus. My mother had also changed slightly and often seemed under pressure, doing a juggling act between me and my stepfather while she sought to adjust to the end of her busy working career as a nursing sister and the beginning of her new life as a farmer's wife. I sensed the strains and I was often sent to town, for long periods, to stay with my grandmother. I was too young to understand why.

Then, one evening, in what would be a turning point of my life, I noticed my mother packing some of my clothes in an overnight bag.

'You're going on a holiday,' she said, when I asked what she was doing. She then immediately enfolded me in a big hug and burst into tears.

*

The miles sped by. I was perched on the front seat of a green Holden farm ute, which came with my stepfather. Ted, my koala soft toy, was in my lap. I nodded off occasionally and dreamed of being on holiday – of waves breaking on beaches and being chased into the water by my mum and my new father. It seemed an impossible dream that we were having a holiday together.

We stopped in town to say goodbye to my grandmother.

'Grandma, Grandma we're leaving on our holiday,' I said, bursting into her kitchen where I'd spent so many happy years.

She swept me into her arms and held me for what seemed an eternity.

'I've made some things for you.' On the table was a brown paper bag. I looked inside and saw about a dozen date scones, still warm. She was always baking things for me. Hand in hand, we walked to the front door as I babbled on about seeing the ocean for the first time.

'D'you think I'll see a whale, Grandma?' I asked.

On the front porch, she stopped. My stepfather was waiting in the car. He hadn't come inside. My mother stood on the porch motionless, looking distraught.

'I'm sure you will. Now come here and give your grandma another hug.'

She held me very tight, and I was surprised to see tears running down her cheeks. 'Grandma, what's wrong? We're going on a holiday. It'll be fun.'

'Be strong, little man,' she said. 'Your grandma'll miss you very much. I'll say a prayer to Saint Anthony for you every day.'

Mum looked at her, then turned and walked to the car. I ran after her. Grandma stood on the porch crying into a handkerchief as we drove off down the street. I waved out the rear window of the ute to the grey-haired figure on the porch who waved her hanky in farewell. She had one hand over her mouth. I watched her until we turned the corner and she was out of sight. I was confused now. Something was happening.

We reached the town of Orange, turned off the highway and wound slowly through the town. We headed up a long, straight road to an imposing building, barely visible as we climbed the hill.

'Where are we going?' I asked my mother, who was very quiet. She looked away from me out the window. She didn't answer me and I could tell by the silence in the car that something was amiss.

'What's wrong?'

'Nothing. Nothing. We're just calling in to see someone. We won't be long.'

We drove through a set of gates under a timber arch that proclaimed 'Croagh Patrick Boys Orphanage'. For some reason, this made me feel very uneasy. At the head of the drive was a magnificent mansion. I wondered what this place was.

We drove around a circular driveway the centrepiece of which was a large fountain that sent spray over an immaculate rose garden. My parents stopped the car and got out, my mother visibly trying to compose herself. She had her hanky out and was wiping her eyes.

I went to follow but was told to wait in the car. My mother and stepfather climbed the steps of the verandah and pushed an old-fashioned ivory doorbell button. Somewhere deep inside the building the bell rang dully. The door then opened and a nun wearing a very strange-looking headdress escorted them inside. I was alone.

I fidgeted in the ute in front of the building, which seemed to me like an empty tomb. The wrought-iron filigree work wound around the verandahs; a bull-nosed roof shaded the second-storey balcony. Time ticked by. I was impatient to get going on our holiday and to see the ocean.

It was very quiet. I wondered who lived there. Occasionally a far-away car horn would sound, the only sign of life in the town at the foot of the hill, walled out by a dense planting of hedges and cypress pine. A boy aged in his early teens who was raking leaves off the driveway caught my attention, and I decided to investigate. I slid out of the car and walked over to him.

'Hello. My name's Kieran,' I said, dangling Ted by one leg. The boy ignored me and kept raking, so I followed him as he worked.

'This looks like a really nice place. Is this your house? D'you live here?' I asked, trying to start a conversation.

'I live 'ere but it's not me 'ouse. Who are those people ya come with?' he said, nodding towards the ute.

'Just my parents. We're goin' on a holiday.'

He looked at me and laughed. I smiled, although I didn't know what was funny.

'Well, you're a liar. Boys who come 'ere don't 'ave parents, and you don't come 'ere to go on 'olidays.'

I was hurt and angry. 'They are so my parents. I've just got a new father.'

'Boys come 'ere 'cause they got no parents, or their parents don't want 'em. This is a orphanage, ya little deadshit. Get it?' He pushed me hard in the chest with a finger to make the point.

'And they won't let you keep that 'ere either,' he said, pointing at Ted.

'Well, I'm *not* staying here. I'm goin' on holidays, and I'll keep Ted,' I shot back, my face going red.

Looking up, his expression changed and he suddenly began raking hard and moved away from me. I turned to see that my parents had emerged on to the verandah of the building, accompanied by the nun who had greeted them. I ran to my mother and was shocked by her face. It was red and puffy, as though she'd been crying. I sensed there was something terribly wrong and I became very frightened.

'Mum, Mum, what's an orphanage? That boy said this is an orphanage. I hope we aren't staying here for our holidays.'

Everyone looked at me. 'Don't worry, Mrs Kelly. We'll take good care of him.'

'Mummy, what's happening? Aren't you coming on holidays, too?'

'No, I'm not. You're going to stay here for a little while. This is Sister Byrne; she's the Mother Superior and she's going to look after you.'

Mum took me in her arms and I could feel her body heaving. Loud sobs came from deep within her. Dad arrived back from the car with my suitcase.

'But I don't want to stay here. I don't know anyone here. I want to come with you.' I started crying. 'What about our holiday?'

'No, you have to stay here. You'll enjoy it here. There are other boys your age to play with and it won't be for long.'

I started to panic. 'Please, please don't leave me here. Please.'

I had my arms around her neck and I wouldn't let go. Sister Byrne gently pulled my fingers apart and prised my arms from around my mother's neck.

'Come on now, stop that crying. Big boys don't cry. Stop that now.'

I began shrieking. The nun held me with one arm as I struggled and fought, until finally my legs went from under me and I was half lying on the verandah, tears and snot running down my face. I had no idea what was happening. My mother bent to say goodbye, tears also streaming down her cheeks. Dad had gone to stand by the car, the door open, looking back.

'I want you to be brave now. This is very hard for me. It'll be best for you in the long run.' She gave me one last long hug.

'Goodbye. Remember, I love you very much.'

With that she was gone. Through a mist of tears I saw the back of her head through the window of the ute as it drove off down the driveway.

I stood on the verandah with Sister Byrne, howling and watching them go. 'There, there. Come on now. Stop that blubbering. You have a new home now.'

I was bewildered and, for the first time in my life, really scared. I felt totally abandoned and was engulfed by a wave of loneliness. Sister Byrne picked up my suitcase, took my hand, turned, and led me inside along a maze of dark corridors lined with grim religious statues.

'This is the refectory, where meals are taken. And there is a shower room, where you will have your shower.' I didn't take any of it in. The place was spotlessly clean and tidy, but spartan compared to my grandmother's house. And it smelled different. My grandmother's house was suffused with the smell of baking cakes and biscuits. I couldn't believe – didn't *want* to believe that I would be staying here. I was in a state of shock. Holding me by the hand and carrying my suitcase, Sister Byrne led me across a small courtyard that had views of the farming paddocks and an orchard, and what looked like a dairy. Some boys were herding cows.

'Who are they?' I was still sniffling and rubbing my eyes.

'They are some of the boys who live here. They are bringing up the cows for the morning milking,' she said.

We entered another wing on the far side of the courtyard and began to climb some stairs.

'This is the dormitory. We have dormitories for the young children like you and also for the older boys.' She pushed open a double set of swinging doors which gave onto a large barn-like room. About twenty beds were squashed into the space, each with a small bedside cupboard. Like the rest of the building it was clean but unadorned, with no carpet on the floor, only polished boards. Toilets were at the far end of the room.

Sister Byrne placed my suitcase on a bed and began sorting through the clothes my mother had packed for my 'holiday'. I lay Ted on the bed.

'What's this?' she said, picking up the toy.

'That's Ted. He sleeps with me every night,' I said.

'I'm sorry, I'll have to take that. The other boys don't have their own toys and we can't allow anyone to have special privileges. Everyone here is treated the same.'

She then looked at the paper bag which I'd clutched as a kind of mental tether connecting me to my past life and to my grandmother. She took the bag, opened it and looked inside. 'I'm sorry. I can't let you keep these, either. We'll share them with the rest of the boys at supper.'

Unpacking done, she led me back to a room at the front of the building that we had passed earlier. It looked like a lounge room, with big, cosy chairs and a fireplace at one end. This was the parlour, she said, and told me to sit in one of the chairs while she took her place at a desk facing me. I was still crying and blowing my nose into a handkerchief. The nun, whose full name I would learn years later was Sister Bernard Byrne, a woman renowned for her kindness, began to explain the rules. The sun shone through the slatted blinds behind her, silhouetting her extravagant headgear which reminded me of an aeroplane's wings. It defied gravity.

'Croagh Patrick is a Catholic home for boys. Our patron saint is St Patrick and we are named after a mountain he climbed in Ireland. We rise at 6.45 every morning and after prayers, you will be expected to make your own bed. Breakfast is at 7.30, and at 8.30 we assemble in the courtyard and walk to school in the town. Is that clear?'

'When can I go home?' I asked, beginning to cry again.

'Your mother has put you here for your own good. This will be your home now.' She wasn't being unkind, but I sensed she had been through this scene many times before and it was said matter-of-factly.

'What's an orphanage; is it like a reform school? Have I been sent here because I've been bad?' I'd heard about reform schools as places where bad boys were sent, but I didn't understand what happened in them or at orphanages.

She patiently explained to me that Croagh Patrick wasn't just an orphanage for boys without parents; it also took in and cared for boys whose families were in financial difficulty and couldn't look after them.

'But I don't belong here. I'm not an orphan,' I sniffed.

She gave me a direct look. 'No, you're not. Everyone who is here thinks they shouldn't be here, but all of us have to live with it.' She read out a list of rules – when you could be in the dormitory and when not, silence before and after meals, and chores expected to be done every day, including working in the piggery and dairy. I was listening, but felt lost in my own overwhelming grief.

'How long will I be here?'

'That's up to your mother. You'll be here until she comes to collect you. Boys stay here until they're twelve or thirteen, then they go to St Vincent's Boys' Home at Westmead, in Sydney.'

My heart recoiled at this piece of news. I had never been to Sydney. It seemed impossibly distant, and my twelfth birthday was an eternity away.

A bell sounded in the distance. 'Ah, that is supper,' she said, and stood up.

I followed Sister Byrne through the corridors once more to the refectory where six or seven tables were laid out, with six boys to a table, seated shoulder to shoulder. There was a hush in the room. Every eye followed Sister Byrne as she led me to a vacant place at the table near the wall.

'This is Master Kelly,' she said to the assembled throng. 'He will be joining us; he comes from a farm near the town of Wellington.' Heads turned to look at me as I took a seat at the end of the table.

Towering over me were two older boys. They seemed enormous, although they couldn't have been more than twelve. Across the table was another small boy, about my age, who looked at me curiously. No one spoke.

One of the nuns then led the boys in saying grace, after which a general hubbub of voices and clashing utensils erupted. So began my first night in a Catholic institution, the first night I'd spent apart from either my mother or my grandmother since I was born.

I felt totally abandoned.

My new life began. The first few days passed in a blur, and I couldn't sleep at night with the strange sounds made by the twenty or so other boys in the dormitory. A gulf had opened up in my life, and I tried to understand what was happening to me.

I'd been raised by two women, and wasn't very tough. Now I'd been pitched into a world of boys. I was completely lost. My first brush with the hard realities of orphanage life came a couple of days after I'd arrived.

'So, how'd *you* get 'ere?' It was one of the bigger boys at the table. I had previously been ignored.

'My parents left me here for a while for a holiday.'

'Bullshit. No one who comes 'ere has parents. If you 'ad parents, you wouldn't be 'ere.'

'I do. I *do* have parents. My mother brought me here. I shouldn't be here. My mother will come and get me soon.'

'What a bullshit artist.' This was another of the older boys. 'This is an *orphanage*. That's where kids go with no parents. If you got parents, they must hate ya to send yer 'ere.'

'Oh, no, my mother loves me very much. And my dad's got a farm with horses and sheep and things.'

The arrival of the porridge trolley stopped the argument. Six bowls of porridge were ladled out and passed around.

'Excuse me,' I said to the nun pushing the trolley. 'Can I have some brown sugar for my porridge?'

'What?' she exclaimed.

'I always have brown sugar on my porridge at home.'

'Well, this isn't your home and it's not a hotel either, Master Kelly. Eat it and be very grateful. Think of the starving millions in India who would love that bowl of porridge.'

The trolley trundled away. With loud slurping noises, everyone went at their bowls except me. I sat there looking at the porridge.

'What's wrong with you?' the boy sitting next to me said, glowering.

'I can't eat this. It's got no brown sugar on it.'

'Eat it, you bullshitting little twerp,' he growled.

'I can't.'

'We'll see about that,' he said. He looked around to see that no nuns were in sight, then grabbed a handful of the hair at the back of my head and slammed me face-first into the bowl of scalding porridge. A cracking noise was my nose breaking as it collided with the bottom of the bowl, although I didn't know it at the time.

'See how ya like eating it through ya nose,' I heard a voice say. I struggled, scratching the back of his hand which was keeping me pinned face down. I couldn't budge him. I tried to scream as the burning porridge went up my nose and down the back of my throat. I felt his hand start to ease up, then he leaned his elbow and forearm across the back of my neck, pressing down harder and driving my head deeper into the bowl.

'He's eatin' his porridge now. That'll shut the little prick up. Teach him to bullshit about havin' parents,' he said.

I heard someone start to bawl. It was the small boy sitting opposite me.

'Shut up you, snivelling shit,' I heard.

My face was pressed flat in the bowl, my lungs bursting. The pain of burning skin throbbed in my brain. Just when I thought I would pass out, my tormentor yanked me up by the back of my hair into an upright position. I sucked in air and porridge, and the hot gruel went down into my throat and lungs. I coughed it up all over the table.

'Ah, ya little bugger! Look what ya done!' the big boy said. 'Here, clean it up and clean yourself up, too.' He threw me a rag used to clean the tables. I wiped the muck off my face.

'What's going on here?' The nun who had been pushing the porridge trolley and who had briefly left the room, had returned and spied the commotion.

'Sister, he wouldn't eat his porridge because there was no brown sugar and spat it all over the table,' one of the boys said, pointing at me.

'Is this true?'

I was crying hard as I held the rag over my face. Blood from my nose ran down onto my shirt. I was too shocked to speak, but shook my head and looked at her imploringly. My face was on fire. 'Please help me . . . my face . . .' I choked out.

'I'll help you, alright. We won't stand for that sort of behaviour here. Some discipline will cure you of these notions, young man.' She pushed the boys aside and rubbed my face with the rag. 'Now go and clean yourself up, then report straight away to Mother Superior.'

Sister Byrne seemed more concerned than the other nun about my burnt face and swollen nose, but nevertheless gave me a savage scolding. I was to carry slops to the pig farm for the next fortnight. I would keep my mouth shut and try to become invisible, I decided.

In line before school the next day, I heard a voice behind me.

'What did you say?'

'Nothing. I didn't say anything.'

'Just as well. You dob, and that'll be the end of ya.'

'I won't. I won't dob.'

'Good, and shut up your bullshit about your parents. You ain't got no parents, right?'

'But . . .'

'Right? *No parents*. Right?'

'Yeah, that's right.'

'Say it.'

'I haven't got no parents.'

A small burning pit of anger suddenly welled in me. It was the birth of my anger towards and resentment of authority figures. I wished I could do something to my tormentor and this would grow over time as a need for revenge for hurt.

'Good.'

He then punched me in the lower back. It wasn't a hard punch, but with his middle finger curled into a knuckle, it hurt and knocked me over. I said nothing, dusted myself off and shuffled forward as the line started to move. Inside me the incubus of anger was fanned to flame and would burn for decades.

The weeks turned to months, and the summer left the slopes and freezing autumn blew in. My face was raw after my initiation, but gradually the burnt skin peeled and the pain abated. I learned to cope. I never spoke out of turn, and I never talked to the bigger boys unless they spoke to me. I became invisible. My mother wrote to me every week. I was one of the few boys regularly to get letters, but I never mentioned them to the others. I would lock myself in a toilet cubicle and read Mum's letters over and over. Then I'd hide them in my socks.

It was a very confusing time. I'd been told that I'd be going on a short holiday and would soon be home and that my mother loved me despite sending me to that place. From the certainty of my place in my grandmother's house, I now felt that I didn't belong anywhere or to anything. The other boys did their best to assure me that once you went into Croagh Patrick, no one ever came and got you; you were there forever. It was a terrifying prospect.

Each morning after breakfast, we were formed into lines, two by two, and made our procession from the orphanage down the hill to St Mary's Primary School in Orange. I remember the lonely nights in the cold dormitory and the silent, watchful presence of the nuns, who tried but could never take the place of a mother. I remember the violence, too, seeing how the older boys handled themselves, tearing into each other. For the first time, I heard the sound of knuckle connecting with bone. We little kids tried to shrink ourselves into becoming invisible, bug-eyed with fright and terrified the big kids would turn on us.

I learned another lesson as the weeks went by. None of the boys talked about where they came from, who their parents were or why they had ended up where they did. It was a strange feeling living every day with the same boys, some of whom were my age, and to know nothing at all about them. This reserve persisted, so that by the time I left Croagh Patrick, I knew nothing about any of the other boys who lived there. I now realise this was a self-defence mechanism and I subconsciously adopted it as well. I realised the blunder I had made on my first day when I started discussing my parents and the reasons that had brought me there and why I shouldn't have been there. I couldn't have made a bigger mistake. If our personalities are largely formed by the time we are seven years old, then a cornerstone of my personality became a reluctance to ever talk about myself, especially to other males, and to never reveal anything about my past. It became a tenet of life at the orphanage and I have stuck by it ever since.

Finally, after what seemed an eternity but was in fact less than six months, I was asked to the parlour. As I walked down the long hall, I saw through the front door my mother standing with Sister Byrne. At the sound of my footsteps they both turned to look at me. I tore down the corridor and wrapped my arms around my mother, who enveloped me in an enormous hug. For reasons I'll never know, because I was too frightened to ask, Mum had arrived to take me home.

Home was back on the farm with my stepfather, who I think secretly despised me, and my mother, whose guilt at having had a child out of wedlock was now compounded by having agreed to have me sent to an institution. I don't think either of us ever got over my time away. If I had felt like a marginal outsider in my small country town before I was sent away, I felt like a complete one when I came back. I was the only kid in my class who knew what the inside of an orphanage looked like, but I never mentioned the experience to anyone. Sticking to the script, I said I'd been away on holidays.

These thoughts tumbled end over end as I sorted through all my reasons for taking up mountain climbing. *Maybe illegitimate children spend the rest of their lives trying to gain legitimacy,* I thought to myself as I packed Mum's copy of *Annapurna* into my travel bag. *Maybe Amelia's right, and I just want some recognition, some acknowledgement, that I belong somewhere, that I'm the same as everyone else. Trying to convince myself that I'm a worthwhile person is a very poor reason for risking my life high in the mountains. I must sit down with Amelia and explain it all to her when I get back.*

I finished packing, pondering on how our children can sometimes hold a mirror up for us to see some unpalatable truths.

'Bye, Dad. Have a good time.'

'Bye, Caps. Look after your mother.' I hugged my youngest child as she stood in the driveway. She was still recovering from Schoolies week and the realisation that school was finally over.

'I hope you're not going to try and smuggle your bong through Customs, Dad. You might never get into New Zealand.'

'Very funny. The bong stays home, Caps.'

'My dad, the crazy mountain climber. I think you're just an old hippie going to sit in the mountains, blowing a few cones.'

'Don't you touch my stash, Caps.'

She laughed as I slung my pack into the back of Prue's car and waved as we backed out of the driveway. I loved her dearly. She had had a smile on her face and given me cheek her entire life, and thankfully had none of the torment that had boiled inside me at her age. The relationship between me and my daughters couldn't have been more different from the one I endured with my stepfather. They probably thought I cuddled them too often.

As we headed for the airport, Prue broke the silence. 'I'm really not happy about this, not happy at all. I think you're too old. Your reflexes are slow and you can't concentrate. You'll start thinking about something else and just drift off. Anyway, don't come back a quadriplegic. I don't want to spend the rest of my life nursing a quadriplegic.'

'You won't. Mountaineering either sends you back whole or minus a few fingers and toes, or it doesn't send you back at all. There's not much of a halfway house.'

I was fairly convinced about this. Unlike competitive horse riding, which seems to go hand-in-hand with neck injuries and quadriplegia, with mountaineering I had a much better chance of not coming back at all than of coming back in a wheelchair.

We lapsed into silence again.

Prue and I said our farewells on the footpath of the International Terminal at Sydney's Kingsford Smith Airport. I slung on my pack.

'This is arse-about, you know,' I said. '*You've* got the athletic skills, and I'm the one going mountain climbing. It doesn't make any sense. If life worked the way it was s'posed to work, I'd be organising base camp for you while you knocked off a big peak in the Himalayas. That'd play to each of our strengths. I'm good at *organising* stuff and you're good at *doing* stuff. Me going to New Zealand and you staying home doesn't play to either of our strengths.'

'Yes, except that I don't *want* to go mountain climbing. Now, you be careful. You've still got a family to think of,' she said.

'Guess you're right.' There was no point debating it further. We'd been through it so many times already over the past eighteen months. I kissed her goodbye and headed through the sliding glass doors to the Air New Zealand check-in counter. I had to admit, as I checked in my pack, that I envied Prue's certainty. She knew she had the skills to do what I was going to do, she knew she had skills I didn't have, but she didn't feel the need to prove anything to herself.

I wish I had that much self-assurance, I thought, as I watched my pack disappear. But I didn't and it was too late to change that. My wife couldn't have guessed at the demons that haunted me. I hurried to the departure gate.

Chapter 4

'Are You a Mountaineer, Bro?'

All men dream: but not equally. Those who dream by night in the dusty recesses of their minds wake in the day to find that it was vanity: but the dreamers of the day are dangerous men, for they may act their dream with open eyes, to make it possible. This I did.

T. E. LAWRENCE, *THE SEVEN PILLARS OF WISDOM*

The cultured voice of the captain came over the intercom to update passengers on our Air New Zealand flight from Sydney to Queenstown. I was reading and only half paying attention, when he said something that jolted me from my reflection.

'We are on track to being on the tarmac in Queenstown at 12.30 pm. If those passengers on the right-hand side of the plane care to look out the windows, you will see one of New Zealand's best-known landmarks, Mount Cook, poking up through the clouds. It's the highest mountain in New Zealand and attracts mountain climbers from all over the world.'

I looked out the window and for a moment I could see nothing. A vast plain of dimpled cloud stretched as far as I could see, looking entirely like a grey, woolly sheep's back. Then far off on the horizon, a rough, saw-toothed ridge stabbed through the cloud, catching and reflecting the sunlight as we flew by. I could only see the very top of it. It looked impossibly steep and exposed. A great sense of relief came over me. *Thank God I don't have to climb that!* I couldn't see any way that people could get up there and was comforted that Alpine Guides had assigned me a lesser mountain to climb.

I sank contentedly back into my seat and watched the impossibly sharp summit ridge of Mount Cook slide by. I felt almost smug. Minutes passed and the captain's voice came on the radio again.

'We will shortly be commencing our descent into Queenstown. I'll be turning on the fasten seat belt signs, but those on the right-hand side of the plane who look out the window now will see another landmark of the Otago region, Mount Aspiring. Known by the local Maori as *Tititea*, "the glistening one", it's considered by many to be the most beautiful peak in New Zealand. Climbers also come to this mountain from all over the world.'

None of the other passengers seemed interested and at best gave a brief, bored glance out the window before returning to their books or magazines. One passenger, however, had sat bolt upright and now had his nose squashed flat against the perspex, desperate for a first view of the mountain. It was terrifying. Up through the clouds punched a cylindrical, silver cow's horn. Off the end of the plane's wing tip, it glistened in the sunlight. I knew from photographs that I was looking at the summit and the top of the southwest ridge.

I'll never be able to climb that. This is a very dumb idea. Amelia is right. I'm going to get myself killed trying to prove that I'm a worthwhile person.

After my orphanage stint, and having spent my early years being brought up by Mum and Grandma, I desperately wanted to be like everyone else. I now had a father, like other boys, and I wanted to feel normal. This was my chance to start over. I didn't really know what a stepfather was, but I presumed our relationship would be just like my mother's and mine, and so I should treat him the same. And I did.

Each night, before Mum put me to bed and read me the obligatory story, I would put my arms around Alec's neck as he sat at the kitchen table having a last cup of tea, give him a cuddle and say goodnight. I soon got used to how different a father was – the feel of the stubble on his chin, the look of his thick neck, and the manly smell of sweat after a day's physical labour. I was getting to like having a father. Finally, I had someone to look after me and protect me. This person would be my guide through life, I thought. He'd help me shape my image of myself. Even at that age, I realised that no matter how much my grandma and mother loved me, there were some things only a father can teach a young boy.

A month after my return from Croagh Patrick, I went to put my arms around my new father to kiss him goodnight as usual. This time, to my surprise, I felt his hand press against my chest and he gently but very deliberately pushed me away. My fingers, intertwined behind his neck, slowly unwound and I stepped back. No words were spoken. He didn't even look at me. He sat motionless at the table and stared ahead. I stood rooted to the spot, bewildered and unsure of what had just happened. My mother led me away and began to sob quietly. It broke my heart to see her cry.

'Don't cry, Mum. Everything'll be alright.'

'You'd better just say goodnight to Alec in future. Don't kiss him goodnight.'

'Alright.' I pulled the blankets up under my nose and whimpered. 'I'm not going to get sent away again, am I? Please don't send me away again.' This had become one of my greatest fears, and would remain so for many years after.

'No. I promise you, I'll never send you away again.'

Mum was really crying now, tears flowing down her cheeks on to her chin and then dropping on to the blankets. She wiped them away with the back of her hand. I was frightened and confused, disturbed that Mum was so distressed, and sensing that something momentous had just happened, though I didn't know what.

From that night on, I did as Mum had asked. I was lucky that my stepfather never bashed or abused me, but there are other ways to brutalise a child. After that night, the only physical contact I ever had with my stepfather was to shake his hand when I went to and returned from boarding school in my teenage years. I never called him 'Dad' again. Thereafter, he was 'the old man'.

To my feeling of having been abandoned was now added rejection. I thereafter sought solace, and larger-than-life role models, in the world of books.

I stared through the broken cloud, snatching at pieces of memory and catching glimpses of different features of Aspiring's southwest ridge, summit and eastern face. It looked impossibly sheer, but pristinely beautiful basking in the sunshine. The lower part of the mountain was shrouded in cloud and mystery. My first sight of this glistening alpine peak, known as the Matterhorn of the South after its famous European cousin, reminded me of the time, long before, when I had seen the sun rise on Kanchenjunga and got my first view of Annapurna after rain.

The magnitude of what I was taking on continued to hammer away at me and I wondered why this trip, and Amelia's chance remark, had ripped the scab off wounds I'd thought had long healed. I had seen so many photos of Mount Aspiring that I expected to be unmoved by its physical reality. Instead, I was rattled. What I was looking at wasn't a photo in a book; this was *real*. I might get killed doing this. And for what? If Amelia was right, I was only trying to prove to myself that I was a worthwhile person; that I really did deserve to be here; that even bastard boys can find a place in life, despite being an 'accident'.

For the first time, I considered that I mightn't be up to this; that I might fail and be shown to be a coward. *What if this challenge proved to me that I wasn't a worthwhile person? What would I do then?* Uncertainty and doubt tumbled around in my head.

As I sat back in my seat, I thought about the practical consequences of a fall from a peak like those I'd seen out of the window, and I thought about Dave Lucas's claim that guides never fall. I had phoned the affable Bryan Carter, managing director of Alpine Guides, just before leaving Australia, and he had been as definite in his opinion as Dave Lucas had been. The clients never belay the guides, and the guides don't fall. Unfortunately, I knew from my research that this just wasn't true.

Three years earlier, on New Year's Eve 2003, a tragedy occurred involving guides on the South Island's Mount Tasman, when David Hiddleston, Paul Scaife, another guide and three of their clients were swept 500 metres down the side of the mountain by a small avalanche. Only two of the six climbers survived, and Scaife and Hiddleston, popular and experienced Wanaka guides, weren't among them. Mountaineering seems to be a quick and indiscriminate killer, and no respecter of experience or care. The guides in the Mount Tasman accident knew the mountain well and had been attempting to set up anchors to safeguard their clients. The avalanche wasn't a big one. They were just unlucky.

If I was honest with myself, I was desperately frightened that something like this might happen to me; that an accident like that on Mount Tasman might kill both me and my guide. Added to this was the doubt that lurks in the heart of most men, that when placed in a position of grave danger they may falter and fail. More than most, I needed to succeed on this climb in order to slay some of the demons that had been tormenting me since I was deposited on the steps of an orphanage for boys almost 50 years earlier. I was frightened on a whole lot of levels as the plane descended into Queenstown.

I walked down the gangway onto the tarmac and my senses wound back 25 years. The last time I'd been here was for my honeymoon, when I'd been under tremendous pressure. While trying to come to terms with the fact that I was finally married, and fearful of the responsibilities it would bring, I was also trying to come to grips with the news I'd received just before we had boarded the plane: my mother's terminal illness might claim her before our return. I was so distracted on that previous visit that I hadn't noticed the Remarkables, the giant pair of peaks that tower over Queenstown's airport. They were now dusted with snow, although winter was long past. As the other passengers filed past me, I stood on the tarmac, registered the chill in the clean air, stared about me, and remembered.

Outside the terminal, where I had a 45-minute wait for a bus connection to Wanaka, I struck up a conversation with a hire car driver waiting for a passenger. He nodded to the trekking poles strapped to my pack. 'Come to Kiwiland to do some tramping, bro?'

Tramping is the New Zealand term for trekking or hiking. The accent told me straight away I'd left Australia.

'No, mate. Going climbing.'

'Climbing, eh? Mount Cook?'

'No, Aspiring. Gunna have a go at Aspiring. Just waiting for the bus to Wanaka.'

'Aspiring, eh? Tough mountain . . . steep. So, are you a mount-aineer, bro? You done a lot of climbing?'

'No, mate. This's my first go.'

He tilted his head and shook it from side to side, then laughed. I grinned back.

'You been up there, mate?' I asked.

'No, bro. But me and me brothers, we tramped into Aspiring Hut a few years ago. That's on the Matukituki River up there, eh. Pretty country, but rough. We could see how rough it was up there beyond Aspiring Hut. Pretty steep up there, too, bro. You sure this is your first climb?'

'Yeah, mate. But I've got a guide.'

'Guide from Wanaka, eh? Some good guides there.'

My bus pulled into the carpark and I prepared to leave.

'Well, you take care, bro. People come here to Kiwiland and get killed all the time, eh.'

'Thanks, mate. I will.' I slung my pack into the bus's luggage bay and climbed aboard.

As we headed north from Queenstown across the rolling hills of Central Otago, I marvelled at how beautiful the countryside was and how much it had changed in 25 years. When last I visited here it was sheep farms. Now, grape vines ran in serried, orderly ranks across the rich valley floors. The driver chatted amiably about the region's history and as there were only a couple of others on the bus, I plied him with questions. I asked about the snow still on the Remarkables.

'Does this happen often in summer?'

'No, it's been an amazing winter. It's hardly stopped snowing. It's *still* going. We only usually get snow resting on the Remarkables in winter time, but we've had such hard westerlies this year.' I'd already learned from conversations with Alpine Guides that the mountains of southern New Zealand were having a very unusual season.

'So, what brings one of our friends from across the Tasman to Wanaka?' the driver asked, looking at me in his rear-view mirror.

'Aspiring. I'm going to have a crack at Mount Aspiring.'

'Oh, so you're a mountaineer then?'

I was reluctant to answer that. 'No, I'm not. Not really. I haven't climbed before.'

The driver looked at me again in the mirror. I felt ashamed, like I was an impostor. 'You'll be needing a guide, then. You're not planning to climb up there on your own, I hope?'

'No, I've got a guide.' I was getting the feeling that the locals were very protective of their mountain. The conversation died and I gazed out the window, deep in thought.

I felt very alone there in the bus, in a foreign country trying something so disconnected from my life experience as mountain climbing. It had been the same when I returned to primary school in Wellington after my stint away in the boys' home.

I was tormented at school constantly about being an 'orphan'. No one believed my carefully crafted story about being away on holidays. I was miserable and lonely. Finally, it came to a head a couple of months after I'd arrived back, sometime before my eighth birthday. Several boys standing in a circle taunted me during a break that my mother was a 'slut'. I didn't know exactly what that meant, but I knew it was a very bad word and was being directed at my mother. I somehow had to defend her.

For the first time, a red curtain of rage danced down in front of my eyes and I lashed out, hitting one of my tormentors solidly in the mouth. It was the first time I'd hit anyone with a closed fist. The boy staggered backward and his mouth dropped open as if he were going to abuse me once more. I hit him again and a cough of blood goobed out of his mouth and splashed on his blue shirt. To my surprise, a black bloody hole now occupied the space where his two top front teeth had been. He stood there howling.

Seeing how the older boys at Croagh Patrick had reacted to slights had frightened me, but it had also planted the notion in my brain that problems can be solved with violence. The older boys' apparent credo of 'retaliate first' seemed to be effective. A bad temper and violence seemed to be necessary survival tools in a Catholic orphanage, and I brought them home with me.

The parents of the boy I hit laid a complaint and I was hauled up before the head nun at the school to explain myself. As my mother was out on the farm, my grandmother was summoned. She stepped resolutely and fearlessly onto the school verandah, coming to my defence as she always did, and I burst into tears when I saw her. She gave me a big hug, and told me everything would be alright before opening the door and going inside.

I heard muffled voices and occasional shouts from the father of the boy I'd hit. Eventually, I was asked to come inside. My grandmother was warned that if there was any more of this sort of behaviour from me I'd be attending school elsewhere. The boy's parents glared at me as they left. I was asked to explain my side of the story and, mortified with humiliation, had to repeat the dreadful word used about my mother. Strangely, after I'd told my side of the story, my grandmother settled it all behind closed doors and I never heard anything more about it. It was another of the many things in my childhood that I didn't understand.

The incident was a turning point, as I was never again teased about being an orphan and no one ever referred to my mother in that way again. However, my long-held hope of having a normal life was jettisoned forever. It was replaced by a seething anger and a preference for my own company and the company of books.

I never spoke to anyone about my past. I locked it away and tried to become like everyone else. As part of this defence I never really trusted anyone, especially people I had just met. I had no idea that by suppressing part of myself, part of my personality was closing down. I know now that you can hide things from everyone else, but you can't hide from yourself. I wouldn't confront these issues for another 50 years, and many people close to me would suffer as a result.

The bus dropped me at Matterhorn South lodge in Wanaka at 4.30 pm. I was an hour late. A tall figure, who appeared to have been sitting on the lodge's front fence for some time, rose slowly and walked towards me. At about 190 centimetres, he towered over me. I noticed that he was lean, bordering on skinny, and that he walked on the balls of his feet.

'Anton Wopereis?' I asked, extending my hand. He nodded. 'Sorry I'm late,' I said. He had a climbing helmet and a big pair of plastic boots that looked like ski boots in one hand. Tucked under his other arm was a big brown paper package. I followed him as we walked up the footpath to the front door of the lodge.

As a resident of Otago, Anton was very different from what I'd expected. I'd played rugby for three winters in London in the 1970s for a New Zealand rugby club. The men of Otago who played for the club were wider than they were tall, with a propensity to have no necks and knuckles that seemed to drag along the ground. They were either dark from their wild Scottish blood or dark from their Islander heritage – sometimes both. Superb sportsmen, who have provided generations of All Blacks, the Otago players liked a drink and were not to be trifled with late at night after celebrating a win against one of the English rugby clubs. Anton was different. His tall, lean frame looked like it wouldn't support a heavy backpack. He reminded me of a Norwegian cross-country skier, rather than a typical Otago behemoth.

It was more than a quarter of a century since I'd stayed in a hostel like the Matterhorn South. Its simplicity and neatness reminded me of all the youth hostels I'd bunked in during a long trip across Asia and Europe in the 1970s. After I had been allocated a room, Anton dumped the contents of the brown paper bag on my bed. This was the gear I'd ordered from Australia. The Macpac shell jacket fitted well, as did the gloves and inners and the storm-proof overpants. The climbing pants were far too big. We had no time to get more, so I'd be climbing in my light nylon khaki trekking pants, with thermals underneath. Next the helmet – too small. The boots also were too small.

'Gee, they're heavy,' I said, as I tried to walk in them.

'Have to be. Climbing boots take a lot of abuse and they have to be stiff enough to take crampons. I'll go back to the house and get another pair of boots and a bigger helmet. Sort through the stuff in your pack and put everything you want to take in a pile and I'll check it.'

Check it came out as *chuck it*, but he didn't have nearly as thick a Kiwi accent as some of the blokes I'd played rugby with.

'Anything that isn't essential, leave it behind. You might have to carry it out, so you don't need any unnecessary weight. Did you bring some joggers to walk out in?' I pulled out the heavy Keen trekking sandals that I'd planned to use. He took them in his hands, weighed them up and shook his head. 'Too heavy. I'll get you a pair of runners. Pile all the stuff up and I'll see you in an hour.'

With that he was gone. It was hard to read this man who I would be entrusting my life to for the next six days. He was quiet, no-nonsense, reserved and obviously knew his stuff. While I couldn't read him well, he did give me confidence straight away. The flipside was that he'd somehow let me know in the 30 minutes we'd known each other that he was the boss. I might be paying the bills, but only one person would be making the decisions and no correspondence would be entered into. This was hard for me, as

I had organised a lot of expeditions and always had a big say in how they were run.

I dumped everything out of my pack on the bed and began sorting it into two piles, the stuff to take and the stuff to leave behind in Wanaka. Some of it was easy. The harness, the Macpac jacket, the thermals – upper and lower body, and three pairs of socks all went in the pile to take. I wouldn't take a change of underwear or a spare shirt. Shaving gear and toothpaste would be left behind. The leather utility belt that I always travelled with was a bit more problematic. The GPS unit and long-bladed knife would stay behind. I had a heavy brass Francis Barker and a light Silva base plate compass. The Francis Barker went in the discard pile. My leather match case, Leatherman tool in its leather pouch and my enamel cup were all coming. My Nikon F80 camera with long lens was also in the travelling pile. I don't know why I didn't think a bit more about this. The camera and case weighed 1.5 kilograms. That camera had bounced along on top of a camel right across central Australia, so it was coming climbing with me. It was only later, on the slopes of Mount Aspiring, that I realised how heavy 1.5 kilos can be when you are carrying it on your back. In reality, I had no idea what to take on a climb. I was inexperienced and out of my depth. I would only know what to take after I'd returned from the climb.

Lastly, on the bed sat Mum's tattered copy of *Annapurna*. I sat and leafed through its pages while I waited for Anton to return. The dusty smell of the pages, the rough texture of the yellowed paper and old colour photographs that looked more like bad paintings brought back rich memories of life in a sad, sweltering farmhouse long ago. It also brought back other memories. This book had been to the mountains before.

Twenty-nine years earlier, in January 1977, I had left Australia aged 25 to seek my fortune. Like many boys of my generation from poor families, I chose accountancy as a career. It was ideal for boys with no parental money or connections because it was easy to get into at university and scholarships could be won if you worked hard enough. But despite graduating with distinctions, I endured three years of miserable work and postgraduate study before pulling the pin on the day I qualified. Confused about what I was going to do with the rest of my life, I headed off to see the world and experience some adventure. With a small hoard of savings, I was determined that I would never work as an accountant again and that I was going to see the high Himalaya.

Three months later, dawn found me on top of Tiger Hill above the Indian hill station of Darjeeling. I had caught the train from the seething, overcrowded cesspit of Calcutta (now Kolkata) the previous day.

Darjeeling, in West Bengal, was gifted to the British East India Company in 1817 and became one of the pearls of the British Raj. At 2134 metres (7000 feet) above sea level, it's everything that sea-level, rat-infested Calcutta isn't – cool, clean and uncrowded.

I rose before 4 o'clock on my first morning in the Darjeeling youth hostel and set off on foot on the eleven-kilometre trek to Tiger Hill, the famous lookout perched above the town. I wanted to see the sun rise over Mount Kanchenjunga and take in what is justifiably regarded as one of the front-row seats for viewing the Asian alps. When I arrived it was still dark and very cold. I shivered in the early morning gloom, so different from the swelter I'd experienced in my trek across Southeast Asia. It was deafeningly quiet.

Soon the first rays of the sun coming up behind me shot overhead and turned the twin peaks of Kanchenjunga a pink colour, which slowly turned to orange as the massif emerged from darkness. My first sight of the mighty Himalayas is one I'll never forget. I'd expected to see just Kanchenjunga, but soon the whole mountain range was visible while darkness still clung to the valleys. There were dozens and dozens of massive peaks.

I became aware that I wasn't alone on the hill. There were two trekkers about my age; both seemed to be speaking German.

'G'day. Do you blokes speak English? Can you tell me what we're looking at here?' They were poring over a map and pointing to the distant ranges. They looked at me curiously for some time.

'You are English or American?'

'Neither. I'm Australian, mate.'

That seemed to spark their interest and they took great pains then to point out the different mountains as they became visible. As well as Kanchenjunga (third-highest in the world at 8565 metres), they pointed out Makalu (fifth-highest at 8462 metres or 27,765 feet). First climbed in 1955 by the incomparable Lionel Terray and his fellow Frenchman Jean Couzy, Makalu is a legendary peak familiar to me from my reading. I could hardly believe I was seeing it for real.

But my biggest surprise came when one of the trekkers said, 'You see that one wid da little bump? Dat is Everest.' I was shocked. It looked so small, just a little knob on the horizon surrounded by massive peaks. I was looking at the highest mountain in the world. It was about 160 kilometres away and looked nothing like its 8848 metres (29,028 feet). My companions also pointed out that some of the mountains we could see were in far-off Tibet. Kanchenjunga, the mountain I'd come to see, paled a little surrounded by this mountain magic. There are fourteen peaks in the world at 8000 metres or higher, and in the space of one sunrise I'd seen three of them.

I chatted with the trekkers. They were from Switzerland. Both were mountaineers doing their national service and had come to Darjeeling for instruction in climbing at the town's famous Himalayan Mountaineering Institute. We decided to have breakfast and I told them over *tsumpa* (porridge made from baked barley) and tea that I planned to leave the following day on a trek into the mountains north of Darjeeling to the villages of Sandak-phu and Phalut.

I had been unable to talk my new Swiss friends into accompanying me, so the following day I set out alone on the first genuine adventure of my life. Ten days later I staggered back into Darjeeling after a feast of sumptuous mountain views framed by a profusion of blooming rhododendrons, and nights spent in mud-walled, smoke-filled shepherds' huts living on a diet of rice, potatoes, dhal, bananas and more *tsumpa*. I had covered about 180 kilometres in ten days with adventures beyond counting, including looking down into Nepal and the closed countries of Sikkim and Tibet, while still standing on Indian territory. For a boy from western New South Wales on his first trip outside Australia, it was an extraordinary experience. At one point, my exploring instincts had overwhelmed my better judgement and I crossed the Indian border, heading for Gantok, the capital of Sikkim, in those days a closed city and a fabulously mysterious place. I was promptly escorted back into India by the Sikkim border patrol. A very serious guard, who could speak no English and wore no boots, convinced me of his intent by shoving his battered Lee Enfield .303 rifle under my nose. To my horror, looking down its barrel, I noticed that he had the safety catch back. But my love affair with the mountains had started, and all thoughts of travelling on to London were shelved. I hurried to pack and leave for Nepal.

I had one last night to kill in Darjeeling before leaving on the long bus ride to Kathmandu and I walked down to the town square known as Chowrasta. On arriving at the wide mall, I noticed a group of men proceeding slowly across the open space greeting passers-by and stopping to chat. They surrounded someone obviously important who attracted many courtly bows and greetings of *namasté*. The bows were accompanied by the

Nepalese salutation of hands pressed together in front of the chest, palms touching and fingers pointed upwards.

Now, who is a big enough deal in Darjeeling, I wonder, to stop the traffic? I knew the answer to my own question, as I'd seen his photo in many books, but I asked a passer-by for confirmation.

'Master Tenzing Norgay, the Tiger of Everest.' His broad Tibetan face beamed with pride as he watched his countryman.

My guess had been right. I'd spotted my first member of mountaineering's royalty. Tenzing, then in his early sixties, had recently retired after several decades as the director of field training at the Mountaineering Institute. He was smaller than I'd expected, but still had an upright posture and looked like he could put on a pack and go straight back up Everest. Here was the son of a yak herder from the Kharta Valley in Tibet, the man who had first stood on Everest's summit with Edmund Hillary and who had held up his ice axe with the flags attached for Hillary's famous summit photo. This was one of the first people whom, as a child, I had thought of as a real hero.

A week later I was bouncing along on top of a bus on a dusty road heading west from Kathmandu to the small Nepalese village of Pokhara. I had met another two Swiss mountaineers, Kurt Kestenholz and Peter Lehmann, in the Kathmandu youth hostel who, like me, were planning to make the trek out to Annapurna. Kurt rode with me on top of the bus. In those years the trek from Kathmandu to Everest base camp was becoming popular and a stream of travellers was heading out to walk, smoke dope or generally get wasted on cheap Nepali hash. I liked Peter and Kurt because they, like me, genuinely loved the mountains and weren't interested in drugs. I wanted to experience something different, and few people then were tackling the Annapurna trek.

I first saw the Annapurna mountain range not from some

romantic hilltop setting at sunrise, but at dusty noon from the top of our bus in Pokhara Bazaar. Baskets of chickens had provided a back rest, and all manner of tethered goats and other animals had competed with me and Kurt for space among the huge amount of luggage that had been stowed on the roof by the Nepali passengers. In my pack, which had served as a cushion for the journey, was Mum's copy of *Annapurna*.

On 22 April 1977, we climbed straight up out of Pokhara Bazaar to the small hamlet of Dhampus, where we spent the night. We aimed to reach the village of Ghandrung the following day. The next morning, we pushed upwards and westwards through driving rain and sleet. It was a bitter introduction to mountain weather, against which my two woolly Australian jumpers and a pair of jeans could provide no protection. Late in the evening we saw on a ridge in the distance the glow of cooking fires at Ghandrung. It looked so close, yet we had to cross a deep gorge to reach it and I was freezing. We descended 500 metres, to the Modi Khola River, which drains the southern side of the Annapurna massif, and forded its waters swollen by the torrential rain. It was then a 1000-metre climb straight up a slippery cliff through the freezing rain to get to the village. I was young and fit, with tireless leg drive and was determined that if my two stout Swiss companions could do it, then nothing would stop me.

We arrived at Ghandrung well after dark, soaking wet, and found refuge in a mud hut that, judging from the smell, had previously been used as an animal shelter. Dinner was potatoes, rice and dahl, and warm milky tea purchased from a villager. My clothes were saturated; my backpack was full of water and my R. M. Williams boots, great for riding horses in Australia, were filled with mud and had provided a refuge for half the leeches in the foothills of the Annapurna range. The wind, rain and sleet beat against the walls of the hut, but curled up in my sleeping bag, I was oblivious. Sometime during the night I realised that it was now quiet outside and I hoped the weather would clear enough for us to catch sight of our goal – the mighty Annapurna.

I was up before dawn eagerly looking to the north. The rain had vanished. Sunrise on a beautiful clear day in the Himalayas showed us Annapurna South and Machapuchare (6993 metres), the spectacular Fish Tail mountain, both so close I felt I could touch them. Annapurna, the alpha mountain of the whole range, wasn't visible, however, being tucked in behind its neighbour, the lower Annapurna South.

Peter, suffering from altitude sickness, headed back down after breakfast, but Kurt and I slogged upwards through the mud and leeches to the 3000-metre Ghoropani pass. Once more we slept in a mud hut, and once more we were up before dawn in order to climb nearby Poon Hill. This spot, now a major tourist destination that can be viewed on the internet, was in those days an isolated outpost and we had it to ourselves, enduring a chilly pre-dawn twilight as we eagerly awaited the first illumination of the peaks to the north. We weren't disappointed. Close up was the now-familiar Annapurna South and just behind it, visible for the first time, the ridges and summit of Annapurna, the mountain that had nearly killed Herzog and Lachenal. Here was the mountain that will forever be part of France but which had reached out and touched a farm boy in far-off Australia. The mountains glistened on the cloudless morning, with views stretching from Everest in the east to Dhaulagiri (the world's seventh-highest peak at 8167 metres) in the west.

'I suppose you've got plenty of mountains like this in Europe,' I said to Kurt.

'No, we have big mountains, but nothing like this. Mont Blanc is our biggest mountain, but it is only 4800 metres. These are really spectacular.'

'Like to climb that one, mate?' I nodded towards Annapurna. Kurt laughed, but didn't reply.

'Well, *I* couldn't do it; I tell you that for a fact,' I said. Standing there on that ridge in far-off Nepal, above the dusty village of Ghoropani where chickens ran around and small children peered shyly at strangers, I realised that only a very special person would even contemplate attempting to climb those mountains. I could see the sheer ice walls that would confront a climber and realised that, with my fear of heights, I would never see the view from the top of a towering peak.

Lacking proper clothing and equipment, we were forced to make a hasty retreat to Pokhara. From Nepal, I headed for Afghanistan. I had some incredible memories, a dose of malaria that would show up in Benares, in India, and a conviction that I would never climb a major mountain peak. While in Europe I learned to ski, and I would visit many minor mountains over the following years to enjoy this pastime, but I forgot about climbing big mountains for the next 28 years.

The sound of Anton's boots clomping down the hall shook me from my reminiscences. He had with him another pair of climbing boots, a pair of runners and a helmet. I tried on the helmet and climbing boots, which fitted well. I also tried on the battered old pair of runners, and they were comfortable enough. They would do the job. Anton then turned his attention to the pile of gear on my bed.

'What's that?' he asked, pointing to one of my leather belt pouches.

'That's my base plate compass. I never go anywhere without a compass.'

'You won't need that where we're going. You can leave it behind. What's in there?'

'That's my matches.'

'You won't need those, either. They can stay behind. What's the cup for?'

'I take that cup everywhere.'

'It can stay behind. There'll be a cup in Colin Todd Hut that you can use. What's in there? Is that a camera? Are you planning to take that?'

'Yeah, I'd hoped to.'

He just looked at me. I couldn't read what he was trying to say, and then he looked back at the camera. He made no further comment. He didn't seem to notice my copy of Herzog's book – or if he did, he didn't say. I wasn't even game to suggest that I put it in my pack. He checked my climbing harness to make sure that it would do the job and then, without further ado he left, saying he would meet me at eight the next morning.

I finished packing. Taking Anton's advice, I left behind my Leatherman knife and the matches, but I shoved the enamel cup and compass in my pack. The battered old copy of *Annapurna* stayed behind. I grabbed the map that Anton had left with me and headed out to find somewhere in Wanaka to have a meal.

While I waited for my dinner of roast lamb and potatoes at Muzzas Bar and Café, I carried out a ritual that I always perform before heading out into the wilderness. I have an unusual talent that I first became aware of at school – I only have to read a page of a book a couple of times and I can store it in my head as a picture. This came in very handy for history and English examinations, where I could regurgitate great slabs of Shakespeare and long history quotations from the reference books studied.

Where this skill was really useful was with maps. I'd discovered during my twenties that I could look at a map, close my eyes, look at it again, concentrate, close my eyes – and *click*, like a camera shutter opening, it would be imprinted in my brain: the rivers, the hills and other major landmarks, and the bearings in-between. In all the time I've been wandering in remote places I've never become lost. I put it down to this unusual gift.

I opened the 1:50,000 Aspiring map supplied by Alpine Guides that Anton had given me. Surprisingly, Mount Aspiring was right on the eastern edge of the map. The relevant peaks and landmarks for a full 360° mental snapshot just weren't there. It was like looking at a photo of someone's face scissored straight down the middle. I had only one eye, half a nose and a bit of mouth to work with – I had only half the story.

I was bitterly disappointed. Map reading and navigation were areas where I knew I could approach Anton as an equal. With only half a map, my chances of retaining some independence and using my skills to make an important contribution to the climb went out the window. I would now be entirely dependent on Anton's knowledge of the high country. I would be entirely in the hands of someone whom I'd only just met. It was very unsettling.

My meal arrived, and as I tucked into the tender local lamb I went through my ritual. I memorised the location of Colin Todd Hut, northwest of Aspiring summit, and north of Bevan Col. Mount French would be a large landmark, about three kilometres south as we tackled the peak. There appeared to be nothing to the north of Aspiring other than mountains and glacial wilderness. Over my healthy dinner and a pint of New Zealand lager, I committed to memory all the major landmarks and bearings.

Chapter 5

Sum of All Fears:
Colin Todd Hut

No other mountain gives me this sense of isolation, of detachment from earthy things. On Aspiring there is no point which can compete, no high neighbour to relieve the aloofness of the place.

PAUL POWELL, *MEN ASPIRING*

James Turnbull Thompson, the chief surveyor of the province of Otago, recorded the following in his field book in December 1857: 'Distant about 40 miles is a very lofty peak which I called Mt Aspiring.'

Mountains are typically named after people, mainly men. Why Thompson chose to name this peak after a human desire to want or seek something of great value is unknown, but it seemed appropriate to the challenge that I knew lay ahead.

As far as is known, Thompson was the first European to sight the glistening one. My first view, from ground level, was on the road ten kilometres north of Wanaka.

Anton stopped his truck and we both got out for a look and to take photographs. He had picked me up at exactly 8 am. After dumping my excess gear in his garage, we headed north around

Lake Wanaka and into the foothills of the mountains. We had only been on the road a short time when we rounded a bend in the lake and there, sprawling across the horizon and piercing the sky, was the icecap summit of our destination, Mount Aspiring.

It's hard to describe what I felt. It looked further away than when I'd seen it from the plane, and I was now looking up from below at its ruggedness. It looked wild and steep, with ridges running up from two sides to a perfect summit cone. It was summer where we were standing, with lush meadows and fat sheep imparting a rural English feel to the countryside. Up there, it was winter. Up there, the blizzard reigned supreme. The mountain seemed to be saying, 'If you're coming up here, you're undertaking deadly serious business and you'd better know what you're doing.' I was still shocked that I was there and planning to climb it. The potential for a fall off any of those ridges seemed enormous.

Anton and I drove largely in silence. This was the part of expeditions that I hated. I would shortly have to trust my life, in extremely trying circumstances, to someone I'd only just met. We hadn't even had the opportunity to sit down over a cup of tea and get to know each other, let alone form any mutual trust. He didn't know me, and I didn't know him. Time is vital in coming to understand someone's strengths and weaknesses, and how they might react in certain situations. This is the basis of mutual respect. I suspected that Anton would presume the worst, presume that I was incompetent, and treat me accordingly.

We drove slowly. Anton had booked a helicopter to pick us up at Raspberry Flat, on the west branch of the Matukituki River, at 10.30 am. He called at a farmer's house to check the helicopter's availability and we then drove on. However, when we finally pulled into Raspberry Flat, all was pandemonium. We arrived just as the helicopter did.

'They're not supposed to be here for another half-hour,' Anton said, pulling up next to the helicopter pad. He bolted out the door and ran up to the helicopter pilot. From the hurried conversation I saw being conducted under the beating rotor blades, I presumed that we would be leaving very shortly. Anton jogged back.

'They're early; they've got to lift four climbers off Bevan Col. He's leaving now. C'mon, we've got to get going.'

He flung open the rear of his truck and we pulled out both packs. I turfed my trusty old Scarpa hiking boots into the back and quickly pulled on the climbing boots. There was no time to lace them. Helmets were strapped on our packs, and Anton handed me an ice axe, short-handled ice hammer and a set of crampons, which I also lashed to my pack. We had been there no longer than five minutes by the time we ran to the helicopter, as I pulled on my Macpac shell jacket. I threw my pack onto one of the skids and Anton lashed it down as I jumped into the front seat of the chopper, grabbed a set of headphones and shoved them on, all the while continuing to do up my jacket. I heard Anton jump in the back and slam the door.

Without further ado, the pilot twisted the throttle grip on the collective stick, the rotors began to pound in that rhythmic thud I've heard many times from choppers used for mustering in the outback, and we lifted off, the helicopter adopting the familiar nose-down aspect on takeoff. The green square of the landing pad quickly fell away. Behind us soared a sharp pinnacle that I recognised from my map reading the previous night as being the Shark's Tooth.

That's good. That'll be my landmark on the way back, I thought. I memorised how it looked and where the carpark was from the summit. The helicopter turned west for a magnificent rush down the sheer-sided Matukituki River valley. We were heading for a small saddle on the southern side of the Bonar Glacier called Bevan Col. It was the low point between Mount Bevan and Mount Joffre, and gave easy access to the glacier from where we would climb to Colin Todd Hut. This famous hut would be home, where we would shelter from the weather, while we organised our attempt on Mount Aspiring.

The journey to the col by helicopter is spectacular – unless, like me, you're frightened of heights. We veered to the north as we flew up to the end of the valley, then began to climb. I had the unnerving feeling which always comes when I sit in the front seat of a bubble-fronted helicopter of looking straight down between my feet at almost a kilometre of air. We were flying straight up the cliffs and gorges of New Zealand's central highlands and were about to land right on the country's spine. From where we had taken off, the rivers flow east into the Pacific. When we landed, the rivers would flow to the west into the Tasman Sea. The cliffs towered above us and quickly shed their mantle of silver beech forest, replacing it with a blanket of ice and snow. As we came up over the top of the New Zealand divide, the wind roaring from out of the northwest, out of Bass Strait, pounded into the helicopter, buffeting and rocking it violently. I hung on, my knuckles white on the overhead hand grip. The pilot had obviously flown this route many times, and wrestled confidently with the controls. I could see the saddle to which we were heading dead ahead – a low cleft between two snow-capped pinnacles.

Suddenly, I spied on the col four people clustered on top of their packs, a small knot of humanity surrounded by whiteness. The chopper yawed and rolled as it took the full brunt of the wind coming across the col, but the figures below us gradually loomed larger and larger and finally, with a thump, we were down. Anton slapped me on the back, flung open the door of the chopper and pointed to a spot near where the climbers had jumped to their feet before running towards the helicopter. Everyone seemed in a mad panic. I was hot on Anton's heels with my pack in my hand. He intercepted one of the climbers, who I presumed was the guide.

'What's it like? Did you get up?' he shouted over the pounding roar of the chopper.

'No, tried the ridge, but it's loaded up . . . Lotta snow. Can't get up there . . . avalanche.'

The rest of his words were drowned out as I ran past, but I clearly heard the last one. I was in the mountains now for real.

Anton nodded, threw his pack on the ground next to mine and then ran back to close the doors of the helicopter while I made sure I had everything. He then sprinted back to where I was waiting as the blades began to *thump, thump, thump* with increasing urgency. We spread-eagled ourselves over our packs and waited face down in the snow. I snuck a peek at the helicopter and to my surprise it had beaten off the col and was only about five metres above us as it fought for altitude against the wind, which threatened to knock it backwards down the valley. I could see the faces of the pilot and passengers peering down. The rotor blades set up a blizzard of whirling ice and snow and made a frightful racket. But the pilot obviously knew his stuff and soon roared over us, out over the glacier, looping back in a graceful arc and thundering overhead before disappearing down into the valley. The *thud, thud, thud* gradually diminished and soon all was silence. We were alone in the wilderness of Bevan Col. My first mountain climb had begun. There was no turning back now.

Anton was all business from the moment the chopper headed out over the glacier. He leapt to his feet and immediately ripped a coiled climbing rope out of his pack and threw it on the ground. Next came his harness, which he put on as I watched and then followed suit. He grabbed one end of the rope and I took the other, and we flaked it back and forth between our feet until we reached the midpoint and had equal-length piles of rope coiled between us. He tied his end of the rope on to his harness with a neat figure eight knot and watched me do the same. When I'd finished, he checked the knot.

'I don't do it that way,' he said. I'd tied the tail end of the knot back on the rope, as I'd been shown in Sydney. Anton took the tail of the rope and fed it back through the figure eight knot once more. 'That's how I like to do it,' he said.

He then began to wind the coils around one shoulder and then under the opposite arm with a whipping motion. I used the method Dave Lucas had shown me, of hanging on to my belt. I did a neat job and was pleased, but as I went to tie a bight in the rope like Dave had shown me, Anton, who was watching closely, said: 'No, you've got those coils too low.' He grabbed the coils and pulled on them. 'They're sitting down near your belt. I want them up a little bit higher, just under your ribcage. Do it again.' I'd had my first, mild rebuke.

I threw the coils on the ground and repeated the procedure, holding my hand a little higher, tied off and then clipped on to my harness. There was now about six metres of rope on the ground between me and Anton.

Anton then pulled a legionnaire's cap out of his pack and threw it to me. These peaked caps have a cape down the back to prevent sunburn – a real menace when crossing a glacier. I unstrapped the long-handled ice axe and trekking pole off my pack and checked that all the straps were done up on my harness and doubled back through the buckles, as I'd been shown in Sydney. Anton checked his pack before slinging it on. I put on my pack and stood waiting for instructions.

'Now, this's what we're going to do. We're going to side-step down here onto the glacier, following the tracks of that group of climbers who just went out. There's a lot of snow, so we're going to have to be careful. I'm going to try to get across without putting on crampons. I want you to carry your axe in your uphill hand and use it like a walking stick. Secure yourself as you go down. Use the trekking pole in the downhill hand. You go first, I'll come along behind.'

As I stood on the col, about to set off with Anton, I wouldn't have changed places with anyone in the world. A dream was about to become a reality. Some of the great names, many long gone, came to mind: Gaston Rébuffat, Lachenal and the great Lionel Terray.

This is fantastic, I thought, standing in the snow with a pack on my back, a harness and rope at my waist, and heavy climbing boots on my feet. For the first time, I felt part of the brotherhood of the rope. I felt I belonged there. Images came to me of brave men climbing steep walls standing on the front points of their crampons, of men roped together bending into a blizzard, of men fighting to get down off a mountain in a storm while desperately trying to save each other's lives, and of the smiling faces of tired climbers sitting over a cup of tea at the end of a hair-raising day. I felt I was now part of those images of friendship familiar to me from my childhood books.

I thought about the great climbs: Eric Shipton and Bill Tilman in 1934 forcing their way up the Rishi Ganga gorge into the Nanda Devi sanctuary; Lachenal and Terray on the Nordwand of the Eiger in 1947; Pete Schoening on K2 in 1953 saving six of his friends from certain death with a thin hemp rope anchored by his ice axe jammed behind a rock. I was now part of this. There were also my countrymen, Greg Mortimer and Tim Macartney-Snape, who made the first Australian ascent of Everest by a new route on the North Face and without bottled oxygen. I had an ice axe in my hand the same as those in all the black-and-white photos I'd seen. I had boots and a harness. And, most important of all, I was tied to someone else with a rope. We were going to live or die together; succeed or fail as a team. In my own small way, I'd joined this elite band of brothers – a band whose lives spread over a century and who had come from many different countries but shared a love of adventure, a pride in physical fitness, and the belief that men and women could be enriched by undertaking difficult challenges with friends. No, there wasn't enough money in the world to induce me to be anywhere else at that moment than on a rope on Bevan Col, a rope that ran from me down through the years to my childhood heroes. I was roped to the brotherhood and my dreams. A circle that had begun in my childhood was complete.

We had been in a blur of activity since setting foot on the col and I had no time to take in the magnificence of our surroundings. Mount Aspiring dominated the view. It was right in our face; everywhere else was a wilderness of snow. Between us and the mountain, down a steep slope, lay the Bonar Glacier, stark and bare, glistening pristine white under a dense layer of fresh snow. To our left was the steep slope of Mount Bevan, but I had scant time to examine it before I was climbing down it. For the first time I felt the time pressure that would become one of my enduring memories of the next five days.

Herzog never mentioned that mountaineering was done in such a rush, I thought as I began side-stepping down towards the glacier. I wanted time to stop and look at the view, to take it in. However, I forgot about my surroundings and did as instructed, gingerly putting each boot into the hole left by the retreating climbers. Anton followed along behind, watching my every step. It was a beautiful, cloudless day. As we descended into the sheltered bowl of the glacier, the wind died and we climbed down onto a still, silent wilderness. On reaching the bottom, Anton took the lead and we set off across the vastness of the Bonar Glacier.

I still didn't get a chance to look at the scenery. I'm sure it was magnificent but I was concentrating on walking exactly in Anton's tracks. Everything felt strange. The climbing boots were stiff and heavy, and with the rope stretching out between us I had to walk at exactly the same pace as Anton. It was my job to pace myself so that the rope between us just touched the ground – too fast, and the rope would become entangled in my boots and I'd end up walking over the top of it. Too slow and the rope would pull tight, and Anton would be towing me.

The sound of my helmet, crampons and ice stake rattling on my pack and the measured pace of my breathing combined with the squeak of our boots on the frozen surface of the glacier to provide a metronomic rhythm as we walked along. I looked only at the ground in front of me. All glaciers are riven by deep crevasses and to go into one can mean a terrible death. This risk of glacier travel was uppermost in my mind, as Dave Lucas had left me in no doubt that a fall into a crevasse would mean I was in the shit no matter which way I looked at it.

I tried to match Anton's crab-like gait. He took very small steps and walked like a duck, but he seemed to cover an extraordinary amount of ground. I had to lengthen my stride to keep up. Anton's eyes were everywhere and he followed exactly in the tracks used by the earlier climbers. Occasionally, he would stop and prod the snow in front of us with the long handle of his axe and divert slightly around a furrow in the snow that signalled a crevasse. Three kilometres away, the tin roof of Colin Todd Hut was a red dot on a bench of the northwest ridge – our destination was splendid in its isolation.

'We'll pull up here. Have a drink. Take a photo if you want to,' Anton said, after we'd been going for an hour. As I sucked on the water from my Platypus bladder, I really took in the mountain for the first time. It towered above us. Anton explained the route of our climb.

'We'll get to the bergschrund at dawn, then climb up that rock band and head straight up the ramp to the ridge. It's pretty easy from there.' He pointed out the route with his ski pole. It didn't look easy to me. The ramp is what is known in mountaineering-speak as the crux of the climb. This word appears in every mountaineering book written. It is the puzzle, or problem – the core challenge of the climb which must be solved or overcome to reach the summit. But the ramp is an unorthodox crux. Most key mountain challenges are encountered on ascent. The ramp has killed more climbers on descent, so once the climber gets to the top of it, he has to conquer it once more on the way down. It is, indeed, a most uncharacteristic crux.

'This is really unusual. Normally, at this time of the year, if I was taking climbers up here we'd be on rock most of the way. It would just be a simple scramble. Because we've had so much snow, and more's expected, there'll be snow and ice cover all the way to the summit. Have to be careful. We'll be climbing it in winter conditions. Look at the ramp; it's covered in snow.'

He pointed out the ramp soaring from the bergschrund high on the glacier rim up to the northwest ridge. Around 50 people have been killed on Aspiring, about half of them peeling off the ramp. I had seen many photos of it, but seeing it for real was a different proposition. It looked wicked – steep and down-sloping, so you could either fall backwards down it or roll sideways off it. I didn't know what to say, so I just stood in silence, taking it all in. I felt conscious of my complete inexperience.

'The thing that really strikes me about this mountain is how it's here on its own. In Nepal the mountains are all jumbled up together, and one's hiding behind another or lost in a maze of other mountains, like Kanchenjunga,' I said, trying to say something sensible.

Anton nodded and continued to stare at the mountain while sipping on his water. From where we stood, Aspiring was an exercise in geometry – a perfect four-sided pyramid of which we could see one side. Two long ridges, the northwest on the left and the southwest on the right, swept straight up to the ice-capped summit and framed the sheer wall of the southwest face. Mountains are usually climbed by their ridges which, though exposed to extreme weather and often comprising treacherous weathered rock underfoot, are less steep. Faces are where reputations are made, notoriety is gained and lives are lost. Often sheer and swept by avalanche and stone fall, they are for experts, not novices putting themselves to the sort of humble test that had brought me here. There is a saying in golf: 'Drive for show and putt for dough.' In climbing, the faces are for show, while the ridges get you the dough.

The ramp was an exercise in bastardised geometry – Euclid after a night on the drink. It was too steep for a ridge and not sheer enough for a face. I found the thought of it frightening and the whole presence of the mountain intimidating. One word could describe those long walls and stony, snow-covered ridges: brutal.

'Unless the wind drops and we get a day or two without snow, we won't be going anywhere,' Anton said. 'We'll probably get some snow tonight. Let's get going.'

I looked around. Other than a few wispy clouds blowing in from the northwest, there was nothing to break the perfect blue that stretched above us from horizon to horizon. *How does he know that?* I wondered. *That's the stuff I've got to learn; how he knows it's going to snow tonight.*

As we resumed our procession across the glacier, I felt the huge presence of the mountain, as if it were watching Anton and me. Not for the first time did I sense an animate spirit in nature. I'd felt it in the desert. There it was benign. Here I felt the mountain was hunting me, watching carefully, waiting for an opportunity to pounce on me. Every facet gleamed in the sun. I should have felt awed by its beauty. Instead, I felt unnerved. I was terrified.

After about an hour we reached the base of a steep cliff running up to the hut. I was surprised, after all the training I'd done, how tiring a slog it had been. The heat radiating from the glacier was ferocious. I swapped one of the trekking poles I was using for the long-handled ice axe I carried on my pack. Anton shortened the rope between us.

'The other climbers have cut steps, so step where they did.'

Anton set off, and I followed. I plunged the axe handle into the snow before taking each step. It gave me a sense of security, and I concentrated on not looking down. We reached the top without incident. I turned and looked back the way we'd come. It was only 200 metres down the slope to the glacier, but the realisation struck me that a fall down even this innocuous slope would kill. This was a very serious business.

The Department of Conservation runs huts right through the remote parts of New Zealand's back country to shelter climbers and trekkers from the often atrocious weather. Colin Todd Hut, on a rocky bench of the Shipowner Ridge, was first built in 1949. It has blown away or fallen down twice since that time. The latest version, built in 1996, commands spectacular views of mounts Aspiring and French and the ice river of the Bonar.

We tramped up to the hut and in through the entry vestibule, pausing on the verandah only long enough to take off our boots and shed the rope. Anton asked me to hang all my 'hard' climbing gear – crampons, ice axe and hammer, helmet and harness – on the pegs provided. I put my heavy boots against the wall. The now neatly coiled climbing rope also went on a hook. Another door opened into a second room containing twelve double-tier sleeping platforms spread along two walls, each covered with a thin foam mattress. A stainless steel bench ran down one side. The room was spartan – unheated with no running water – but it was clean and tidy and well maintained. Huts like this have saved the lives of numerous climbers forced to shelter from the weather. This would be home for us for the next five days. If the weather was unkind, we would shelter here before returning to Bevan Col without making any attempt on the mountain. The weather was one of the great imponderables of mountain climbing.

'Hello, we've got a couple of other residents,' Anton said, pointing at two sleeping bags unrolled on the benches. 'They must be out climbing or somewhere on the glacier.' He peered out though the small hut windows but could see nothing.

'Right, we'll have some lunch. Then we'll go out and spend the afternoon showing you how to use the gear. You've never used crampons, right?'

I nodded. I got the impression that Anton was full of restless energy and didn't sit around much.

Early afternoon we emerged from the hut into a different world. Heavy banks of cloud now cloaked the top of Mount Aspiring and parts of the ridge above the hut were already in flitting shadow. Anton had shown me on the verandah how to attach the crampons onto my boots by clipping up the front toe-clip and rear bail. He showed me how to carry the long-handled ice axe – the French call it the *piolet*, or little axe – with my hand wrapped around the adze (the sharp metal end of the tool), and how and when to use the ice hammer.

Roped up, we began to ascend the slope of the Shipowner Ridge behind the hut. I tried to walk how Dave Lucas had shown me in Sydney. It was impossible.

'No! *Fuck* no. Don't do it that way, that's really dangerous. You're rolling your knee and you've got your points off the snow,' Anton snapped at me early in the session, pointing an accusing axe handle at my boots and the offending crampons. 'You've got to get all points on the snow.' I would try again, but to no avail. My ankles are slightly pronated and as I put a boot down my knee would roll inward and lift the crampon points on the outside edge of the boot off the snow.

'No! I've told you to do it properly – get *all* the points on the snow,' Anton shouted. Never enormously confident, I quickly felt demoralised.

Above the hut, near where we were training, was a small crevasse. Anton stepped lightly over it. As I followed, the points on my lower boot slid off the snow and with a heavy thump I landed on my side with one leg dangling in the black hole and the other lying on the snow. It gave me a fright.

'That happened because you're not using the crampons like I showed you,' Anton said quietly.

Back and forth, and up and down, the slope we went. Anton showed me the basic technique of self-arrest, by sliding on his back down the slope, rolling on to his stomach with the axe across his chest, and then ramming the pick into the snow until his descent slowed. I tried it, clumsily at first. I had to resist the impulse to dig in my boots, which is the kiss of death in a sliding fall. Over and over we practised, until Anton was satisfied. I nearly rammed the adze into my face several times and wouldn't have backed myself to arrest a fall on a very steep slope.

'You ever had to do that for real?' I asked.

'No. You never want to get in a situation where you have to use it.'

We also tried glissading – sliding down a slope on your arse, then pulling up using the sharp point of the ice axe handle. That at least was fun.

We kept at it until late afternoon, by which time the hut and mountain were shrouded in mist and cloud. The sky had disappeared. Grey cloud covered everything, and the wind, out of the northwest, had picked up and started to bite. As we retreated into the hut, it began to snow.

The other two hut residents arrived just as we did. Over a cup of tea, we learned that they were brothers, both doctors from Perth aged in their mid-thirties. Recent graduates from the Technical

Mountaineering course, they were also out on their first serious mountain climb together.

After the tea was finished, I wandered out onto the verandah into the deepening gloom of evening. A storm was clearly brewing. Some of the clouds were black now and the summit of the mountain was visible only intermittently. It had a malevolent look. Extreme apprehension weighed on me, festering from my irrational dread that the mountain was alive and watching me, waiting for me to set foot on its slopes. Anton's sharp tongue in the afternoon had flattened what little confidence I had. I felt every day of my 54 years and for the first time ever felt that I may be facing a challenge that was beyond me. I was profoundly frightened.

At 6 pm, Anton pulled a small ring-binder from his pack, remarking, 'Weather report time.'

A small radio crackled to life under the kitchen bench. I hadn't noticed it previously. The warden at Aspiring Hut in the valley was calling all the huts in the area, such as ours and the one at French Ridge. Anton picked up the set, keyed the mike and reported on the number of climbers at Colin Todd and their plans. The other huts did the same. The radio operator then read the weather report: 'Morning rain then clearing, though isolated afternoon showers possible. Northwesterlies 70 kilometres per hour about high ground easing, and tending west or southwest. Freezing level gradually lowering to 1800 metres.'

Colin Todd Hut sits at 1800 metres, meaning that if the freezing level lowered to 1800 metres, everything would be iced up and slippery as soon as we stepped off the verandah.

While the report was being read out, Anton leafed through a sheaf of meteorological charts in his folder. He thanked the radio operator and then closed his charts. 'Well, we won't be going up tonight.' That was it. I looked at the young West Australian climbers and guessed that Anton had just made a decision for them, too. I regretted my lack of knowledge. I understand the weather of Central Australia like the workings of a fine watch. Here I had no idea what had just happened.

I headed for my sleeping bag with a copy of the Mount Aspiring guidebook that I had found in the hut. I opened it to the chapter on weather. I was surprised, as most Australians probably would be, that at 44°22' south Mount Aspiring is closer to the South Pole than is Hobart. It's in the region known as the 'Roaring Forties'. In years past, courageous schooner captains, sailing from England to Australia around South Africa, raced down into these latitudes chasing the fierce winds. Storms thunder across the globe, passing through Bass Strait or under Tasmania before smashing into the bottom end of New Zealand's South Island. The winds we were experiencing were probably born out in the Indian Ocean and had travelled thousands of kilometres to vent their spleen on the slopes of our mountain. I now understood why northwesterlies were bad. The same weather that has sunk yachts in the Sydney to Hobart yacht race was now pounding on the walls of the hut and would consign our climbing endeavours to oblivion unless it swung around to the south. I switched off my head torch and was soon fast asleep.

Sunday, 3 December 2006, the day of our intended climb, was one of those lost days in my life. Anton stayed on his bunk and read for most of the day. After breakfast, I wandered outside to check the conditions. I was wearing only thin merino gloves as I'd forgotten the shells, which were inside the hut. My hands immediately turned to stone. The wind nearly knocked me over, and the wind chill sucked the warmth out of me. The Perth climbers ventured out into the blizzard to practise some belaying up the slope but were soon beaten back inside, blue from the cold. I retreated to my bunk and crawled into my sleeping bag. Everyone dozed on and off, the monotony broken periodically by a pumping sound, then the hiss of fuel stoves being lit to make tea. It was very pleasant in my down sleeping bag, with a beanie pulled over my ears, even though the hut was unheated. I had no interest in going climbing. Years of reading climbing books had prepared me for the reality that a core element of mountaineering is waiting patiently for conditions to be suitable.

I lay on my back, hands clasped behind my head and stared at the timber base of the upper bunk. Screwed into it were a number of hooks where previous climbers had hung socks, gloves and thermals to dry. My gear now adorned the hooks, and the wool inners and nylon shell gloves swung slightly on their lanyards from the gentle movement of the air inside the hut. The right-hand glove hung straight down, but the left-hand inner and glove were already adopting the misshapen, claw-like appearance of my damaged left hand. I hated looking at that glove; it was a metaphor for a broken life.

I dozed off. Images of Lionel Terray and Tenzing Norgay, in black-and-white photographs, drifted though my consciousness. These men were always smiling. They didn't have to climb mountains to prove something to themselves; they climbed them because the mountains were there and to have fun. They didn't have to search for role models. They had fathers. I had to make mine up, to conjure them out of thin air, out of photos and stories in books.

I looked over to where Anton lay propped up on his bunk. He was reading. I would have liked to ask him why he climbed, but I held my tongue. Anton had said hardly a word all day except when I'd made a mistake and he had corrected me. I hadn't enjoyed what happened outside on the previous afternoon because Anton was reminding me too much of my stepfather. Days like this had sometimes ended badly for me.

As a sixteen-year-old I'd come home one day just before dark, after working since sunrise fencing. It had been a hot, lonely day slamming in steel fence posts with a heavy, iron hand-rammer. I'd shifted and laid tons of fence posts and was dirty and tired but felt I'd done a man's work and there might be some acknowledgement given. I walked though the kitchen without saying anything, into the bathroom, filled the basin and washed the day's sweat and grime from my face. I lifted my head from the basin to look through the bathroom window, out over the verandah. A crazy pattern of lines radiated out from a hole in the middle of the plate glass. I was dumbstruck. It hadn't been like that in the morning.

Jesus, that looks like a bullet hole! I poked my index finger though the hole. Curious now, I walked out on to the verandah and at the same height found a similar hole through the flyscreen.

I was really alarmed now and raced back inside. Sure enough, on the bathroom wall opposite the basin, a similar-sized hole had been punched through the plaster wall. I ran out into the kitchen eager to alert Mum and the old man who were standing watching me and deep in discussion.

'Have you seen this?' I crossed to the kitchen following the trajectory and pointing to where a large gap in the louvered kitchen windows showed that one of the glass panes had been blown out. I strode outside and sure enough shattered glass covered the cement walkway and the remains of a torn flyscreen hung limply. I flew back inside, eager to warn everyone.

I was about to say, 'Someone's taken a shot at us. It's a big calibre. Looks like a .303 or .308. It's gone right through the house.' I never got to say it.

'What do you know about this? Did you take the rifle out with you today?' My stepfather was furious and his face was flushed. This was shouted at me across the kitchen.

'What?' I faced him, speechless.

'Were you shooting today? Someone could've been killed.' The accusation was clear.

'What? D'ya think *I* did this?' I exploded.

'I was just asking . . .'

'Don't you *dare* fucking blame me for this. Something goes wrong and I get the blame straight away.' I burst into tears and stood in the middle of the kitchen sobbing. I'd never used a four-letter word before, let alone in front of my mother. She screamed and ran out of the room leaving just the two of us.

My stepfather stood red-faced and shocked. 'Don't you speak to me like that. I never spoke to my father like that.'

'Well, don't you fucking blame me for things I didn't do. You never blame your own fucking kids for anything that goes wrong.' I stepped towards him, my fists curled in tight balls and I now looked down on him. For the first time I saw fear there, as well as shock and anger. I couldn't do it, even though I felt over-whelmed by a sense of injustice.

I turned and stormed out of the house, banging the door so hard that the glass quarter-pane shattered.

I headed for the garage where the lethal Lee Enfield firearm stood against the wall. I picked it up, pulled back the bolt and no spent cartridge came flying out. The magazine was empty. I sniffed the breech. The unmistakable smell of unburnt gun oil – it hadn't been fired. I placed my hand over the muzzle – it was cold. I looked down the barrel from the muzzle end. Clean – no cordite grains. This was the only rifle we had that was capable of doing damage like I'd just seen. Whoever had done it hadn't done it with this firearm.

I walked out of the garage into the night and kept going. I wasn't going back inside. I walked for miles through the bush and across creeks, climbing fences as the stars wheeled overhead and the moon left the sky. Dawn found me sitting on our wood-heap, waiting for the house to stir. I wasn't game to go inside. I felt like I didn't have a home anymore and didn't belong anywhere.

I felt like a piece of human crap, as emotionally dead as the chain-sawed logs on which I sat.

I was frightened of what would happen. I thought there was a chance I'd be sent away again. But the injustice of it ate away at me. A man who'd never brought himself to have more than a short conversation with me dumped a shocking allegation at the feet of someone who by sixteen was already a crack shot and had learned firearm safety from an expert – my stepfather. It was the only thing we'd ever shared and he knew how careful I was. It was the ultimate breach of my trust and shattered my self-esteem.

Just after sunrise, Mum found me still on the woodheap. She came and sat next to me and we talked. I railed against the injustice, while she told me, that for her sake, I had to apologise. I didn't want to. We never learned who blew the holes in the wall, probably an illegal shooter some miles away. I screwed up the courage to apologise. It was never acknowledged and it was never the same again. Some of the respect had gone and the farm would never again be even the modest home it had been until then. From then I was alone, as I realised Mum had to juggle her other children and her relationship with her husband as well as with me. An impossible job.

The hatred of authority and injustice and of being spoken down to that had been implanted at Croagh Patrick was now firmly established and would persist through my life. I didn't like catching the edge of *anyone*'s tongue, especially someone in authority and especially when I was giving my utmost at something. Anton had reminded me of this and I now had a battle on my hands, a battle with my demons. The scolding I received as a child in Croagh Patrick for getting my head planted in a bowl of porridge was bearing bitter fruit.

I tried to banish these thoughts and to understand the client–guide relationship. I'd paid Anton to get me to the summit and down again. That was it. He had no interest in me as a person, had not asked me one question about myself – the obvious one being why I suddenly wanted to take up mountaineering at 54. He didn't know what I did for a living, didn't know if I was married or not. Of my kids, he had no idea. He knew that following the climb he'd never see me again and so he wasn't interested in any form of bonding or friendship. Likewise, he offered no information about himself. I found it curious that two men who were about to risk their lives together wouldn't get to know each other a little. Amazingly, he didn't try to find out how I'd react in a crisis. My inexperience had the potential to kill him up on the mountain. Why didn't he try and find out what he was dealing with? His quiet presence dominated the hut.

Another weather report came at 6 pm. Anton hunched over the radio, this time writing down what was said. I only caught '. . . the southwest flow over the park is weakening as a high over the Tasman Sea extends to a ridge over the South Island.' I thought a high over the South Island indicated fine weather, but I wasn't sure. I looked at Anton for a sign. Nothing. Outside, it continued to blow a gale. A trip outside to the toilet shed perched on a rock twenty metres from the hut was a matter for an emergency only. It was easier to hang on.

After dinner, Anton slung a rope up to a hook attached to the hut ceiling. He then instructed me to set up the rope the way I'd been shown in Sydney and to climb it. He saw me clip on the tibloc slings Dave Lucas had made. 'You don't need those,' he said. 'Just use prusiks.'

'Can't, sorry. I can't manipulate the knots. This is easier for me.'

No comment.

He then showed me how to tie the Kiwi coils, whipping the rope around himself in a blurring motion. I tried his method and just couldn't manage it because of my left hand and reverted to the slower method I'd learned in Sydney.

'Too slow, but if you're happy with that, then use it.' He checked my harness fit and that I knew how to strap it on properly. The two Perth climbers watched us intently, particularly Anton's way of tying a figure eight knot and his method of tying off the coils to the karabiner on his harness. He spoke with quiet authority from long experience, and we three novices just watched. I don't know if they felt it, but I sensed the vast gulf that existed between Anton and us. He belonged to a proud tradition.

The first mountaineers who pioneered the sport were mostly from the British professions, such as doctors, lawyers and professors. They had two vital ingredients for amateur mountain climbing: money and leisure time. Usually men of intellectual achievement, they sought the challenges and dangers of mountains as a counterpoint to their sedentary lives.

They learned rock climbing in Britain, but were under-done for the higher peaks of the continent. Undeterred, they hired local guides, ultimately forming some famous climbing partnerships. The combination of English, French and Italian gentlemen and alpine guides produced plenty of first ascents, such as the first summits of Mont Blanc and the Matterhorn, but would reach its finest moment on Annapurna in the partnership between Maurice Herzog and the Chamonix guides Terray, Lachenal and Rébuffat. It was, and remains, a more complex relationship than ever exists between employer and employee. As I was finding out, I was paying the bills, but there was no doubt who was boss.

As the clients gained experience, they no longer needed the guides who then turned to inexperienced tourists for employment. Many an overweight client, whose climbing ambitions far exceeded his athletic ability, was dragged, panting and terrified, to the top of a famous peak for a summit photograph. This was the category to which I belonged. No experience or skills, just the financial resources to buy a guide and get him to put his life on the line.

When Europe's gentlemen mountaineers moved on to the conquest of mountain ranges in far-flung parts of the world, particularly the Himalayas, many hired local peasants as porters and taught them the basics of climbing so that they could make meaningful contributions to a mountaineering campaign. This encouraged the development of a new type of mountaineer, the Asian mountain peasant. Born and raised in high mountains, these men had short stocky frames, lungs like furnace bellows, and blood that soaked oxygen out of thin air, making them uniquely adapted to load carrying at high altitudes. The Sherpas of Nepal became the world's most hardy and enduring mountaineers. They would be immortalised by my boyhood hero, Sherpa Tenzing Norgay.

The pinnacle of guiding prowess traditionally was membership of the French Company of Guides at Chamonix. Anton belonged to the more modern International Federation of Mountain Guide Associations (IFMGA). These men, and more recently women, ply their trade up where the mighty peaks punch the sky and the blizzards rage, making mountain guiding one of the world's most dangerous professions. Even though I thought he couldn't communicate and he reminded me unnervingly of my stepfather, Anton's quiet authority shone out in the hut that night and he held everyone's attention during this impromptu lesson.

At the end of the training session, Anton said to the Perth climbers, 'If the weather clears, we'll be going at 4 am and I want you two to wait half an hour to give us a head start and I don't want you climbing round above us on the ramp. That way you can follow in the tracks we make. Understood?' They nodded without argument. What we all felt was Anton's concern that two novice climbers were a good chance of coming off. If they peeled on the ramp and we were in the fall-line below them, all four of us would perish. Without warning, two roped climbers would come hurtling out of the darkness, down the face and before we had time to move they'd sweep us off as well. The rope in this situation becomes a scythe – a lethal cord between two heavy human missiles sweeping all life below them off the mountain. Anton was also backing his skill to keep *us* on the wall so *we* didn't fall back on *them*.

Later, as I helped Anton pack away the rope and gear in the vestibule, I had one of those lucky breaks for which there is no accounting. Hanging on the wall were the Perth boys' harnesses. They had the latest gear and it was the best that money could buy. Hanging from a gear loop on one of the harnesses were two Black Diamond Turbo Express ice screws. I had never seen an ice screw except in books and gingerly lifted one out of its plastic sheath.

'How do these work?' I asked Anton.

He took the 22 centimetre screw from me and, using his fingers to represent a wall of ice, he pulled a small handle down on the end of the screw and wound it in, then back out. 'Simple, you just turn the handle. They're easy to get in and out. These look like they've never been used.'

He replaced the screw in its sheath on the harness. He then picked up a set of Petzl twelve-point crampons hanging next to the harness and examined them closely. They were also like new. He indicated the wicked-looking, fang-like front points. 'Too aggressive for this. These are better for ice climbing; we'll be going on mixed ground, snow and ice.' With a wisdom born of years of experience, he turned over the crampons in his hands, assessing them with the certainty of a sage old carpenter comparing different hammers and saws. He was a craftsman of the mountains, of that I had no doubt.

When I went to bed a half-hour later, I had no idea whether we would be going up in the morning. I hoped not. I fell into a deep sleep.

Sometime later I was awoken by Anton walking lightly past my bunk and heading out of the door of the hut. I was immediately aware that something had changed. In my half-sleep I realised that the noise of the wind pounding on the walls and roof of the hut had died. It was breathlessly quiet. I heard the outer door of the hut reopen and Anton once more stepped quietly past the sleeping benches. I waited. I heard him rustling around in the dark but I couldn't tell what he was doing. I knew that if he got back into his sleeping bag, we wouldn't be going up today. I waited. No sound. Then I heard something that truly terrified me. It was the *pump, pump, pump* of a fuel stove, followed closely by the flare of a match. I briefly saw Anton's face lit by the flame as he bent over the stove. He was about to brew tea. I looked at my watch – it was 2 am. Dread clutched at my chest and I felt like an anvil had been deposited in the pit of my stomach. We were going. The light in the hut came on.

I wriggled out of my sleeping bag and pulled on thermals. Something deep inside me, something steely that had never been broken, relished getting up in the hours before dawn and buckling on greaves and breastplate as warriors had done since time imme-morial. Despite my fear, some part of me relished the contest that lay ahead.

'Morning, Anton. Seems like the wind's dropped,' I said softly, trying not to wake our companions.

'Good morning. Yes, the front came through during the night; wind's got around to the south. We'll have some breakfast. I want to be away by 4 am sharp.' Anton made porridge and pancakes and I wolfed them down while trying to organise my pack. The next two hours went by in a blur.

Spare thermals, spare head torch, spare inner gloves were jammed in my pack along with two full water bladders. Anton had advised me to wrap one bottle inside my thermals to prevent it from freezing. I jammed the big Nikon camera into the top pocket of the pack, then hauled it out on to the verandah.

I'll never forget my first sight of Aspiring that night. The clouds were gone and a billion stars silhouetted the immense mountain. A full moon gave a luminous glow to the northwest ridge and summit. The quiet and stillness added to the mountain's intimidating presence. *Let's get it on!* the mountain seemed to be saying, and the audience had gone quiet. It was like a night at the theatre after the lights had gone down and the audience was poised in anticipation.

Anton joined me on the verandah, where he checked and double-checked everything I did – from clipping on my crampons, to buckling up my harness, checking that all the straps were doubled back through the buckles, to tying the rope into a figure of eight onto my harness. He was leaving nothing to chance. I zipped up my jacket and pulled a woolly cap down over my ears. I took one last look at my watch – it was 4 am. I pulled on my glove liners and the outer windproof glove shells over the top. I was ready to go. Anton switched on his head torch and began to tramp towards the hut steps. His boots made a dull thudding noise on the timber planks of the verandah, followed by the clank of his crampons on the metal steps. I followed him out into the dark, where I would have to confront my most deeply ingrained fear – my fear of heights.

As I walked off the verandah, I was surprised to find myself praying for the first time in years. *God, don't let me be a coward. Don't let me make a fool of myself. Don't let me get stuck up there, frightened out of my wits and not able to go up or go down. Let me do a good job. I want to pull my weight, make a contribution. Most of all, let me handle the fear, let me handle the heights. And God, don't let me injure the guide.* This from a person who would claim to be irreligious, who hadn't spoken to God since his teens when six years of Catholic boarding school finally reamed out all the religion. I wondered if God would be listening. Probably not. It had been a long time.

This was the compilation of all my fears, but the coming battle with heights weighed most heavily.

I tramped across the snow-covered ledge, following Anton's bobbing head torch in the dark. The things I should have been concerned about – a fatal fall, an avalanche, the cold, being killed or injured – never crossed my mind. Somehow, I had presumed Anton was looking after them.

My stomach was tight with fear and doubt, my mouth already dry. I wished I had never organised to do the climb. I cursed the demons that made me do these things while other men my age were at home safely tucked up in bed. Those same demons wouldn't even allow me to consider backing out and I plodded after Anton. Everything was black beyond the narrow cones of our head torches. I stole a glance upwards above Anton's head. There, visible only because it blocked out the stars, was the vast bulk and summit cone of Mount Aspiring. From the ledge above the glacier, it once again reminded me of a blunt cow's horn.

We descended the steep cliff below the hut, following our tracks of two days earlier. I could see nothing in the blackness of the glacial bowl and could only dredge up from memory the space underneath us. My head torch followed the line of the rope as it snaked down to Anton then up to his harness.

We reached the base of the glacier with no problems. The snow was frozen and crisp and our boots made the now-familiar squeaking sound. With Anton in the lead we headed southeast, walking across the contour of the glacier. Anton wove back and forth around any suspicious indents in the snow. Sometimes he would stop and prod with his ice axe, and I would hear the words 'Crevasse, walk over here' or 'Crevasse, step over there'. On and on we went in the dark.

After about an hour, Anton changed direction and we began to climb steadily northeast. The image of the map memorised back in Wanaka scrolled through my consciousness as we trudged along. I tried to judge speed and direction, recording our passage in case something went wrong and I had to back-track on my own in the dark. I could tell we were heading up the névé of the glacier, up the side of the bowl towards the start of the climb proper. The gradient continued to increase and we climbed on. My breathing was regular despite the increasing steepness and I was grateful for all the training I'd done.

Time passed and I was absorbed in the darkness and the task when, without warning, Anton stopped and began chopping with his ice axe. I waited for some time. I could see that he was carving out a large ledge in the side of the glacier, which had now become very steep. 'Step up here,' he said finally, and I moved to the ledge where he now stood winding in the rope.

In front of us, running from right to left out into the dark on either side, was a deep black crack. I realised immediately that this was the Mount Aspiring bergschrund, the place where the glacier broke away from the mountain. I looked down into its gloom but could see nothing. 'How deep's this?' I asked.

Anton rounded on me angrily. 'Don't you worry how deep it is; you just worry about getting across it and not falling in. Now, get those tools into the snow and get a good stance.'

I was shocked by his response but managed to bite my tongue. Anton, my stepfather and I may have possessed very short fuses, but the last thing Anton and I needed was to be cursing each other with the engulfing blackness of the Bonar Glacier below. I backed away.

Anton had taken off his pack and unbuckled the helmet lashed on the back. He took the helmet from my pack and handed it to me. He also untied my short-handled ice hammer and slammed the trekking pole I'd been using to cross the glacier into the snow near the lip of the bergschrund. We seemed ready to go and I followed Anton's lead, switching off my head torch and stashing it in my pack. Darkness closed in around us.

After issuing me with final instructions, making sure I understood what was required, he slung on his pack, stepped up and over the bergschrund and was gone. For a brief moment I saw the moonlight glinting on his crampons as he moved up the wall before the night swallowed him up. I was alone with my thoughts. Far, far below, in the stygian blackness, two tiny pinpricks of light moved slowly across the glacier. The head torches of the two Western Australian climbers, who had dutifully given us a head start, showed they were following the tracks we'd made earlier. The bobbing lights were the only sign of life in the gloom after Anton's departure and provided stark proof of how high we had already climbed.

Chapter 6

The Ramp: Between Earth and Sky

On ascents of any real difficulty the guide's life is a perpetual adventure, as is shown by the relatively large number who have been killed at their work. With a client thus more or less at the mercy of events, the leader's concentration must not lapse for a second. I couldn't count the number to times I have seen my second 'peel' at the very moment when he looked perfectly at ease.
LIONEL TERRAY, CONQUISTADORS OF THE USELESS

I tackled the second pitch, trying to drive with my legs, ice tools and crampons propelling me steadily upward to where Anton squatted on a small ledge he'd cut in the wall. I was conscious of the vast space starting to develop under me, but I didn't look down or behind me. As I approached Anton's stance, he widened the ledge with his axe.

'Stand in here and clip on,' he said, indicating the ledge. He'd cut a box and twisted a screw into the ice and had clipped on with a tether to his harness. I did as he asked, clipping on to the same screw. For a moment we were both safe, secured by the spike driven into the side of the mountain. I was surprised by the sense of security that slim piece of metal and a 60 centimetre tether gave me. I took from my harness the gear that I'd cleaned off the top of the first pitch and handed it to Anton. It disappeared among the other gear on his harness. I was chuffed that I'd managed to clean it out and bring it up to him without incident. I felt like I was pulling my weight as a team member.

I thought about mentioning how lucky it was that he'd shown me the previous evening how to use the Black Diamond screws. If it hadn't been for that chance conversation, I would still be 50 metres down the slope trying to work out how to get the screw out of the ice. But he looked like he had a lot on his mind.

'This's too slow. We're going to move together from here,' he said. He picked up the rope that had joined us together, which now lay coiled in a neat pile on the ledge, and he began whipping it around his shoulders – making Kiwi coils – just as he had shown me the night before. In less than 30 seconds he had coiled the entire rope around his shoulder in a uniform set of neat loops, all the while disregarding the space below him. He formed a bight in the rope, passed it around the coils, tied a hitch around all of it, and then clipped it onto his harness with a karabiner. This was the same technique we had used when crossing the glacier some hours earlier, but now Anton was carrying the whole rope. A tail of about three metres of rope extended from the bight in his coils to my harness.

Anton was setting us up for the classic mountaineering 'short roping' technique. We would climb the rest of the way unbelayed – no anchors. If I fell I would have two chances. I could dig the picks of my tools into the snow and stop my fall with a self-arrest. However, the chance of a novice like me performing a self-arrest on the ramp was practically zero. My backstop was Anton. If I couldn't self-arrest I would have to rely on his ability to stay on the wall and absorb the tremendous force of my weight as it hit the end of the rope. Thus, Anton was keeping the rope short so that he had some hope of holding on before the acceleration of my falling body made this impossible and he too was pulled off. If I did peel, he would need to react instantly, plunging his tools into the snow and using his crampons to get purchase, and hopefully getting a loop of rope around one of the tools so that his body didn't absorb the full shock of the impact.

If Anton fell, we were both doomed. He would pull me off, as I would never be able to hold him. We would both tumble down the ramp together over the rock buttress and into the bergschrund, a mass of rope, arms, legs, packs, crampons and ice tools. I was about to experience the fellowship of the rope for real.

I had complete faith in Anton's skills and his ability to hold me in the event of a fall and so save my life, but my mind raced with questions. *Why do it this way without an anchor when it's so much harder for the guide? Why not give me half the coils and let me share the weight of the rope? I'm only roped on in one spot – my harness. You're roped in two places – on the coils and at your harness. Won't I suffocate in a long fall?*

I burned to learn the technical aspects of mountaineering; to understand all that was happening. But I kept my peace. Halfway up a dangerous wall with air underneath our arses and nothing much else wasn't a good place to conduct classroom lectures. He had his hands full just keeping us alive.

'I want you to follow right behind me. Kick your crampons *into* the holes I make, not beside them. Understand?'

I nodded.

'And move up *with* me. Move when I do.'

Again, I nodded.

Seeing I was secure on my stance with a good grip on the tools, he unclipped my karabiner from the ice screw and handed it to me. I was now unanchored. I kept a firm grip on the axe, which I had slammed into the ice, let go of the hammer, which was also jammed into the ice, took the karabiner from Anton and clipped it onto my harness. He unwound the screw and placed it on his harness. With only a quick look up the slope, we were off.

I had only moved up a few metres when I realised how difficult it is to move up a steep slope while short roped to another climber. It's like being part of an organism with four hands and four legs, all of which must work in unison, for connecting this disjointed whole is three metres or so of rope that must be kept tight. This is the critical part. The rope must be kept tight enough that the lead climber knows where the second is, can feel immediately if he falls – but not so tight that the lead is hauling the second. The movements of both climbers must be smooth and coordinated. I was determined to do my bit. It was hard.

As Anton moved up, he would pull one boot out of the small pocket he had kicked in the wall. I would move up and put my boot in the same hole that he had vacated, but my step up had to be coordinated with the left-hand, right-hand movement of his hammer and axe.

Anton worked silently, kicking and moving, kicking and moving, his ice tools punching into the wall with a perfect dagger technique. His movements were economical and rhythmical. I was going okay, but I've never concentrated so hard in my life. The rope ran from my harness up my chest, past my nose and up beside Anton to the coil of rope wrapped around him. I watched it like a hawk. As Anton moved and the rope swished back and forth, I took great care to swing wide with the tools so as not to hit the rope. Modern climbing ropes are miracles of engineering, combining the strength of a steel cable with the elasticity of a bungee cord. They are frozen and thawed, saturated with water then baked dry in the sun, exposed to UV rays, and dragged over rock and ice, yet they continue to perform and to save lives. However, they can be sliced like butter if they are stood on with crampons or hit with tools. Our tools had razor-like picks, so I always looked for the rope before I swung them. I also took notice of where Anton's legs were. If I swung too high I would bury the sharp picks in the back of his lower leg. This was one of the practical dangers of climbing together which had never been mentioned in books and Anton's reaction to an unexpected blow in his calf muscle from a wayward tool didn't bear thinking about.

There was a lot to manage – the rope, the tools, getting my boots into the toe holes and moving with Anton – but I thought I was handling it. Although the slope on which we climbed was still deep in shadow, the darkness was fading and as the light slowly came up I saw for the first time the vast sweep of the ramp above us and the many rocky crags and the séracs that defended it. It was inspiring. I felt like I had left the cares and worries of everyday life back in sea-level Sydney and was now perched like a bird between the earth and the sky. I was starting to feel confident enough to consider taking a look down behind us.

I wonder what the view's like? I thought, almost absentmindedly. *We're climbing northeast, so Mount French is due south of us. That'd be over my right shoulder. The north face of French'll be getting the sunrise soon . . .*

For the first time since we roped together I took my eyes off Anton's boots and stole a quick glance over my right shoulder. It was breathtaking, and reminded me of being on Tiger Hill watching the sunrise light up Kanchenjunga 29 years before. While Mount Aspiring's summit and the slope of the ramp were still deep in shadow, three kilometres away the first rays of the sun struck the pinnacle spire of Mount French, turning it a soft pink colour. The effect flowed down onto the top of the Bonar Glacier and the area known as the Quarterdeck. Lower down, Mount French was still clothed in blackness, but fingers of light shone down the glacier illuminating the high points.

Gee, the summit of Aspiring must be lit up now. Can't see it, though. Sun comes up a lot softer here than it does in the outback. That big yellow ball coming up like thunder. Long, straight horizon . . .

A jerk on the rope broke my reflection. Anton looked down to where I clung just beneath him and roared:

'You *fucking* come up! Don't you *fucking* pull me off!' My split-second loss of concentration could have been a disaster. His face was livid with rage and it shocked me.

As Anton had attempted to move up, I had stayed still for a moment taking in the sunrise. The rope had jerked tight on his coils, threatening to topple him backwards and downwards. This was exacerbated by the pack he was carrying. He was suspended there with one boot out of its secure hole but unable to step up and kick in, as I was a dead weight on the rope. If I had pulled him off he would have landed on me and we would both have plunged down the ramp.

'Sorry, mate,' was all I could think to say. Both he and the mountain had given me a hell of a fright.

This was the core of mountaineering, the awesome battle against one of nature's most fundamental powers – gravity. A human body drops 9.8 metres in the first second of a climbing fall off a steep wall, and the speed accelerates from there. In just three seconds the climber is falling at a rate of 98 kilometres per hour, almost the speed of a car on a freeway. The belaying climber – usually the guide – has virtually no time to react. The flip-side of acceleration, and the really deadly part of the climbing/gravity pirouette, is mass – the faster a body falls, the heavier it gets. After falling only five metres, a climber of my weight exerts a 500 kilogram force on the rope he is attached to. That's why a climber in a peel from any decent height often tears out the anchor and pulls the belaying climber off with him. The lead – again, usually the guide – cannot afford to let the second fall far and pick up acceleration and mass; hence, the very short roping lengths on steep slopes.

'Right! I'm gunna *really* short rope you now.' Anton pulled savagely on the rope as I climbed up next to him. He whipped several more turns of the now slack rope around his shoulders, undid the bight around his coils, then retied around the new, expanded burden he carried and clipped on to the karabiner on his harness. This was achieved with effortless speed and economy while we clung to the wall. Only two metres of rope now separated us.

'Now pay attention and come up with me, or you'll pull us both off,' he said. I was shattered. I knew what I'd done and the years of reading climbing literature left me in no doubt of the consequences of a fall. We were especially vulnerable as Anton wasn't belaying off an anchor – we were climbing free, roped only to each other. Any mistake I made directly threatened his life. One tiny slip in concentration and I'd nearly mucked up the whole thing.

Our spider-like progress up the ramp resumed. I had learned a hard lesson about mountaineering. It's not like a desert expedition or a really hard bushwalk, where nature can be savoured at your leisure. The relationship between man and desert is a gentle one; between man and mountains a savage one. This was war – we struck the mountain with our tools, kicked her with our heavy boots and crampons, drove ice screws into her, chopped chunks out of her for toe holes, and generally visited on her every form of violence necessary to keep us alive. But the mountains fight back. The crevasse, the avalanche, rockfalls, weather and steep slopes like the ramp are her weapons of war. Mountaineering is all about speed and pressure – get to the summit as quickly as possible and get off as quickly as possible. It's not about looking at the scenery.

While I'd had my little piece of purgatory, for Anton the climb was about to get immeasurably harder. To climb as we were doing it, kicking footholes into the snow for support, is slow and exhausting for the lead climber and usually turns are taken to establish the trail. Due to my inexperience we didn't have the luxury of alternating the lead. To attack a mountain the way we were doing it, the snow must be soft enough to allow the boots to be kicked in, yet firm enough to support the weight of the climber. As we climbed higher, conditions changed from firm snow-pack to a thin layer of snow over rock-hard ice.

Anton could no longer kick footholds into the mountain as he'd been doing. For him, this wasn't a problem. He could've climbed using just the front points of his crampons. These would have held him, even though he couldn't kick in the toes of his boots. For an inexperienced climber, though, this presents real difficulty – front pointing over any distance exhausts the calf muscles and stretches the Achilles tendons, and there is always the risk that the points will slip out and the climber will begin to slide feet first down the mountain.

Since Anton could no longer kick steps in with his boots, to assist me, he now had to cut them, using the adze on his ice axe like a small mattock. He had, on occasion, done this lower down the mountain, whenever we'd hit a patch of ice. From the time of our shortened rope at the top of the second pitch, he did it continuously.

The rhythmic swing of his ice tools became *chop, chop, chop*, with the adze of his axe. *Chop, chop, chop* for the right boot. Move up. *Chop, chop, chop* for the left boot. Move up. *Chop, chop* for the right boot. He worked in complete silence. A shower of ice chunks and loose snow cascaded down on me, as my head was just below his boot.

'Make sure you step into those holes,' he said.

I was concentrating hard. Each time he stepped out of one of the little foot holes, I stepped into it. I felt like a complete bludger as Anton toiled away, his arm rising and falling.

'Wish I could help,' I said. He didn't reply as we inched our way upwards.

I then made my next big mistake.

Determined not to fall, and surmising (correctly) that we would use these same steps on our afternoon descent, I raked each one out with my crampons as I stepped into it. This cleared out any loose ice and snow, and enlarged the step from a hole barely big enough for my front crampon points and toes to a hole deep enough to take each boot up to the ball of my foot. I jammed my boots in.

This was a more secure stance. However, it had an unforeseen drawback. Because of the crampons, I couldn't rip my boot out of the hole as quickly as Anton did. I was a fraction slower. I was also more brutal than him in my treatment of the mountain. He moved lightly, gently placing the picks of his tools and the toes of his boots into the snow. It was like watching a fly climb a pane of glass. I slammed the tools in, using all the shoulder leverage of my overhand Chouinard technique. Because I was frightened and inexperienced, I was burying the tools up to their handles in the mountainside.

As Anton climbed I had to rip one boot and one tool out and go. Sometimes I ripped the tools out with such force that I would almost topple over backwards into the void. Desperate to ensure I didn't repeat my earlier mistake, and to give myself some extra time on each step, I began to anticipate Anton's movements – I began to move up just *before* I thought he was going to. This ensured he wouldn't have to tug on a tight rope as he stepped up. Then the inevitable happened. He went to move up, hesitated, then stepped back down to enlarge the step he was working on. Simultaneously, I stepped up and ended up almost beside him. This gave him a tremendous shock, as he'd been concentrating on chopping and moving and presumed I was just below him on the rope. He rounded on me again.

124

'Don't come up *yet*!' he shouted. 'Ah, fuck! Look, you've got the rope slack.' His face was only about two feet from mine as he turned on me, and was a frightening study.

In attempting to help, I had made another serious mistake by overcompensating. Anton took it out on the mountain. His right arm suddenly whirled in a frenzied bout of activity, sending ice chips tinkling and bouncing off my helmet before they bounded wildly down the void of the ramp towards the glacier. My gloves and ice tools were soon plumed with snow from Anton's attack on the slope.

Chop, chop, chop. 'Fuck! Fuck! Fuck!' he shouted at the mountain, his voice in perfect cadence with his arm. His axe pounded the ice. When his right arm tired, he changed the axe to his left and went at it again.

Chop, chop, chop. The ice chips flew. Steps materialised in the blink of an eye as we climbed higher and higher. This scared me a little, as I thought he would exhaust himself and collapse in a heap. I would have been even more scared if I had known that he was still recovering from a reconstruction of his right shoulder necessitated by a fall into a crevasse on his Everest attempt in 1990.

Another dread came over me: that he would suddenly stop on the ramp and say, 'That's it. I can't get a climber like you to the top of Aspiring; we're going back, there's too much risk.' But Anton persevered. He seemed to calm down and quickly resumed his metronomic chopping. We both continued climbing, and I was determined to make no more mistakes. I felt considerable guilt at what Anton was going through to get me up the mountain. Whenever he paused momentarily for breath and we both hung there silent and motionless, the remorse was even worse. He ignored me during these rest stops and stared resolutely up the slope.

It seemed like hours since we'd arrived at the bottom of the ramp. From about halfway up, the slope dog-legs slightly to the left. As we came up this second section, we could see the saddle that marked the junction of the ramp with the northwest ridge. We inched towards it.

The rocky crags along the top of the ridge towered over us. Here the wisdom of climbing early was rammed home. In the pre-dawn hours the cliffs and upper slopes are frozen solid. No rock-fall or avalanche would pound down upon us. The blizzards from the north had dumped tonnes of snow on the other side of the ridge. To climb there would be fatal. The ramp offered us safe access to the northwest ridge from the southern, or lee-side, so we were unlikely to be buried in a snow avalanche. Our principal enemy was rocks. A boulder the size of a cricket ball bounding down a slope as steep as the ramp would have smashed Anton's helmet and knocked him out; a boulder as large as a house brick would have decapitated him. The result for me would be the same. Mountain cliffs often calve rocks as big as refrigerators and hurl them down their slopes. Travelling at 100 kilometres an hour, a rock this size would obliterate us, smash us off the mountain and deposit us in the bergschrund, a pair of broken, unrecognisable bodies roped together. This was the objective danger of moun-taineering. No matter how experienced the guide, these are the sorts of dangers that climbers must expose themselves to and which years of training can mitigate but never eliminate. For as long as it was freezing, and the sun stayed off the ramp, we were safe.

With the dawn came relief that we could finally see clearly, but it also triggered the start of a desperate race against time. We had to get to the summit and then back down the ramp before the sun thawed the rock, allowing it to unleash its missiles at us. The clock was running and I understood why Anton seemed under pressure. We climbed on. Anton's eyes constantly focused on the ridge.

'Doesn't seem to be getting any closer,' I said lightly.

'We're getting there – slowly,' Anton gasped, pausing briefly in his chopping. 'I'm going to have to cut steps all the way to the top.' He sounded both exhausted and exasperated. We had about 50 metres to go.

'Wish I could help,' I said again.

Mountaineering as Anton and I were doing it offends one of the notions I hold most dear – a belief in teamwork. It's supposed to be the fellowship of the rope, but so far I'd done nothing to assist in this climb. I hadn't done anything, because I *couldn't*. Anton was risking his life and turning himself inside out to get me to the top. If I'd known how much risk the guides put themselves through, I never would have attempted the climb. What had seemed a good idea at home now seemed nothing more than an exercise in conceit and reckless selfishness. Anton must have been thinking the same thing, because he suddenly broke the silence.

'If I was coming up here on my own, or with an experienced climber, or even with a good amateur, we'd free climb. I wouldn't have to cut any steps, wouldn't even need a rope.' He peered across the slope, checking the snow condition and looking up at the cliffs as we neared the ridge. He resumed chopping. Finally, after what seemed an eternity, the slope gradually gave back and Anton's chopping stopped. Suddenly he pulled his tools out of the ice and stood up. He turned and looked down to where I clung with my points and axes driven into the snow.

'Right, we can walk from here,' he said. He whipped off a few coils of rope, lengthening it to about five metres, and we set off on a steep though relatively safe walk up the saddle. I wanted to turn around and look back down the ramp to see where we had climbed, but I was too frightened and rattled. I looked resolutely ahead and followed exactly in Anton's tracks.

I estimated that he had cut over 200 steps in the three hours it had taken us to climb the ramp. His earlier rage seemed to be forgotten. It was as if nothing had happened. It was uncanny how much he reminded me of my stepfather – a quiet man who worked hard without saying much, but who would suddenly unleash a terrifying explosion when something went wrong. Unlike my old man, Anton seemed to get over it quickly, all forgotten and no grudges held. My stepfather would sometimes not speak to us for weeks after a blow-up.

Chapter 7

Death Cookies and the Northwest Ridge

Money can't buy you a summit. I feel that it's my responsibility to make sure not that the clients get to the top but that they get home. Everything else is secondary. They're hiring me for my leadership and judgement, not for a double-your-money-back summit guarantee.

ED VIESTURS, RENOWNED AMERICAN GUIDE AND CLIMBER,
NO SHORTCUTS TO THE TOP

As we crossed the level saddle at the top of the ramp, firm frozen snow crunched underfoot. The rock buttress that had threatened us during the climb stood mute on the left as we tramped past, its craggy magnificence coated with a frosting of fresh snow. On the right, séracs – soaring blocks of ice – leaned on each other in a state of tottering frozen confusion.

The walk out on to the northwest ridge of Mount Aspiring is a wondrous natural pageant. My first shock was seeing the summit, which had been hidden all morning by the ramp and then by the séracs. The northwest ridge ran steeply and uniformly all the way to the top.

Steep, but I can get up there. Only about 45°. Not nearly as steep as the ramp, I thought.

A rooster-tail of snow blew off the summit in a plume extending to the north. I didn't need to be told what that was. Cold wind howling out of the south, out of Antarctica, was blowing snow off the top of the mountain. 'Lot of wind up top,' Anton said.

I looked up with fear and uncertainty born of inexperience. *How fast was the wind on the summit? How cold would it be up there? How hard does the wind have to blow before Anton aborts the climb?* Questions assailed me as I examined our intended route. I cursed my lack of experience in these most basic of mountaineering matters. It was noticeably colder walking across the saddle than it had been on the ramp. The wind hit me between the shoulder blades.

Another surprise was the glittering pancakes scattered all the way from where we stood up the entire northwest ridge as far as I could see. The sun was fully up now, and transparent, flat pieces of ice, about ten centimetres across, flashed like diamonds. They looked like clear frozen pikelets of ice scattered randomly across the slope.

'Death cookies. They're rime – frozen rain,' Anton said when I pointed them out. I guessed that this was moisture that had fallen over the last couple of days as rain, or water that had come out of clouds or fog, and had frozen when it hit the ground. I didn't ask why they were called 'death cookies', but I presumed that if you stepped on one, your crampons wouldn't bite and your boots would slide away downhill. The cookies weren't integrated into the snow. Death cookies. They look good, but like a lot of things in the mountains they concealed murderous possibilities.

We trudged out onto the saddle, me following Anton, careful to keep the rope between us just touching the ground and determined not to step on it. The wind remained at our backs. Unbeknown to me a southeasterly gale had been howling all morning, but the southwest ridge ran adjacent to the ramp and sheltered the slope from the worst of the weather. The long ridge that I'd seen earlier as we climbed had provided perfect shelter and I hadn't even realised it was doing so.

We were now standing on top of the saddle. If we walked further, we'd start to walk down the sheer northern side of the mountain. I could see it was loaded with snow. 'We'll head down off here a bit and get out of this wind. We'll have something to eat and drink,' Anton shouted over the roar of the wind.

'Fine with me,' I shouted back, and we started to walk over the northern slope of the ridge into a small bowl filled with snow. The wind had dropped the temperature sharply on the exposed saddle, but with my modern thermal gear and shell jacket, combined with the exercise, fear and adrenalin, I was very comfortable and not too cold. But I suddenly realised how thirsty I was.

When we reached an area partly sheltered from the wind, Anton dropped his pack. I followed suit, watching his every move. I whipped out the drinking tube to the Platypus water bladder I carried on the outside pocket of my pack. As expected, the long drinking tube contained nothing but ice. The water in the top half of the bladder was also frozen.

'Won't be getting anything out of there,' I said.

Anton also inspected it.

'Try the one wrapped in your pack,' he said.

I undid the pack straps and reached gingerly inside for the bottle. I didn't want to pull spare thermals or my fleece out of the pack, as I thought they might blow away. I eased the bottle out, all the while kneeling on the pack. It too had chunks of ice floating in it, but I crushed these in my fingers and managed to make it drinkable. I sat on my pack and poured the cold liquid down my throat. I was parched, and although the water contained slivers of ice, it was a wonderful feeling to do something as human and familiar as drinking water. At least here was something that I had control over. It was comforting and reminded of my many water stops on desert expeditions. Life's great pleasures are often very simple things.

'Have one of these.' Anton handed me a muesli bar that he had retrieved from his pack. I sat on my pack munching on the muesli bar. The rough grains were hard to get down my dry throat and the last thing I felt like was eating, although breakfast had been a long time before. I knew I had to eat or face running out of energy. I persevered and forced myself to swallow.

I used the break to take stock. Anton stood and slowly sipped water, walking back and forth in a restless manner. He seemed completely unaffected by his ordeal on the ramp. He didn't seem to need to sit down, but just looked at the view. I guessed it was about 9 am; we had been climbing for five hours. It was clear that this break was for me, not him, and that he was keen to get going again.

Below us was one of the great views of the New Zealand alps. I clicked the map light on in my brain and went over the sections I'd memorised. It was all there. The cliffs of the northwestern face of Mount Aspiring fell sharply away from our perch straight down to the Therma Glacier. I could see for miles up the northern side of the Haast Range – a wilderness of snow-covered peaks. The names came rolling back: Mainroyal, Skyscraper and Stargazer, little brothers to Mount Aspiring, but all challenges in their own right. I'd never seen a sight like this before – snow-covered wilderness with peaks marching off to the horizon, and we were looking *down* on them. I thought of telling Anton that all the names of the peaks were sails on a square-rigged ship. Someone with a nautical bent had been out here. But I guessed he would have known that, and instead I munched on my muesli bar in silence.

The view was arresting but didn't fill me with the joy that the sight of wilderness usually does. Mountains filled me with a certain dread – the lack of vegetation, the glaciers, the sheer snow cliffs and unyielding texture of the ice underfoot showed me an implacable, merciless, fierce side of nature that you don't often see in Australia, except during a bushfire.

Anton began repacking his gear and adjusting his coils. 'Got to get going. No telling what the weather is going to do. Don't like the look of that.' He pointed the handle of his ice axe towards the south, where large black clouds were building over French Ridge about five kilometres away. He cast a critical eye over the summit snow plume, way above our heads.

'It'll be windy up there – maybe 50 or 60 kilometres – and cold,' he said. I followed his gaze but I didn't comment. I was already intimidated by Anton and didn't want to ask questions showing my lack of experience.

The journey up the ramp had convinced me that Anton was a great guide and climber, probably a brilliant one, but he was as merciless as the mountains he climbed – merciless about mistakes and very sparing with words of encouragement. In time, I would see this as an advantage, but I couldn't see it then. I had come to the mountains to conquer my fear of heights, but I'd been too scared of Anton to worry about heights so far.

I stood up, repacked my water bottle, checked that everything was in place, and struggled to do up the waist strap of my pack without compromising the rope, karabiners and gear attached to my harness. To my great relief, Anton wasn't aborting the climb. He seemed to be preparing to head up.

'What's our turnaround time?' I asked, as I wrestled with my gear. This was the time when we would have to turn back no matter how close we were to the summit.

'At eleven we head back down.'

That meant we had only two hours to get to the top. 'We got time?'

'Yeah, we'll make it,' he said.

I was enjoying this brief burst of conversation, and my excitement was starting to build at the thought of tackling the ridge and, possibly, getting to the top. *Dare I hope for the summit?* I asked myself, beginning to feel that, with the ramp behind us, it was possible.

'Get off the rope! Get off the *fucking* rope!' Anton's sudden shout broke into my reverie.

'What?' I still had my head down, checking that all my harness straps were doubled back through the buckles. I looked up and he was pointing at my feet.

'You're standing on the rope!' Anton shouted. I looked down. Sure enough, the rope ran from the figure eight knot on my harness down to my left boot, under the crampons and across the snow to where Anton stood.

'Oh, fuck,' I said. I jumped off the rope in fright and began to coil it up out of harm's way. Anton charged over and, picking up the rope where I'd stood on it, examined it closely by running it through his fingers.

'Look, you've damaged the rope!' he said accusingly. He bent the rope over his index finger and, sure enough, there was a tiny cut in the mantel sheath where the points of my crampons had nicked it.

'The rope's our lifeline!' he stressed. I knew how grave my error was. We were using a modern kernmantel climbing rope constructed with a core, or *kern*, of braided nylon fibres and a tightly plaited sheath. The core gives the rope its strength and the sheath its protective layer. The protective mantel makes the rope less vulnerable to internal damage by dirt or sand, but makes it more difficult to inspect, particularly to check if there's damage to the core.

If I had nicked the core of the rope, it would have been useless and I think Anton would have aborted the climb. Even if he only suspected that the rope was compromised, he couldn't trust a client's life to it. We still had to get up the ridge and back down the ramp. Because of their complex construction, kernmantel ropes are also more expensive than hawser – or twisted fibre – ropes, which had been used by mountaineers for decades.

'Brand-new bloody rope, too,' he muttered. His voice seethed with rage and frustration. I suspected, and it was later confirmed, that as a guide Anton had to supply, out of his own pocket, everything for the clients: ropes, boots, crampons, helmets – the lot.

'Sorry, I won't do it again,' I said lamely.

He stepped away.

Maybe the work on the ramp really knocked him around, I thought as he retreated towards his pack, furiously winding in coils. But it also crossed my mind that maybe Anton had had enough of taking inexperienced climbers up Mount Aspiring. Maybe he no longer wanted to risk his life so that wannabe mountaineers could live out their dreams without putting in the years of practice required to do it safely without a guide. Weekends spent climbing with his peers probably seemed a very attractive alternative to guiding others.

I picked up my tools and snugged up the leashes. We then climbed out of the bowl and headed back out onto the saddle. Out of the lee of the ridge, on the exposed saddle, the wind again hit us like a hammer and nearly knocked me over. We trudged across the saddle for ten minutes until we reached where the steep part of the ridge rises from the saddle. Anton stopped suddenly. I waited, keeping the rope length between us just touching the ground, as instructed. I wondered what the problem was. He walked back towards me.

'I'm freezing! We're gunna have to stop so I can put on another layer!' he shouted over the howling gale. He dumped his pack on the ground and threw his coils on top of it. He then knelt on the pack and very gingerly began undoing his outer windproof shell. I realised the risk he was taking.

The wind was smashing into the southern face of Mount Aspiring and the Shipowner Ridge. Trapped by these two giant geological features, the wind had nowhere to go but up and over, and was funnelled up the ramp and into the saddle. It was in this saddle that we were standing. The saddle effectively became a wind tunnel, collecting the gale from the Bonar Glacier and dumping it over the northwest ridge on to the Therma Glacier. We were stuck in the middle.

Anton, like me, had a top-shelf Macpac Prophet shell jacket made of wind-resistant Gore-Tex. After peeling it off, he held it in both hands and then knelt on it. He was now kneeling on his jacket and his pack – if he'd stood up both would have been gone in an instant. He reached into the pack and pulled out a spare thermal jumper, pulling it over his head without much difficulty. Then the fun started.

'Gee, I'm freezing. Should've done this down below,' he cursed at the wind. 'I don't know why I didn't think of it. Should've done this when we stopped for a drink.'

He got his right arm into the jacket, but when he went to put his left arm through, the wind caught the jacket and it flapped around behind his back, making a sound like a flag, snapping in a gale. He twisted and turned, trying in vain to get his arm into the sleeve.

'I'm freezing,' he yelled again as the wind tore at him and he struggled in vain.

'Hang on, I'll give you a hand!' I shouted, stepping towards him while making sure not to tread on the rope at our feet. I grabbed his jacket by the collar with my right hand and took the wayward sleeve in my left hand, trying to guide it to where Anton's left hand was trying frantically to engage with it.

'Hold it down! Hold it fucking down!' he shouted as I wrestled with the jacket, which acted like a sail as the wind drove into it. 'Hold it down. Down there.' He gestured, looking back over his shoulder. He finally got his arm into the jacket and began to zip it up. He then ignored me.

'Fuck you! Put your own bloody jacket on. I hope you freeze to death ya Kiwi cunt,' I cursed. Luckily the wind was so loud he didn't hear me. Later, I would regret my rage on the saddle but I was still smarting from the dressing down I'd received on the ramp and the incident with the rope. But deep down, I had been hurt. I'd come to Anton's aid because he was a team-mate and he needed help, but he had shown me in a very blunt manner that we would never be on the same team.

Also I was confused. I had guessed correctly in Colin Todd Hut that, given the strenuous nature of the climb, two layers of thermals and the Gore-Tex shell jacket would be sufficient for what we were doing. Anton had on the same gear as me. Why did he need to change it now?

'Stupid Kiwi prick,' I said under my breath. As the wind raged across the saddle, I stamped around and cursed and muttered, calling Anton and all his countrymen every name I could think of. I was on the boil and would have set off up the mountain on my own If I'd known how to. 'That's what rest halts are for – to get organised – ya dumb Kiwi fuck. *You're* the one who's supposed to know what he's doing, for fuck's sake.'

Anton heard none of this as I seethed mostly to myself, battling to contain my temper. Fear and rage are a lethal combination on a mountain climb, and I struggled to control myself. An argument between a client and the guide at this point would mean the climb was over. It was too important to me for that to happen, but I was really rattled now. Seeing Anton struggling despite all his experience filled me with dismay. I looked towards the summit where the snow blew off in a straight line.

What the hell's it going to be like up there? What's Anton so worried about? I asked myself. I was battered by indecision. I looked in vain at the summit for answers. I just didn't know what to do, so I decided to change my glove liners.

Modern mountaineering gloves, such as the Marmot gloves I was wearing, come in two parts – an outer waterproof, windproof shell made of nylon, and a separate inner glove made of super-fine merino wool. To allow for varying conditions and temperatures, the inners can be lightweight for warm days or thicker for cold days. I had put on lightweight inners at Colin Todd before we left and they had proved up to the task – my hands were warm, even on the saddle. But Anton's sudden decision to rug up and put on more warm clothing, and the violence of the wind that was assailing the summit, made me doubt my decision.

Will my hands freeze up there? Will I get frostbite? I wondered. I was especially worried about my left hand. The nerves in that hand were irreparably damaged – was the circulation also? *How will I cope higher up if it gets really cold? Will I be able to manage a tool in my left hand, if that hand freezes?* I had no idea of the answers.

'Can you hand me the spare inners?' I shouted to Anton after he was organised and ready to go. 'They're in the top of my pack.'

I kept the spares in the zippered section of my pack to make them easy to get to. He unzipped the pack and handed me the thicker inners without comment. I ripped off the left-hand outer shell glove, which was secured to my forearm with a lanyard. The glove flapped wildly in the breeze, but was in no danger of blowing away. I ripped the inner off my left hand and stuffed it into my jacket. I immediately realised my mistake. The fourth and fifth fingers of my left hand are completely paralysed. It's difficult for me to get gloves on, especially when my fingers are cold, as I had experienced many times while skiing. In the excitement I'd completely forgotten. I could feel Anton's frustration at the delay as I struggled to get the inner glove on my left hand. I felt time ticking by. To my great relief he didn't say anything but just watched as, every time I tried to pull on the glove, my fourth and fifth fingers just curled over or both ended up in the same hole. Finally, despite my mounting panic and frustration, I managed to get all five fingers into the correct holes. Thankfully, the outer shell slid on smoothly. I stuffed the spare right-hand inner back into my jacket. I wasn't going through that again.

If my right hand freezes, too bad, I thought. We set off up the ridge.

Chapter 8

The Summit: 'Give Us a Sec, Will Ya?'

Mountaineering differs from other sports in that there is no contest for glory among men, only between man and the forces of nature, or man and his own weakness. With a few rare exceptions the climber has no renown to hope for, and no audience to encourage him apart from his companion on the rope. Alone among the silence and solitude of the mountains he fights for the joy of overcoming his chosen obstacle by his own unaided powers. No other sport is so disinterested, so removed from human considerations, and it is precisely in this kind of purity that much of its grandeur and attraction lie.

LIONEL TERRAY, CONQUISTADORS OF THE USELESS

The lower part of the summit ridge on Mount Aspiring is broad, about 50 metres wide in most places, and although it pinches in just below the summit it is not an arête as most high alpine ridges are. An arête is like the top of a pitched roof, falling sheer down both sides. It's usually climbed on one side of the ridge cap, with roped climbers often alternating on both sides, to better hold a fall.

140

I looked up the ridge as we set off. *Straight to the top*, I thought. The Italians have a beautiful word for this: *direttissima*. This is the most direct route or line from bottom to top up a mountain. The Eiger north face *direttissima* is an example. Straight up. But there would be no *direttissima* for us.

'We'll traverse over to the left and then turn around, and come back over to the right,' Anton said, pointing up the ridge. This came as a bit of surprise to me. 'We're aiming for that point on the ridge. See, it looks a bit like a picket fence.'

I followed the line of his ice axe handle as he pointed and, sure enough, up near the wind-whipped summit were a series of humps that looked like a cornice over the sheer drop-off of the southern face.

'Hold the axe in your right hand, your uphill hand, and use it like a walking stick,' Anton said. 'Hold the ice hammer in your left, downhill, hand. Just let it hang by your side.'

Anton set off and I followed close on his heels, but here was something different again. It was nothing like a normal walk. I watched closely what Anton was doing. He dug in the ice axe with his right hand, then stepped forward and slightly up the mountain with his right leg before bringing his left boot up and around in front of the right. This was ice axe, right boot up, left boot up and over – again, again and again. Rhythmic small steps, ice axe one, two.

I realised how vital are hands in the simple act of walking. The rhythmic swing of arms and hands enables bipedal man to stand upright and walk. To have a long ice axe in one hand and have to factor that into the rhythm is quite a chore on a steep, snow-covered ridge. It requires coordination and concentration.

After 50 metres my right quadriceps muscle, the muscle in my thigh, was on fire. I was already in trouble. I hadn't factored in the weight of my boots or the strange way we'd be walking, although

Dave Lucas had warned me back in Sydney. A modern, plastic, double climbing boot with crampons attached weighs about 1.5 kilograms. They started to feel like lead. The strange sideways motion also meant that for part of each stride my entire weight was supported by just one upper leg. The fact that neither foot was flat, but angled to the slope of the mountain to get all the crampon points in, added to the discomfort. The upper boot pointed slightly up the slope, the lower boot slightly down. Tendons and ligaments in both my ankles began to shriek in protest. It was like walking sideways up an endless flight of stairs, where each of the treads slopes downwards at a sharp angle.

We got to the end of the first traverse on the northern, or left-hand side, of the ridge. Anton stopped, taking several precise, exact steps almost in the same spot while turning. He kept all his crampons on the snow and ended up facing in the opposite direction.

'OK, change hands with the tools,' he said. I swapped the long-handled axe into my left hand which was about to become the uphill hand. The short-handled ice hammer is of no use in this situation, and I changed it to my right hand which was about to become the downhill hand.

'Step in my tracks as you come around.' He watched me like a hawk as I deliberately and slowly picked up my boots and put them down in his crampon tracks. We set off once more across the face of the ridge, across the glittering field of rime, which sparkled in the sun like ice cubes from God's alpine refrigerator.

The pain in my right leg eased but my left leg, which was now the uphill leg, almost immediately began to burn.

'No, no, no,' Anton said, stopping suddenly. He had allowed me to get slightly ahead and was uphill and behind me. This made it easier for him to belay me in the event of a fall as the ridge got steeper.

'You're taking too big a step. You're walking too fast. Slow down, or you won't make it,' he said. He was right. A mixture of fear and adrenalin, the desire to keep up, and a notion to prove to Anton that I had what it took to be a mountain climber, meant I was walking too fast. He took much smaller steps than me but seemed to be able to cover much more ground.

We plodded on across the traverse, stopping well back from the cornice on the southern side. We changed hands on the tools and turned slowly. The pain in one leg would immediately ease, but then begin in the other as we moved off. Ice axe, crampons, one, two, breathe. I was determined not to ask for a rest and managed to keep up for a couple of traverses before throwing in the towel.

'Just give us a minute, will ya?' I asked. Anton stopped immediately, saying nothing.

'Shit, this is hard. My legs are on fire,' I said, using the axe like a crutch. Anton was immobile.

'You're not used to it. You're using muscles you've never used before,' he said.

'Yeah, but I trained the bloody house down before I came over here.' I leaned on my ice axe, willing the pain in my thighs to stop. Anton looked off into the distance.

'You come from a flat country. Doesn't matter how fit you are, you didn't grow up with it.'

I looked at him, his gaze a mixture of curiosity, contempt and resignation. I felt that he'd been in this position many times before with other climbers, and their struggles had ceased to interest him. He was just doing his job. He stood waiting for me to signal that I was ready to move off. He showed not the slightest sign of any physical exertion.

'This doesn't seem to be knocking *you* around,' I said.

'I do this for a living,' he replied quietly.

We set off again and slowly won metres from the mountain

with this strange walking style where every stride forward was matched with a stride upward.

I couldn't look down the slope. The only way I could judge if we were making progress was to look up. The great lump of the summit ice cap and its wind-blown mantle loomed larger and larger. We seemed to have been going for hours. I wondered how our turnaround time was going, but I was too stuffed to ask. The higher we climbed the more my legs burned, and I was having to ask for rests frequently now. I would swear at each stop that I wouldn't ask for another halt. I'd try to push myself, but the pain would begin to build and enough pain will always overwhelm any amount of pride. 'Give us a sec, will ya?' became a recurring plea. The pain got worse with each traverse and my legs started to wobble. Inside each thigh a molten ball of metal burned. The halts came at shorter and shorter intervals. It seemed that we no sooner set off on a traverse after a rest than I would have to ask to stop again. I felt humiliated. I would lean on my axe, look at my boots and try to collect myself. Every tendon and sinew in my lower legs and ankles seemed to be ripping apart.

The great ice-cap dome seemed to be growing larger and more threatening the higher we climbed. I felt intimidated, like I was the wrong scale to be tackling this great pile. I felt dwarfed by it.

We were approaching 3050 metres (10,000 feet), so the thinness of the air may have been telling on me as we tramped higher, although I didn't seem to be breathing hard. Humans live in a belt of atmosphere about sixteen kilometres deep. If we move up through this layer the air pressure and oxygen content drops dramatically, hence the need for pressurised aircraft. At Balmoral or Manly beaches in Sydney, where I'd done most of my training, the air pressure is about 1034 hectopascals (fifteen pounds per square inch). At the top of Mount Aspiring, it's only about 690 hecto-pascals (ten pounds per square inch) and can be less if a low pressure front hits the mountain during a climb. A climber's lungs, no matter how efficient, may not be able to force an adequate supply of oxygen into the blood servicing the large quadriceps muscles that I was now calling on for greater effort. In extreme cases, even at 3000 metres, altitude sickness may set in, resulting in fatigue, shortness of breath, headaches and vomiting. I felt only extreme fatigue.

The fitness tests I had completed before I left Sydney indicated I shouldn't have had any problem utilising the lower oxygen content of the air. Fine in theory, but it didn't seem to be working here on the mountain.

You should'a done more training before you came over here, you lazy prick. You've lost your leg drive. The proud, competitive part of me started to get stuck into the other, more human part. I thought I'd done enough. I wished I'd done more.

I began to get lost in the monotony. Ice axe, three, four, traverse and then change tools. Ice axe, three, four, right foot, left over, pain. 'Give us a sec, will ya?' During the enforced stops, Anton stood impassively. To his great credit and my great relief, he never pushed me on but stood there waiting for me to regain my strength.

After what seemed an eternity we reached the picket fence, which was really a cornice high on the southern side of the ridge. The summit loomed above – an unyielding cold helmet made of ice and rock.

I was done. *I can't do this. I'm finished. I'm too old to be up here*, I finally admitted to myself. The pain in my quads was now so intense that my legs were shaking and I had difficulty controlling the placement of my boots. I wanted just to sit down in the snow for five minutes to ease the pain in my thighs and ankles, but we didn't stop. As we set off across the extreme top of the north ridge, I struggled to stay on my feet, to keep up with Anton, to look up, not down. *I can't do this*, a voice in the back of my head kept saying.

I called for another halt. Finally, there on the cusp of the ice cap, the desire to sit down became overwhelming. It was all over for me; I couldn't go any further. I no longer cared about reaching the top. I just wanted to sit down.

But I *didn't* sit down. Leaning over my axe, I looked up to where Anton stood waiting. His face was like stone, giving no clue as to his thoughts.

'Anyone ever quit on ya? Just refused to go on, or asked to start going down?' I asked. He looked at me. He knew I was almost *hors de combat* – out of the fight.

'No, I've had a few turn back on Cook. It's a longer walk in and you're up at midnight, so they're climbing for a lot longer. Never had anyone turn back on this climb.'

'Gee, I'm amazed. I thought I was pretty fit, but this is tough. There must be a lot of people come up here who aren't fit enough.'

'Not really. Most clients are active people, and a lot of them are good climbers. They're younger than you, too. If they're not fit, they don't come up here.'

He waited for me to make a decision. I understood why he was impassive. He'd leave it up to me. If I wanted to push on, fine. If I wanted to go down, that was OK too. Amelia had been right; climbing mountains is a very strange way to get recognition. There was no audience here. I was in a battle with myself.

Anton didn't encourage me to continue or suggest I turn back. Nor did he criticise my frequent halts. It was my call. The only iron-bound rule was that when his watch said it was 11 am, he would announce 'That's it – we're going down' and it would be all over. We would retreat no matter where on the mountain we were or what I was doing. I felt under tremendous pressure.

I looked up at the ice cap. I didn't see how I could reach it. I was desperate for an energy recharge, some inspiration, something – *anything* – to overcome the poverty in my leg muscles.

Luckily, although my body was exhausted, my brain wasn't and chose this moment to enter the fray. I recalled Dave Lucas's quiet words: 'Try to break it down into little bits. Just take it ten steps at a time, otherwise the mountain will overwhelm you. Don't worry about how tired you are, or where the summit is, or if you're going to get to the summit. Just concentrate on the next ten steps.'

I steeled myself for one last go and followed his advice. I took one step, then concentrated on taking another, until I reached ten steps. I then started to count again, and on we trudged.

Blissfully a fog of exhaustion came over me somewhere below the summit cone. Some part of my brain stopped registering the pain in my legs, which were now on auto pilot. I was beyond pain; I was oblivious of anything except Anton's crampon tracks. Despite my mental stupor I was conscious that Anton wasn't turning back from the traverse towards the left hand, or northern, cornice. I didn't care; I just followed blindly along behind him, stepping in his tracks. I didn't look up at the summit or down the ridge. In the dim recesses of my brain I registered that we had stopped walking sideways in our strange crab-like crawl and had turned and were now facing up the mountain. Anton was again kicking in steps for the first time since we had left the ramp. The mountain had suddenly steepened again. We had started up the towering summit ice cap.

One thing that still worked was my sense of direction. I realised that we had walked off the line of ridge that we'd been following all morning and were climbing up somewhere above the northern face of the mountain. We were going straight up.

If I looked left and down now, I'd see the north face dropping right to the glacier. It would be a terrifying sight, I thought. I didn't care, didn't look. I followed Anton's crampon tracks, and counted to ten. My ankles were screaming, my legs felt shot to pieces, but I realised I hadn't asked for another halt.

Keep going . . . Keep going, I said to myself over and over. *I wish I'd done more training*. Thoughts tumbled around in my head as I looked at my snow-covered boots with their lattice of yellow crampon straps. Up and up, we went. Lionel Terray was right – mountaineering is a battle only between a man and his own weakness. Strangely, the fact that we were going straight up – like climbing a ladder, like the climbing we'd done on the ramp – saved me. It allowed my ankles and thighs some relief. Different muscles came into play, especially in my feet.

Anton stopped momentarily. 'That's it,' he said.

'What?' I looked up and he had stopped about three metres in front of me on a small, flat section of the mountain. He started taking off his pack.

What the hell's he doing now? Like a sudden train smash, I realised that our 11 am turn-back time had come and Anton was aborting the climb. We were done; we were turning around. Time had beaten us in the end.

Anton was reorganising the rope again. I stood there mute and beaten, awaiting his instructions.

'The summit! Come up,' he said. He started to dig around in his pack, looking for water. His words took a moment to sink in. I climbed up the last few metres and joined him. There was no more up. Every direction was down. It was an unsettling feeling. We had arrived.

I've read in a lot of mountaineering books about what it's like to stand on the top of a big mountain after battling up its flanks. Euphoria, triumph, excitement, dumb exhaustion and relief are all to be expected. I felt only the exhaustion and a sense of dread.

The summit of Mount Aspiring is about the size of four pool tables, arranged end to end. I was stunned to see the lip of the southern face only about three metres away. The human body will sometimes survive a fall of 25 metres, depending on what it lands on: 50 metres will always kill. In front of me, so close that two long strides would have brought me to the edge, was the lip of Aspiring's southern face. I knew from studying the maps and photographs and from our walk across the Bonar that it was about 700 metres straight down to the glacier. No one could survive that sort of fall, no matter how good their self-rescue techniques or crampon work. Death was the only outcome if one stumbled over the edge. Its closeness really bothered me; my old fear of heights.

A thin, sharp arête ran off to the west. *That must be the southwest ridge*, I thought. It was one of the toughest routes on the mountain. Anton confirmed my thoughts.

'If you did the southwest ridge, that's where you'd come up,' he said, pointing down the arête. He had done it many times, I presumed. The wind howled out of the south. I didn't follow Anton's example and take off my pack. I knelt in the snow, exhausted and overwhelmed by our journey. I wasn't taking any chances that either me or my pack would blow down over the northern face. With the lip of the southern face in front and the northern face so close behind, kneeling seemed to be the safest option.

The view should have inspired me. To the south I could see all the way down the Matukituki River valley. 'That's where we'll walk out tomorrow,' Anton said, pointing. 'That's Shovel Flat down there.' It was about ten kilometres away but looked like it was in another world – green and grassy, and the Matukituki River a silver thread running along the warm valley floor. I should have felt elated, should have felt excited, but I didn't.

The hard part starts now, I thought. The words of the Australian climber Sue Fear rang in my ears: 'Mountains are harder to climb down than climb up.' I felt the power of the mountain under my boots; felt its cold, merciless mass – a million tonnes of schist and snow and ice eager to destroy anyone who ventured upon it.

149

I've got you by the balls now, you bastard. Let's see you get down, it seemed to be saying.

'Gee, I'm late already – 5.45 and I have to be in Terrey Hills at six. See you tomorrow,' I said to our receptionist, as coat in hand I headed out the door. It was March 2005. Gunning my car up the freeway through peak-hour traffic, I wondered what tonight would bring. *Australian Geographic* magazine, which had sponsored several of my past expeditions, was holding a cocktail party to welcome the new editor, Dee Nolan, and give various adventurers an opportunity to share some memorabilia of their trips.

I roared into the *Australian Geographic* carpark at 6.30 and ran into the foyer through a garden bedecked with Black Boys and flowering palms. The voice of a speaker drifted down from the reception hall. *Bugger, it's already started*, I said to myself. The room was full and I squeezed in down the back. A small, slim girl wedged against the back wall stood aside to make way for me. Our eyes met briefly – hers were bright blue-grey in a tanned face. She wore her hair in long plaits. The blue eyes and tanned face were a startling contrast. *Gee, that face has seen some weather*, I thought, as I found some space beside her. Her reed-thin body also spoke of a life of hard work outdoors. I turned my attention to the speakers.

After a while, my mind started to wander and I looked around the room at some of the exhibits brought by the adventurers. I happened to glance over my shoulder and there behind me was a two-metre-high poster of Mount Everest with a dotted line up the northern ridge, the ridge that comes in from Tibet. The line went to the summit.

Across the bottom in big letters was 'Sue Fear Mount Everest, 1992'. On the bottom was a photograph of a girl in climbing gear. I looked closely. I'd seen that face before. It was the girl standing next to me! Sue Fear was at that time one of Australia's most successful mountaineers, only the second Australian woman to climb Mount Everest – all the way without oxygen.

As the speeches wound down, I introduced myself and, extending my hand, congratulated her on her climb. Her hand was small, but the handshake was firm. She regarded me carefully, almost warily. 'That's me over there,' I said, pointing to a stand with a map on it showing the camel track across the Tanami Desert that I had completed in 2002 with Andrew Harper. She wandered to the stand, picked up a copy of my book and looked at the photos. That I was a fellow adventurer seemed to reassure her somewhat, and she began to talk about the travails of being the only female on an all-male climbing trip to Mount Everest. I plied her with questions.

'What's the hardest part of climbing Everest?'

'Coming down. You're tired and crook from the altitude, and you've used a lot of energy just getting up there.'

'Is that why fatalities usually occur on the way down?' I asked.

She thought for a while. 'Yeah, partly. On the way up you're facing in, so it's easier to dig in with your tools and boots. On the way down, you're often facing out and you're in a sort of a controlled fall anyway. The mountain's behind you.'

'I suppose the lack of oxygen really starts to tell, too?'

'Yeah, it slows your reflexes. And everyone's dehydrated by that stage, and that starts to make you wonky.'

'Well, you made it,' I said. I told her about my discovery of Herzog's book *Annapurna* at a young age, and about taking it up Tiger Hill, above Darjeeling, to watch the sunrise on Kanchenjunga and my attempted trek into the sanctuary at Annapurna.

'You should've been a climber,' she said.

'Nah. Too late. And I'm really afraid of heights.'

'*Everyone's* frightened of heights,' she said.

'Not like me, they're not. I'm terrified.'

We were interrupted by one of the *Australian Geographic* staff who wanted Sue for photographs, and to meet some of the dignitaries. She was the celebrity in the room, although this wasn't a role in which she seemed entirely comfortable.

'I've got three teenage daughters and I'm always trying to inspire them,' I said as she turned to go. 'I think you're a great role model for young women. They need inspiring figures like you. Well done.'

'Thanks,' she said. She seemed almost embarrassed. We shook hands and she disappeared into the crowd. I never saw her again.

Australia's first successful mountaineer had been a woman. Freda Du Faur was the first woman to climb Mount Cook and Mount Tasman, New Zealand's toughest climbs. At the turn of the twentieth century, she had worn a frilly shirt, tweed skirt, puttees, leather hob-nail boots and a driving veil. Tools at the time were primitive, including ropes made of manila hemp. That Freda had been considered a daft eccentric, and Sue was an admired example of what a modern woman can achieve, is a sign of how far women had come in the 100 years that separated them. Had they met, Sue Fear and Freda Du Faur would have found much in common.

It was the first time I had spoken to a real mountaineer, and for weeks afterwards I rehashed our brief conversation with my wife and daughters. They seemed underwhelmed by my brush with a climbing superstar.

Fourteen months later, at the end of May, 2006, I was in my car, running late for work and cursing the traffic. The radio was turned to the ABC's 8.30 am news broadcast.

TONY EASTLEY: While the Australian mountaineering community is celebrating the survival of climber Lincoln Hall, they're coming to terms with news that Sue Fear, the second Australian woman to climb Mount Everest, is missing.

The 43-year-old from Sydney and her Nepalese Sherpa climbing partner reportedly fell into a crevasse after reaching the summit of Mount Manaslu in Nepal.

Ms Fear's climbing partner climbed out of the crevasse and told authorities she was missing, presumed dead.

Sabra Lane, an ABC journalist, took up the story describing Sue's twenty years of mountaineering experience and how she had set out a fortnight earlier with her Sherpa climbing partner and got within 150 metres of the summit of the eighth highest mountain in the world before turning back. Undeterred, the pair had made another attempt, successfully reaching the top before both fell into the crevasse during the descent. The journalist briefly described Sue's work as an ambassador for the Fred Hollows Foundation.

I had pulled into a side street, where I sat listening to the awful news. I was gutted. I couldn't believe she was gone, and that a mountain had taken her, on the way down, after the hardest work was apparently done.

I thought about Sue Fear again as I knelt on the summit of Mount Aspiring.

'Come on, we've got to get out of here,' Anton said, stuffing my camera back in my pack. He began busily reorganising coils and lengthening the rope for our descent. 'You'll go in front. Follow the tracks we made on the way up.'

I nodded, but was surprised by this arrangement. The reason soon became apparent.

'Put the axe in your left hand. Use it for support,' Anton said.

There were no last lingering looks around, no poetic notions of having conquered the mountain. All I was conscious of was fear of the coming descent, and the need to get off the mountain as quickly as possible. *At least it will be easier on my legs*, I thought.

Coming down the steep section above the north face, then around on to the ridge, forced me into a brutal confrontation with my fear of heights. On the way up, I had looked at my gloved hands on the tools, at my boots or at Anton's back. I had studiously avoided looking at the view, and especially at anything below me. In this way, I had managed to get right to the summit without exposing myself to the void. Cowards can climb mountains, but there's no way you can get down one without having a look.

'Oh, crap,' I said out loud as I made my way slowly off the summit. Dropping away beneath my boots was the entire Mount Aspiring panorama. Below us was the north face, then the sweeping slope of the northwest ridge and, finally, the Therma Glacier. In the distance, the Haast Range stretched away into infinity. It was a wilderness of snow and frightening peaks.

My feet started to slide from under me.

'Stay on your feet! Keep moving!' Anton roared over the shriek of the wind.

'Give me one good reason why I wouldn't want to stay on my feet,' I said under my breath.

My problem, once again, was my crampon technique, combined with a subtle change in the snow conditions. I religiously put my boots down in the crampon tracks that we had made earlier, but because the slope was so steep and my technique was faulty, my lower leg kept sliding away and I went close to stumbling sideways on several occasions. I couldn't get the outside points of my crampons into the snow. The mechanics of my pronated ankles were trying to kill me.

'Use your axe to support yourself. Stay on your feet. Don't roll your knee in,' Anton shouted. He was behind and slightly above me, watching me intently, waiting to belay what he must have thought would be an inevitable fall.

I had a lot of problems with the axe. I tried to get a rhythm going with my boots, and when the snow was hard and just the tip went in, the axe gave me support, like a walking stick. Every five or six steps, however, I would hit a patch of softer snow, lean on the axe, and the handle would slide right into the snow, threatening to topple me forward. When, as often happened, I pushed the axe in with my left, uphill hand and my right boot slid away down the mountain, my only contact with the mountain was the crampon points on my left boot. I stumbled, slid and wobbled, righted myself, took a step, slid again and recovered. When this happened I would pause momentarily to collect myself, but stopping in such an exposed place invited disaster and I understood Anton's frustration.

My heart in my mouth, expecting a fall at any time, I staggered around the summit cone and eventually, somehow, we crossed over onto the top of the ridge.

Other than shouting at me to stay on my feet, Anton didn't say anything. He kept a tight grip on the rope and a look of somewhere between rage and intense concentration on his face. My legs were shaking with fright and exhaustion when, somewhere near the picket fence on the southern cornice, Anton called a halt.

'You're rolling your ankle and not getting all the points on the snow. It's really dangerous. The crampons will slip out from underneath you.'

'Yeah, I know,' I shouted back over my shoulder. 'I can't seem to control my legs. And the snow seems to vary – one minute it's hard and the crampons bite in, and the next it's really soft and slides away. I'm finding it really difficult to stay on my feet.'

'If you were stronger, one leg would hold you if the other one slips away. Your leg muscles should balance you, no matter what the conditions. Let's keep going over there.' He pointed towards the northern cliffs. We began the downhill traverse by following the tracks we had made earlier. He was right. Because my legs were tired, my balance was badly affected.

Sue Fear's warning was spot on. When descending a mountain, the only things between you and an uncontrolled fall are a strong pair of legs and your crampons. The long-handled ice axe is not nearly as helpful on the way down as on the way up, I was discovering. The short-handled ice hammer was of no use whatsoever.

And so we proceeded, Anton behind and slightly uphill; me treading carefully in this morning's tracks. *Ice axe one, two, get to the end of traverse, change hands, change direction, ice axe one, two . . .*

About halfway down the ridge we met the two Perth doctors struggling up the tracks we'd made earlier. I passed the first climber and nodded at him. 'G'day. How's it going?' He didn't reply. He had his head down in a determined fashion and was taking very small steps. He seemed to be exhausted. Some way behind, and making harder work of it, the second of the brothers stopped as we drew near.

'G'day. Everything alright?' I asked.

'How far to go?' he asked Anton breathlessly.

'Ah, a bit of a way,' Anton said. 'You've got about an hour ahead of you. A couple of hundred metres.'

'God, I'm stuffed,' he said, and leaned on his ice axe.

I know how you feel, mate. I wondered if they would get to the top. They were climbing unroped in that section of the climb, so were obviously confident. I resumed walking. 'See ya. Good luck,' I called out over the wind as we continued down. I took some comfort from the fact that, although they were at least twenty years younger than me, they were just as buggered and looked just as scared.

Further down, the ridge began to flatten out. Anton stopped and said suddenly, 'We're going too slow. I want you to face out and walk straight down like this.' He coiled the rope in his hand and then took three huge strides straight down the mountain, launching out and landing on the rear points of his crampons, his heels striking the slope first and arresting his downward momentum.

'You have to walk a bit like a duck, feet poking out slightly. It's a lot quicker,' he said from a spot about five metres below me. He had covered an enormous amount of ground with each stride, practically bounding down the mountain. Unencumbered by a novice client, he would have reached the bottom of the mountain in no time.

'Now you try it,' he said, climbing back to me with the rope in his hand.

I set off lunging down the slope with long-legged strides. This was a completely different caper. Climbing up, we'd had our backs to the airy spaces. Now I had to embrace them, step fearlessly out into them, trusting that my heel crampons and leg muscles would pull me up. Anton followed close behind, still watching me carefully. We were certainly descending more quickly, but I still found the varying snow conditions difficult to judge.

'This is a lot quicker. Not so hard on the quads,' I shouted back over my shoulder to Anton.

My confidence grew with each stride, but confidence is a dangerous attribute in the apprentice mountaineer. I decided to take a look at the view. We were about halfway between the summit and the saddle marking the top of the ramp, walking straight down the spine of the ridge. I had been focusing intently on the placement of my ice axe and boots, heel strike and crampons. I'd lunge with my left leg and immediately plunge in the ice axe with my left hand. My right leg would swing through, and slam down heel first. Then I had a peek. It was all there, the majesty of Mount Aspiring. Straight in front was the saddle; beyond that the Haast Range ran off to the right, the Shipowner Ridge to the left, peaks, glaciers, vast airy distances and 'death cookies' everywhere.

While I was looking around me, my left boot heel hit the slope, followed by the point of my axe handle. Unfortunately, on this occasion, the spike on the tip of my axe handle broke through the hard crust of snow and sank in, causing me to lurch to the left. Simultaneously, my right boot swung through on its journey down the mountain and the inside crampons on the boot clipped the gaiter on my left leg. The steel points snagged momentarily on the gaiter, but with my forward momentum arrested I was left standing on my left leg and there was only one place I was going – straight down.

I saw a flash of blue sky, then the saddle below, then the glittering rime as I fell head-first down the ridge. Things started to slow down. You're supposed to shout 'falling' when roped to another climber. There was no time.

The classic self-rescue technique in this situation is to land with your head pointing up the mountain, on your back, then roll onto your stomach and get the pick of the ice axe into the snow. All your weight must be over the head of the axe. There was no time. Anyway, I was going to land with my head pointing down the mountain, and it is difficult even for an experienced mountaineer to recover from there. I took the only option available. The axe handle was already halfway in, so I pushed it all the way. Simultaneously, I let go of the ice hammer in my right hand and grabbed the top of the axe, pushing it even further into the snow. To my great relief, I felt it plunge like a sword deep into the muscle of the mountain. I rode the axe, using my weight to drive it in. With a tremendous thump that knocked all the wind out of me,

I landed on top of the axe. I felt the top of the axe drive into my lower left rib through my jacket and thermals.

Hanging on to the top of the axe with both hands, I ended up wrapped around it at the hips, with my upper torso pointing downhill and my legs splayed across the slope. I could hear Anton's comment, spoken in a very loud voice. 'That happened because you weren't fucking paying attention. You're not here to look at the view.'

I looked up to where he sat about five metres above me on the slope. As I'd fallen, I felt the savage tug of the rope as it jerked tight on my harness when Anton had driven upwards and backwards with his legs to gain purchase. He ended up sitting in the snow, his legs braced against my weight on the rope.

He sprang to his feet and began shouting directions. 'Now get your boots downhill. Dig your crampons in!' As I began to move, my weight shifted slightly on the axe and my head ended up even further downhill. Mass and gravity were taking over.

'Get your *legs* downhill, I said! Not your *head*.' With Anton using all his strength on the rope, I managed to wriggle around until I was lying with my legs pointing downhill, front points dug into the snow. I still clutched the top of the axe, which protruded about 30 centimetres out of the snow. I slowly got to my knees, then to my feet, facing uphill. I was shaking with fright and humiliation. The fall had knocked the breath out of me, and a sharp pain in my side suggested I may have broken a rib. I was gasping for breath, and somewhere under all those thermals my heart was pounding.

Anton came down to me, his face in a fury. 'I want you to pay attention. Mountaineering's a serious business.' I nodded, feeling gutted.

I had been here before, whenever my stepfather had raged at me for some mistake I'd made while trying to do my best. Fear and humiliation – old ground for me, and for a moment I was sixteen again. Then, as now, I was unsure how to react and what to say. I felt Anton's scorn and buried my humiliation deep inside, as I always had, and said nothing.

I thought I'd left all this behind as a teenager. I don't want to go through all this shit again, not here on the mountain, I thought.

Uncertain what would happen now, I stood silent and shaking, frightened and angry, but gritting my teeth. I was determined not to lose my temper and lash out, especially as I had razor-sharp tools in both hands. I gathered up the rope, not bothering to apologise.

At that point, my stepfather and Anton merged in my mind. Both were very capable in everything they did, immensely practical, but short on patience and sparing with encouragement. Unwittingly, Anton was opening some very old wounds. I pulled the ice axe from the snow, wrenching it up by the adze. I retightened the wrist leashes on both the axe and hammer and turned back down the mountain, taking a deep breath and trying to collect myself. I couldn't stop shaking. My heart was pounding blood through my temples at such pressure, I could hear the noise in my head over the howling wind.

I stepped off as instructed. 'Head that way,' Anton said, pointing with his axe towards the left-hand side of the saddle we had ascended earlier. 'In mountaineering, we take the line of least resistance down the mountain.' Down we went, Anton calling directions over my shoulder as I re-focused my attention on my boots. The view went by unheeded.

Chapter 9

No Place for an Atheist: The Ramp Again

Courage is resistance to fear, mastery of fear – not absence of fear.
MARK TWAIN

Anton led me down to the top of the snow slope we'd climbed early that morning. It ended in a short, abrupt lip. This was the top of the ramp proper. Although I couldn't see, I knew that just below us the cliff fell straight down for several hundred metres, then dog-legged around to the right before plummeting onto the Bonar Glacier. Our tracks from the morning's climb led from the lip of the ramp up past the small depression where Anton now called a halt.

'Here will do,' he said, taking off his pack and leaning it against the wall of the depression. We remained roped together. I looked at the giant séracs – crags of ice, each weighing many tonnes – towering menacingly over us. They were deep blue at the edges, where they refracted the sun's rays.

Anton fished sandwiches out of his pack. I uncoiled the tube on the Platypus, desperate for a drink. The water had thawed considerably and I was able to free the tube by squashing the trapped ice with my fingers. The day was really starting to warm up now; I could feel the sun scorching my face as heat radiated off the snow. The great silence of the mountains enveloped us as we sat on the snow eating our lunch. Despite the morning's shared struggles, there didn't seem to be any bonding occurring between Anton and me. It was very stiff and formal, just like when my step-father and I had stopped after a long morning's hard work and eaten our lunch in silence. I'd hoped to have a yarn with Anton over lunch, hoped we'd end up mates at the end of all this, but that now seemed unlikely.

I'm the boss. You do what you're told, seemed to sum up our relationship so far.

I suppose, given the circumstances, it can't be any other way, I thought, looking absentmindedly at the giant ice towers.

Hoping to open the batting, I asked: 'How'd ya know they're not gunna fall over on top of us?'

He looked up at the séracs. 'Don't worry, they're frozen. They won't fall on you.'

I thought I could detect a note of contempt in his voice, when I had a genuine interest in knowing. I'd asked him about the depth of the crevasse earlier in the day because I wanted to know how far a bergschrund goes down a mountain under the snow. He'd taken that question as a sign that I was afraid. Similarly, I wanted to know why there were séracs well above the glacier. Séracs are unstable towers of ice, some as large as a house, and are usually found in ice falls – equivalent to a waterfall – where a glacier plunges over an under-lying cliff. Sometimes they occur where two glaciers intersect. We didn't appear to be in an ice fall. We were above the Bonar Glacier, so what were the séracs doing up there? I had wondered about this as we'd walked past them in the morning. The world's most famous sérac field, the Khumbu ice fall on Mount Everest, has killed more climbers than any other mountain feature on earth. I genuinely wanted to know how glaciers are formed; how they tear the ridges off the mountains to form buttresses. I was full of questions. Sure, I was frightened, but that's not what motivated my questions. Anton didn't seem to get that.

As we finished our lunch, eaten mostly in silence, I tried to see climbing from his point of view. In 25 years of alpine guiding he had probably been asked every dumb question about mountains and mountaineering – probably the same questions many times over. And how many times had he sat under the giant séracs and been asked, 'Are they going to fall on us?' I had to admit it would drive me crazy too.

'Time to get going,' Anton said after about ten minutes. I stood up and slung my pack on, looking over to where Anton stood about three metres away.

Where's the rope? I thought.

As a matter of habit now, every time I stood up I hooked the rope with my ice axe handle and pushed it away from my boots. I followed the course of the rope from my harness across the axe handle to where it snaked around behind Anton. I stopped dead – I couldn't believe my eyes! He was standing on the rope. I had to stop myself from laughing. *What would it prove?* I asked myself. *We've got to get down the ramp together. Don't be a dickhead.* I let it pass.

'We'll step sideways down to the top of the ramp. Then I'll get you set up for the descent,' Anton said, after he'd finished organis-ing his pack, the rope and the two tools – a snow pig and snow stake – which would be critical for our safe descent of the steep snow slope in declining conditions. Indicating that he was already considering the descent, he removed the snow pig from my pack, where it had been strapped since we left Colin Todd Hut, and strapped it within easy reach on his own pack. The pig is a type of snow stake used as an anchor in soft snow conditions, where a conventional stake would not hold.

I nodded and led off, side-stepping carefully down the slope, and concentrating on getting all the crampons on both boots into the snow, which was becoming sloppier by the minute. The slope started to steepen, and soon we reached the top of the lip. I forced myself to look down that terrible slope to where the buttress, the rocky outcrop marking the bottom of the ramp, was a dot in the distance.

'That'll do,' Anton said. As he began to prepare the first anchor, my mind wandered to the tragedy that had occurred below our stance less than two years earlier.

In January 2005, Marc Freedman (aged 22) and his mate Giovanni Trambaiolo (23) had stood where Anton and I now prepared for our descent. They were accomplished mountaineers from Sydney on the last leg of a year-long mountaineering tour. They had planned one last climb before returning home – Mount Aspiring. Freedman, a former Sydney Grammar student and one of the most gifted climbers in the University of New South Wales Rock Climbing and Mountaineering Club, went first. Trambaiolo followed him down. They were unroped, choosing to back their experience and fitness against the wiles of the mountain and the deteriorating mid-summer snow conditions. Unlike Anton and me, they had reached the summit by the technically more difficult southwest ridge. They were seeing the ramp for the first time as they climbed down it.

Freedman surged ahead, descending strongly and getting well in front of his friend. He soon disappeared from sight. Somewhere between where we stood on the lip of the ramp and the buttress far below, a tragedy had occurred. Trambaiolo was unaware that his friend was gone, as he had heard no sound. He reached the bergschrund shortly after 10.30 am expecting to find Marc, who was nowhere to be seen. After a search along the base of the ramp, he became concerned and retreated to Colin Todd Hut where he raised the alarm on the Department of Conservation's radio. As the coroner's inquest would subsequently show, a frantic Trambaiolo then ran into a bureaucratic minefield. Asked by the radio operator whether he had seen Freedman fall, he had to answer in the negative. Freedman was thus considered only to be overdue, and so a search couldn't be instigated straight away. It wasn't until about seven o'clock that evening that mountaineering rescue experts arrived at the hut. Freedman's body was found in a seated position above the bergschrund about two hours later. The coroner would report that he had sustained massive injuries and died instantly. Ten days later, demonstrating how ruthless the ramp can be, a 28-year-old German climber also fell to his death on descent.

I watched Anton setting up and was curious to know what technique he would use to get us both down safely. He had three choices, I reckoned. We could down-climb, facing into the mountain, short roped – the same as we had done in the morning, only in the opposite direction. *Highly unlikely*, I thought. The snow had deteriorated underfoot, and was noticeably softer now. If we were down-climbing, I would be going down first. And if I fell, Anton would find it hard to hold me without an anchor, as his momentum would also be in the downward direction.

An alternative was to place an anchor, such as the snow stake he carried on his pack, which Anton could use to belay me as I climbed down. This was the reverse of the technique we had used on the first two pitches in the morning. The downside to this technique was my inexperience – the snow was treacherous, and Anton knew my legs were tired. Also, down-climbing stresses the Achilles tendons and calf muscles, especially if the descent is down sustained pitches. We would have to climb down five, possibly six, lengths of rope. As my legs tired further, I might lose control, fall and shock-load the anchor, tearing it out. Anton would then have to rely on his own stance on the snow to hold the fall after the anchor went. On a steep pitch such as the ramp, he would be keen to avoid having to do this at all costs.

Anton started to cut a small box in the snow and then removed the ice stake from his pack. The ice screws he'd used earlier would no longer work, as the mountain had turned treacherous. He began to pound the stake into the snow, the arm holding the ice hammer rising and falling rhythmically. *Looks like I'm down-climbing belayed off that snow stake*, I thought.

Another alternative was that I would abseil off the stake, which was fine with me; I'd practised the technique many times in Sydney.

Which method Anton chose would depend on his assessment of the worsening snow conditions and his confidence in my climbing and athletic ability. It turns out he had no confidence in either.

'OK, step up here. I'll get you set up. You're going to abseil down,' he said.

'Great,' I replied. 'I've practised this heaps of times.' I stepped cautiously up to where he had set the anchor. I reached for the stitch plate – a friction device – and prusik sling to attach to the rope. These tools would allow me to control my descent and lock the rope if I started to fall. At worst, if I slipped or lost control of the descent, I'd be left dangling off the anchor. Anton saw me reaching for the tools on my harness.

'You won't need those. I'll control the rope,' he said.

My heart sank. This was a fourth alternative I hadn't even considered. In a genuine abseil the climber controls his descent. What Anton was proposing was to lower or rappel me off the anchor. All I would have to do is climb backwards and downwards and not stumble. In technical mountaineering terms I would have stopped climbing, as my weight would be on the rope which he'd control.

Bugger it. I'm gunna get lowered like a sack a potatoes, I thought.

He must have sensed my disappointment. 'This is the safest way to get an inexperienced climber down here,' he said matter-of-factly. I nodded in agreement.

I squatted below the anchor. The rope ran from my harness to an Italian hitch on a karabiner attached to the snow stake cable. The rope then ran through Anton's hands. He'd tossed the coil down the mountain so it wouldn't snag. He also tied himself onto the anchor. He then knelt in the snow and got a grip on the rope.

'Now, this is what's going to happen,' he said. 'You're going to step down in the tracks we made this morning. When the rope's run out, I'll call "five metres". You'll stop, cut a stance, get secure, dig your ice tools in and call out "safe". Make sure you cut a good stance. I'll bring the anchors with me and down-climb to you, and then we'll do it again. It's important that you follow the line we used this morning. Understand?'

I nodded.

'When you're ready,' he said. I squatted just below the anchor and we looked at each other. I thought of trying to change his mind – to let me down-climb under my own steam, with him belaying me off the anchor but not holding my weight or controlling the descent. I didn't think for long. Clearly, either he felt that I couldn't get down under my own power, or he wasn't prepared to risk me falling and taking the anchor and him with it. Didn't matter; the result was the same. I was going down under his control.

He watched me while I deliberated. Even though this was a very secure method of descending, it took me a moment to summon the courage to step backwards. I looked down over my left shoulder where the slope fell away for hundreds of metres. It was like stepping backwards for the first time off the abseiling platform in the Sydney gym. The floor was a bit further away here. I squatted there, thinking about it for a moment.

Anton was becoming impatient, and I think misread my hesitation. 'You're going to have to stand up sometime to get down,' he said. I nodded. There was no point in discussing anything further. I took up the slack in the rope, testing my weight against the anchor.

'That's me,' I said. Anton gripped the rope tightly.

'Abseiling,' I said, and stepped out and down into the first of the footholes we'd made during our ascent. They were now full of snow and barely discernible in some places. Looking over my shoulder, I began to descend. Down and down I went, treading gingerly, kicking into the foot holes where I could. After about 25 metres I hit my first snag. The loop of rope fell down the mountain. When I reached it, it was doubled over. To avoid stepping on it, I would have to step across about a metre, as well as down at the same point. If I was going to fall and muck this up, this is where it would be. I made sure my right crampons dug in and then I stepped over the rope and down into the next foot hole. I was clear of the rope. To tread on it and cut it at this stage would have been catastrophic. Down I went, placing one foot after the other, looking constantly at the snow just over my left shoulder and trying not to look down the ramp.

After what seemed a long time, I heard 'five metres' from above. I stopped. Digging my crampons into the snow and taking my weight off the rope, I began to wield the large ice axe. I used the adze this time, not the pick – just as I'd seen Anton do on many occasions during the day. *Chop, chop, chop*. Now I was doing it.

First, I dug a horizontal piece out of the wall about 60 centimetres long. I tried to use the same economy of movement that Anton had used. Next, I chopped the vertical foothole. I raked the loose snow and ice out until I had a clean, neat position for my boots, then I stepped into it. I spreadeagled my feet so that the insteps of both boots hugged the snow and the toe points were buried deep in the flesh of the mountain.

'Safe,' I called. Anton immediately sprang into action.

The rope between us ran up the mountain – a straight line on the snow from my harness to the anchor. As we were descending in full daylight, I could see exactly what Anton was doing and watched him curiously. He unhitched himself from the karabiner attached to the snow stake, placed the karabiner on his harness, then pulled the stake out of the snow and strapped it to the side of his pack. Neither of us was now anchored to the mountain.

'Off anchor,' he shouted.

He began his descent. I now had a front-row seat from which to watch a great climber strut his stuff. He was facing into the mountain, using his tools once more in the dagger technique. *One, two* with the tools, *three, four* with boots and crampons, stepping methodically into the steps he'd cut earlier. Unencumbered by a short-roped client, he moved effortlessly, almost swaying down those giddy heights. Climbing as Anton was doing it sits somewhere between gymnastics and ballet performed on a high trapeze without a net.

Watching him, I knew that great athletes are born, not made. As he swayed down towards me, I also realised there was a problem with the rope. As the whole 50 metres of it was uncoiled on the mountain, it slid downwards as Anton descended. About a metre to my right, it wound down the fall line like a giant 'U' running from Anton's harness down past me before running back up to my harness. The further he descended, the deeper the 'U' went down the mountain. I realised after he had taken only a few steps that this would happen and that I should try to grab the rope. But if I took my hands off my tools, I would risk toppling backwards off my stance. I watched the rope continue to skid down the mountain.

Anton said nothing as he reached my stance. He climbed about two metres above me, then across to my left side, so that if he fell he wouldn't land on me and knock me off my perch. He pounded in the ice stake again. He then needed to gather in the rope to secure himself and set the abseil.

'I've gotta flake 50 metres of rope. It's all the way down the mountain,' he said in an exasperated tone.

'I'd thought of trying to grab it, but I couldn't reach it without taking one of my hands off the tools. Sorry.'

He continued silently to wind in the rope until it formed a neat pile where he knelt.

After he'd set up the anchor and hooked me on, I set off down the second pitch, stepping over the rope halfway down. I took great delight in cutting my second stance. I was really warming to the work and felt the joy of swinging the long axe to cut a ledge that could save my life.

'Safe,' I called. Again, as Anton began to descend, the rope whizzed down, tantalisingly close this time. But still I couldn't reach it without letting go of the tools. Again, Anton wound in the rope when he reached me, wordlessly this time.

During the third pitch, several things happened. We were about halfway down the ramp now. Anton began to pound in the snow stake. I'd noticed on the previous two pitches that it took him at least fifteen solid whacks with the ice hammer to get the long stake buried deep in the snow. This time, it slid home with six hits. I noticed as he hit the top of the stake that the metal was beginning to curl and deform from the concussion.

'No good, too soft,' he said. He reattached the stake to his pack and took out the snow pig. He pounded this new anchor a few times, then he pulled on the cable. Again he shook his head and pulled it out.

'Too shallow. It'll just slide along under the snow if you put any weight on it,' he said. He pulled the pig out, then banged it in again at a slightly different angle. The pig is a last resort tool for when the snow is so soft it won't hold even a conventional stake. The pig is put in at an angle to the snow, so that as a climber's weight is put on it, it buries itself under the snow like a diving submarine. The only catch is that it has to be put in at *exactly* the right angle, or it will pull out – with catastrophic results for the climber rappelling off it. Anton pulled on the cable, testing to see if it was secure. He seemed satisfied and, after rigging up the rope, nodded to me to descend.

I set off again, gradually warming to the routine as my confidence grew. I cut my stance as usual. It gave me great satisfaction to step on to these tiny ledges I'd cut myself. Anton was half a football field above me on the slope. I felt I finally owned part of the climb.

If I fall here, I've got no one to blame but myself. This is great, I thought. I revelled in being momentarily alone. I felt excited by the height and danger, relieved that Anton wasn't looking over my shoulder. I watched him climb down the third pitch and the rope again slid past me down the mountain. I debated with myself whether I should try to grab it. I felt that Anton was doing all the work and I was doing nothing. At the same time, I didn't want to risk falling. *It's Anton's problem. He can wind the rope in when he gets down here.* Finally, I couldn't stand it anymore. I took my right hand off the ice hammer, keeping the leash round my wrist for safety and grabbed the rope. I flaked it into a pile resting on top of the ice tools, as I wound it back and forth. My left hand remained grimly attached to the long ice axe, the handle of which was buried right up to the adze in the snow. My toes were jammed as deep into the mountain as my crampons would allow.

About 200 metres below me was the rock buttress that had ended Marc Freedman's life. He would have hit those rocks at over 100 kilometres an hour, then been spat out into space before landing near the crevasse below the buttress. I thought of what it must be like for a climber's loved ones to get that fateful call; what it would be like for my wife to get such a call. The first that she would know would be the New Zealand accented voice of an anonymous Wanaka policeman calling to say a family member had been killed and instructing them to make arrangements to collect the body. That's how it would be for Prue and my daughters if anything happened to me. I felt very selfish there, clinging on to my tools on that deadly slope. Other than my mother a long time before, I'd never experienced the death of a close relative. I had never given my own mortality much consideration, until I was forced to face it on that cliff of ice and snow, surrounded by the ghosts of Marc Freedman and the other climbers who had lost their lives there. I confronted the grim reality that death was only a second away – if I let go of the other tool, if my boots slipped or my crampons broke, I'd smash into the rocks below. There was no maybe about this. No *maybe I'd only suffer severe injuries*. There was a definite reality about those black rocks and the crevasse lurking beneath them. With 50 metres of rope out, Anton would have no way of holding a fall like that.

Is this what my family deserves? I wondered.

I had told my wife that – with Catherine leaving school and Hilary leaving university – my childrearing responsibilities were finished. 'Now it's my turn,' I'd said. 'Now it's time for me to enjoy myself.' But now, I wasn't so sure. Do a parent's responsibilities stop just because you stop writing the cheques, stop standing on the sidelines at sporting matches, stop looking up exam results? Do you stop being part of a family just because the children are grown? I had to conclude, the answer is 'no'.

Mountaineering is a selfish pursuit. Climbers take with them their own fears and anxieties but also leave a load of dread and apprehension for all their family members left behind. They don't know what's driving the climber to climb. They may not even know on what day a summit attempt is to be made. They can only imagine the worst possible outcomes of falls, crevasses and avalanches. It must be torture every time the phone rings. A call in the middle of the night would be shattering.

This is really self-indulgent. My kids deserve better than this. No man's life is his own to chuck away if he feels like it. I've got a lot left to live for, I thought.

While I'd agonised during the first couple of pitches about flaking the rope, I had also weighed up the consequences of a fall. The prospect of falling was now uppermost in my mind, as I had time to consider my situation and had screwed up the courage to look down the mountain. I wondered what it would be like to fall. Would everything just stop? How would I handle the dreadful realisation that I was about to die? My parents had a strong belief in a better life in another place after death. For them, death would be a release from the struggles of their daily lives. During my high school years spent in Bathurst, the Vincentian fathers had burned any religious faith out of me with their tolerance of the brutality practised in boarding schools run by male Catholic clergy. They took away from me a safety net that I now badly needed. Flogged into attending mass every day of high school, I tried hard to talk to God and listen to what He might have to say to me. Nothing. He never talked back. By the time I left boarding school at age eighteen, I was convinced that God didn't live in churches. He probably didn't live anywhere. So for me, a fall down the ramp had a calamitous and terrifyingly final dimension. There is no upside for an atheist on a mountain climb. I had everything on the line. If I fell, it would be all over; there *was* no afterwards. But on that wall – on that animate, pagan pile of rock and snow – I was so scared, I knew I needed help and I wasn't so sure anymore that there was no God, whatever that means.

Anton climbed surely and steadily towards me. When he arrived on my level, he spied the neatly flaked pile of rope. 'Good. That's what mountaineering's all about – teamwork,' he said. Despite my fear I felt pleased with myself, like I was finally part of the team, and talking to Anton relieved some of the fear as it gave me something close at hand to concentrate on. After five pitches we had climbed down past the rock buttress and the breadth of the glacier was visible. The bergschrund was a gaping black crack 50 metres below us.

'You should get down on this rope. I want you to step exactly in our tracks from this morning. Go to the edge of the bergschrund and cross where we crossed. Just step over backwards and make yourself secure.'

I nodded.

'See your ski pole – head for that,' he said.

I looked down to where he pointed. Sure enough, the black handle of my trekking pole, with its dangling leash, poked up over the lip of the bergschrund below us. It was almost like a welcoming committee, something familiar in the wilderness. It was a strange feeling to see it just where I'd left it in the dark, in what seemed an eternity ago. I would have to step down and to the left to reach the pole.

'Abseiling,' I said, and set off on the last pitch following our tracks. Everything went well until I reached the lip of the crevasse. *Oh, crap*, I said to myself. I looked up at Anton. He was looking down at me but was going to be of no use. He was too far away. I looked back over my shoulder.

The ice bridge we had crossed in the morning was no longer there. I paused to gather my thoughts. The gap was too wide to step across backwards where we had crossed previously. Anton could probably do it, but I wasn't confident I could do it and hit the bottom lip of the crevasse on my first go. I looked to my left.

The crevasse was just a gaping hole. To my right, about six metres away, a small ice bridge crossed the bergschrund where it narrowed. Would it hold my weight?

'Hold on. I can't cross here,' I shouted up to Anton, warning him not to play out any more rope. If he did, I risked stumbling back into the hole. I stepped sideways towards the ice bridge along the upper lip of the crevasse, taking care to stay well away from the hole.

On reaching the bridge I twisted around and poked it with the long handle of my axe. It seemed firm. Here goes, I thought. 'Crossing,' I yelled to Anton, and took as big a step backwards as I could. My right boot landed on the lip of the crevasse just where the ice bridge joined the crevasse lip. My left foot followed and I dug the axe in for support. I was over. I moved to where the ski pole jutted out of the snow and drove in the tools.

Now it was Anton's turn. He descended the last pitch with the tireless rhythmic swing he'd used on all sections of the ramp. But it was here that the mountain showed us its sneaky side and demonstrated why anyone who climbs in New Zealand without a helmet will eventually make a trip to the undertaker. It also showed me that while we were off the ramp, our stance on the lower lip of the bergschrund was still a long way above the floor of the glacier. A fall from here would still be a killer.

As Mount Aspiring is an alpine peak, it's continually freezing and thawing. During the day as the temperature rises, snow and ice melt and water pools in the rock crevices. When the temperature drops at night, this water freezes, expands and cracks the rock. This process of gradual disintegration goes on constantly, with the mountain perpetually shedding its skin of ice and rock – but especially in spring. Spring is avalanche season.

I took my stance but quickly realised that an ice cliff about 100 metres above us, which we'd passed on the way down, was now raining missiles. Projectiles the size of golf balls were pouring off the cliff. I estimated it was around 3 pm and that this side of the mountain had been in sunshine for at least five hours. Most of the missiles disappeared into the bergschrund, but some went flying over the top on the long journey down to the glacier below. Then I saw one fall from the cliff in a shower of snow and begin its journey. It looked the size of a bowling ball and began to bounce as it picked up speed and seemed to grow as it congealed with more snow.

'Watch out!' I yelled up to Anton. Whether he heard me or saw the missile, I don't know. He was concentrating intently on his boot placement as he had done all the way down the mountain, looking down his chest and between his legs to see where to kick in his crampons. He was looking down, not up, and was hence very vulnerable. To my great relief, the missile shot down between us, cleared the bergschrund and bounced out of sight down onto the glacier. I couldn't imagine what it would be like to be hit by one, especially if the climber didn't have a helmet. At best, it would fracture your skull.

'Don't follow the tracks – the bridge is gone,' I called to Anton when he was only ten metres above. 'I crossed over there to the right.' I pointed. He looked around and summed up the possibilities. I knew he would make his own decision about where to cross. He was soon down on the ledge beside me. I breathed a sigh of relief. I had descended the ramp without making any mistakes and upsetting Anton. I was very relieved. The hard part was over. Or so I thought.

Chapter 10

'Maurice, You Lying French Prick'

'George, we knocked the bastard off.'
SIR EDMUND HILLARY, TO FELLOW NEW ZEALAND CLIMBER
GEORGE LOWE ON HILLARY'S RETURN FROM THE FIRST
SUCCESSFUL SUMMIT OF MT EVEREST WITH CLIMBING
SHERPA TENZING NORGAY, 1953

Once Anton reached me on the south side of the bergschrund, it was all business. He dumped his pack against the ice wall and told me to do likewise. The rope had gone too wide for me to grab on the way down, so I began to haul it in starting from my harness. It snagged around a small ice protrusion further down the glacier and I couldn't bring it in. Anton saw me struggling. I didn't want to pull too hard, frightened that I would damage the rope in some way. I was terrified of that rope. Anton grabbed the other end. We now had each end of a 'U' that ran from our harnesses, 25 metres down the mountain and round the ice dome.

'OK, now pull,' he said. We both heaved, and the rope pulled tight around the ice knob. I knew Anton would have to climb down to free it and then climb back up, if this didn't work.

177

Nothing happened at first as the rope stretched, but suddenly the knob broke and we hauled in the rope, flaking it in a neat pile. Anton quickly measured out half of it and made a pile at my feet. The other half was flaked near him. He whipped the coils around himself, clipped a bight onto his karabiner and was now roped for glacier travel. I'd seen Anton do this many times by now, but watching the speed with which he coiled half a rope length around himself still amazed me. In less than half a minute, he had perfectly uniform coils of identical length wrapped around his right shoulder and under his left arm. I tried to do the same, but because of my hand I was much slower. He came over and helped me organise the coils, then tied off and snapped the bight onto my harness with the karabiner.

We drank some water, tied our helmets and ice hammers on our packs, and donned the peaked legionnaire's caps that would protect our necks from the burning sun.

'Crikey, it's hot,' I said, feeling the heat reflecting off the snow and ice. While the tempest may have been raging in the mountains above us, down where we stood, sheltered in the bowl created by the surrounding peaks, nothing stirred. Unlike the first two days the glacier was now breathlessly still; not a breath of wind disturbed the silence. I was vaguely aware that I had started to sweat under my thermals. I considered taking off my jacket and a layer of thermals, but the thought that it might increase my chances of falling from the stance and making the long tumble to the glacier was sufficient reason not to bother.

How hard can it be from here? I can see Colin Todd, I said to myself. I knew we were less than two kilometres from the hut – a small red dot on the Shipowner Ridge. In the Australian outback on foot, I'd have covered that distance in less than twenty minutes. *It won't take long, and there's not much climbing. It can't be too bad. I'll take everything off back at the hut.*

I left the bergschrund wearing glove liners, two layers of thermal jumpers under my storm jacket, thermal long johns and windproof outer shell pants. I would pay dearly for this miscalculation. This was now becoming a familiar pattern in my short mountaineering career. I would go through a period free from mishap, start to gain some confidence, and then do something stupid and end up in the doghouse again. I felt like a boxer who gets cracked hard on the jaw every time he struggles up off the canvas.

'OK. I'll go first. You follow exactly in my footsteps,' Anton said. 'The glacier's a lot more dangerous than it was this morning. The snow's softer, and ice bridges that gave us support won't be there now. You'll have to pay attention.'

I nodded.

'Use your long ski pole in your left hand on the downhill side, and use the axe for support on the uphill side.'

'OK. Right,' I said.

I had a quick look around; it was a truly amazing sight. We were standing at the top of the Bonar Glacier névé, literally the birthplace of the glacier. As we'd crossed the bergschrund we were technically no longer on the mountain, but on the mass of hardened snow piled up on its flanks. It's this mass, and the compaction caused by years of snowfall and avalanches cascading off Mount Aspiring, that makes the glacier flow and produces the awesome pressures that tear into the mountain.

To our left was the church steeple spire of Mount French; away over the far side of the glacier was Mount Bevan. I could see where we had landed on the col. Far down below, on the blinding white wilderness of the glacier, was the spot where we'd had a water halt on our walk in and Anton had explained to me the geometry of the mountain. It seemed an age ago. To the west – on our far right – the Shipowner Ridge formed another barrier. Perched on top of it was the tiny red dot of Colin Todd.

From our perch on the névé we were looking down into the Mount Aspiring corrie (from the Gaelic *coire*, for cauldron) – a steep-sided amphitheatre whose floor was the glacier. We were standing on the northern rim of the corrie; on the western rim was Colin Todd Hut. Walking around the rim of the bowl to reach the hut was too dangerous. It would be safer to climb down into the basin, cross the floor formed by the glacier, then climb up the other side. The Mount Aspiring corrie was nature at its most magnificent. This is what I'd come to experience.

I took a last look up the face of the ramp. It was intimidating. When last I'd stood at the lip of the crevasse in the pre-dawn twilight, I hadn't been able to see what we were about to tackle; now I couldn't believe I'd done it. The proof was there. Our tracks, a neat line of steps, formed a ladder far up the face. A uniform line of punctures created by ice tools driven in for support followed the tracks until both disappeared into the snow glare.

I wouldn't have had the guts to go up there, had I seen it. I'm glad it was dark, I said to myself.

I stared up the ramp, awed by its sweeping grandeur. Was this it? Had I achieved my goal? Could I finally relax and stop driving myself to take risks before I was crippled or killed? I began to relax and think about the journey home.

Twenty-five years before, I had flown back to Sydney from New Zealand to be with my dying mother at the palliative care hospital in Kirribilli. I sat with her for the last two days of her life, watching her gasp for breath as lupus slowly suffocated her. And finally, we had the conversation we had avoided having all my life.

'Why didn't you ever tell me about my real father? I don't even know his name.'

She stared at the ceiling, her breath coming in wheezes. It was

My mother, Alma Eileen Muss, with a newly minted member of the Esteemed Company, in Wellington, New South Wales, early 1953.

My grandmother, Mary Maude Muss, a tower of strength and support in my early childhood.

Sister Gertrude Cooke and three boys at Croagh Patrick Orphanage in the late 1950s, around the time of my stay.

My first sight of Mount Aspiring up close from Bevan Col before our descent to the Bonar Glacier.

Below: A water break on our journey across the glacier. Mount Aspiring is in the background. I felt the mountain was hunting us.

The verandah, Colin Todd Hut, after Anton had introduced me to crampons for the first time.

Below: Mountaineering is about waiting and patience. We waited inside Colin Todd Hut for the weather to clear.

Anton Wopereis, my guide on Mount Aspiring and a craftsman of the mountains. His quiet authority shone through the hut.

Below: Sunday afternoon in Colin Todd Hut, with Anton and two Perth climbers.

A man of many talents
– Anton cooks breakfast
at 2 am before our
climb.

Below: Anchor, first
pitch on the ramp.
The Clove hitch on the
right secures Anton to
the anchor. The belay
plate (centre) allows
him to haul in the rope
as I climb but lock the
rope if I fall. He has
added a transposed
karabiner for more
braking friction.
He knew his business.

Our route on Mount Aspiring.

1. Dawn halt Wopereis/Kelly

2. Morning halt

3. Picket Fence

4. Kelly falls on descent

5. Marc Freedman falls to his death in January 2005

Southwest Ridge

Southwest Face

Bonar Névé

Northwest Ridge

Ramp

Bergschrund

To Colin Todd Hut

© Craig Potton Publishing

Above: The sum of all fears. Our second pitch on the ramp just before dawn. The Perth climbers are visible coming over the rock band below me.

Morning halt, northwest ridge. The ice-capped summit of Mount Aspiring, plumed with wind-driven snow, is visible above.

Anton at the morning halt. Unaffected by his step-cutting ordeal on the ramp, he didn't need to sit down. He is holding a snow stake in his right hand.

'Give us a sec, will ya?' A pause on the ascent of the northwest ridge.

Reproduced with kind permission of Barbara Easson

Mates. Australians Marc Freedman (left) and Giovanni Trambaiolo on the summit of Mount Aspiring about 9.30 am, 2 January, 2005. Marc was killed an hour later descending the ramp. His spirit pervades the mountain.

No guard rails! On Mount Aspiring's summit, wondering how do I get down?

Afternoon shadows are already playing across the Bonar Glacier as I descend the ramp with a full length of rope out.

Anton and myself on our return to Colin Todd Hut. Only one of us was tired. Mount Aspiring is in the background.

Above: The loneliest privy in the world at Colin Todd Hut, looking towards Rolling Pin peak in the Haast range.

Anton and his Kiwi coils on the cliffs above the Matukituki River. 'The walkout's a killer.'

The first of the bridges across the Matukituki River.

Trying to find a path through the boulders in the riverbed.

Below: The serene beauty of the Matukituki River valley.

The spring-heeled terror of the West Matukituki. Anton is about to give me a lesson in how fast you can walk with a heavy pack if you really have to.

It ends here. Sitting on the verandah of Croagh Patrick Orphanage, December 2007.

quiet in the room, except for the hiss from her oxygen mask.

'I was too ashamed – ashamed for myself, and ashamed for you. I thought you'd grow up an angry and bitter man. I'm sorry, but I just couldn't bring myself to talk about it with you.'

I didn't know what to say. I was 29 years old, just married and about to embark on one of life's great journeys. I was really still a kid, and had tried to put my past behind me but I did understand a bit about shame.

'I'm not ashamed of you,' I said. 'You've always been great to me. You were the most special person in my life. We shared so much.' I held her hand and felt her frail, thin bones. She gave my hand an almost imperceptible squeeze, her strength fading fast.

I had a host of questions I wanted to ask about my father, things that were important to me. Was he successful? Did he have a uni degree? Was he smart? When, as a teenager, I'd thought about my father, I used to wonder what he'd achieved – not what he looked like, or what he was doing. To help fashion my own image, I had a vision of him as being successful; a famous barrister or a powerful businessman, and I just presumed he would have been good at sport. Deep down, I really wanted him to be someone like Lionel Terray, someone I could admire and of whom I would be proud to say, like other boys did, 'That's my father.'

'I need to know his name,' I said. 'Just in case I've got to contact him for any reason.'

Mum looked at the ceiling, tears streaming down her face and running off the edge of her oxygen mask. I wiped her face with a tissue.

'If I tell you, you must promise me one thing,' she gasped.

I nodded. She turned towards me, her bright blue eyes shining despite her pain.

'Promise me you won't go after him.' She explained that she and her sisters, who knew the whole story and my father's identity, had agreed not to tell me anything until after he had died. They had been too frightened of what I would do to him.

'Mum, I need to know. I need a name.'

She turned to face me. 'Kevin Moraghan,' she said. This gave me a jolt. I'd never heard the name before, but now it was real – a real person existed who probably looked like me, maybe talked like me.

'Why'd he run away?

'He had a wife in Sydney, and he was terrified she'd find out. He said he'd deny everything if I ever told anyone.'

'So he deserted us, both of us, and just ran away?'

She nodded.

'Did he ever offer to help you out financially?'

'No. That's one of the reasons I got married. I thought it would give us some financial security and you a father.' She shook her head, her eyes closed with pain.

A stab of anger went through me. *Oh, mate, you're gunna pay for this*, I thought. Back then I couldn't understand how anyone could leave a woman with a child to fend for herself in these circumstances. I understand desertion of a son by a father even less now that I am a parent.

Mum then asked me to say the rosary one last time with her. It had been a long time since we'd prayed together but I knew it would comfort her and so I agreed. She took great strength from the familiar ritual in her final moments, strength from a church that had denied her the right to have an abortion and then shunned her and me as being beyond redemption. She slipped in and out of consciousness and the beads slowly fell from her fingers.

Later, as I stood by her side after the doctors turned off her oxygen, she slipped into final unconsciousness surrounded by her children. I was stricken with grief for this woman who had shared life's long, hard journey with me. I wanted to wake her one last time and tell her that it didn't matter, that she shouldn't be ashamed, that she'd done her best. Her bastard baby boy had survived this far and would continue to survive. I wanted to tell her that despite it all, I loved her and I wanted to thank her. I begged the doctors to bring her around one last time so that I could tell her. They shook their heads. She was gone. I stood by her bedside holding her hand, sobbing.

'Don't worry, I'll square this up for you,' I vowed as I looked down at her face, peaceful now. 'I'll square this up for both of us.'

I had many questions to ask Anton, but he was already trudging away across the névé and tending to the rope. I dutifully followed. I was in trouble almost immediately. We had previously crossed this section in freezing darkness. The snow, firm and frozen, had made a squeaking sound underfoot. That firm surface had provided support for trekking pole and axe. Now the snow was late-afternoon mush and I continually sank up to my knees.

We'd gone no more than 200 metres and I had to ask for my first stop. Once again, my legs burned from the effort and felt rubbery. Again, I found it difficult to control the placement of my boots.

'I'm finding this stuff bloody hard to walk in. I keep sinking up to my knees,' I gasped during one halt.

'Just step exactly in the tracks,' Anton said, looking back. We stepped off again. It was no good, I kept sinking. I was soon panting, and the sweat ran down my face and under my thermals. I realised I had on far too much clothing.

'Take some snow into the holes as you put your boot down.' Anton demonstrated. I noticed he put his boot just to the side or to the rear of the existing tracks and pushed a pile of snow into each hole, giving him extra to stand on. We set off again and I tried his technique, but I couldn't get my foot to hit exactly on the side of the existing tracks. I'd take five steps, and then one leg would sink in up to the knee. It was exhausting trying to pull my boots and legs out of the holes, and I kept falling over.

'Use the axe to support yourself.' Anton had stopped to watch me getting up after another stumble. This didn't work for me. Sometimes the sharp point of the handle would stick in only a couple of inches and it would act as an effective walking stick. Other times it would sink in a couple of feet and I'd fall over.

After I'd stumbled into a hole, it was incredibly difficult to get out. If I used the axe to push myself up, my weight would force the tool in almost up to the adze and I'd stay put. If I put my hand down, it would go in up to the elbow. Try as I might, I found it almost impossible to get purchase on the snow.

We lurched along like this for over an hour – me panting and falling over, trying to stay on my feet, finding it very difficult to get up out of the sludge.

'Hold on a minute,' I said over and over. On one of my many halts, I paused to look back at the mountain, leaning on my axe and catching my breath. *Aspiring, you were sure more than I bargained for*, I thought. But the mountain summed up my life in some ways: aspiring for financial success, to prove myself the equal of other people and win their respect and aspiring for the love and affection of my family. But this is where aspiration can get you if you're not careful – exhausted and swimming knee deep in fresh snow on a remote glacier with treacherous crevasses all round. My face was burning from the sun's radiation, and I was so overheated it was becoming increasingly difficult to breathe. Then, without warning, I heard *woompf* – a noise from in front, like air exploding out of a burst tyre. I looked up. Anton was lying sideways in the snow, but he had only one leg.

What the hell's happened? I stood and stared. With growing shock, I realised that Anton had fallen into a crevasse. The snow had given way under one leg and he'd gone in up to his hip. His other leg stayed on the snow, and he'd ended up lying sideways. Then, like a cat, he leapt up, landing on both feet. He turned to face me.

'Small crevasse. Now I want you to step over that.' He pointed with his axe. I followed his tracks and came to a faint indent that ran across our path. I looked at him, then stepped over a large black hole the size of a basketball where Anton's leg had gone into the gloom. I was slowly realising why clients are never trusted with even a tiny part of the responsibility for a climb. Anton had fallen into a crevasse and leapt out before I'd even realised. If he'd fallen in completely I would have plunged in after him, still trying to work out what was happening. I had neither the skills, nor the experience or conditioned reflexes, to make a reliable climbing companion. It was another blow to my pride.

I stumbled on as Anton weaved around the dents and undulations in the snow that signalled the increasing number of crevasses. He stopped often to prod a suspicious piece of snow with the handle of his axe and then would change direction. 'Step over that', or 'Cross just here', or 'You'll have to jump over that' was a constant refrain. Sometimes when I jumped, I fell on landing. I seemed to have lost control of my legs.

The reality of a crevasse fall, one of the great objective dangers of mountaineering, was rammed home as we crossed the glacier. Photographs in mountaineering books usually show crevasses as vast open ice canyons, sometimes twenty metres wide, easy to see and easy to avoid – just go around them. If you do happen to fall into one, you get roped out. The reality is starkly different. Many are little more than cracks, up to 30 centimetres or so wide, but the really dangerous ones are twice that width and covered with a light roof of snow and ice. These are just wide enough to accommodate a human body, which, after falling as little as ten metres, could become so tightly wedged that no amount of skill could get the climber out. He would be pinned there in the dark, sometimes upside down with arms jammed by his side, unable to remove his pack or set up the rope. Death from hypothermia is the only outcome.

Somehow, after what seemed an age, we reached the last steep slope of the glacier – the far side of the bowl that led up to Colin Todd Hut. Perched on the ridge, it was about 200 metres above us, up the steep slope we'd climbed on the first day. I was fresh then, exhausted now. I looked up through a fog of pain and aching muscles and the cold, clammy feeling brought on by heat exhaustion. I had stopped sweating and I thought I might faint. Alarm bells rang in my head. I had been in this situation once before. Crossing the Tanami Desert in 2002, Andrew Harper and I had, on an unforgettable day, walked a punishing 30 kilometres through the scrub in temperatures around 39°C. I made it to the evening campsite, but then when my turn came to help set up camp, organise the fire and tend to the animals, I couldn't do it. I passed out and couldn't move for several hours. I felt the same way now. Blood pounded in my temples and I was developing a headache. I knew that if I didn't stop my exertions and get my body temperature down, I would probably faint. The skin on my face felt like it was being fried in oil, just as it had felt all those years ago in the desert.

The problem was due to inadequate hydration, I knew. I just hadn't drunk enough water during the day, especially given the amount of exertion required, the dryness of the air and the altitude. I've learned from numerous skiing trips that I cope much better with extreme cold than virtually anyone I've ever met. A slight rise in body temperature, however, and I fall apart.

'We'll follow these tracks straight up. The steps are well cut and I want you to walk in them. But the snow's soft and it's easy to fall from here, so be careful.' Anton led off. I don't remember much from that point. Time became a blur. I was sick with heat exhaustion – in a kind of detached fog. I remember putting my boots exactly in Anton's crampon tracks, slowly ascending the cliff to the shelf on which the hut stood; remember the last half a dozen steps. Anton climbed them effortlessly – I had to use the long ice axe to haul myself up, almost in a crawl. Through the fog I heard the sound of people clapping. 'Bravo! Congratulations!' It hardly registered.

Dimly I recall the sound of crampons clanking on the metal steps of the hut – first Anton's, then mine – then the duller sound of crampons on the timber verandah. Slaps on the back. 'Well done. You have the summit.'

I slid off my pack; someone took it from me and leaned it against the wall of the hut.

'Don't tread on the rope,' Anton said. It was now wound around on the verandah.

I staggered to one of the long benches and collapsed onto it. Someone thrust a cup of tea into my hand and slapped me on the shoulder. 'Well done, mate,' said an Australian voice.

I looked up. I hadn't seen the man before. I looked around. A dozen or so people were crowded onto the verandah. The hut, empty but for the two Perth climbers when we left in the morning, was now full as climbers who had been waiting in Wanaka for a break in the weather had been ferried up to Bevan Col in the chopper.

'What time is it?' I asked.

'Ten past five,' a host of people checking their watches answered. Thirteen hours had elapsed since we had left the hut and fifteen hours since I had climbed out of my sleeping bag. I had enough presence of mind to keep watching Anton. I wondered what would happen next. On a desert expedition, we would be clearing a place for the fire, getting the animals settled down, putting the hobbles on. Grooming would start if we were using horses. I knew all the rules in the bush; I had no idea what the protocol was after a mountain climb.

Anton detached himself from a group he was talking to. They appeared to be guides and were looking over at me. Anton joined me on the bench and immediately began to take off his crampons. We were sitting on the bench still roped together. Demonstrating how careful he was, Anton had taken no chances and had left me roped up right until I sat down on the verandah and there was no further chance of misadventure. We had shed our backpacks, but our crampons were still attached to our boots and the rope was still tied to our harnesses. I followed Anton's lead.

'Eez dis der person who only had der crampons on yesterday?' I looked up. A new arrival, whom I'd not met, had come over to us from the group Anton had been talking to. It was a mid-European accent, possibly German or Slovakian. He was smiling and looked friendly.

'Yeah, I guess that's me.'

'Dis eez not der mountain you climb first time. You should be climbing der smaller mountains first.'

'Yeah, mate. I think I agree.'

'Still, you have da successful first climb. Very good.'

'Thanks, mate. You're very kind, but there were two people up there today and only one of 'em was climbing.' I managed to smile and tried to make light of what had been a very difficult day.

The man looked confused. 'But you still climbed to the summit, no? You achieved your goal?'

I thought about what my real goal had been.

'Nah. Anton climbed to the summit, mate. I just tagged along,' I said, smiling.

The man seemed puzzled that I didn't appear more satisfied or triumphant, but I felt neither. I felt gutted, and I certainly wasn't about to start heaping accolades on myself, accolades that I felt I hadn't earned. In truth, I felt disappointed.

After Anton had taken off his crampons, I handed him mine. I'd noticed while taking off the left one that I'd had ripped the plastic anti-balling plate almost off the foot-bed. It must have happened when I fell on the descent. Anton looked at the broken plate but didn't comment.

I made a mental note that I should shout Anton a new rope and a set of crampons when we got back to Wanaka. He put the crampons on the verandah to dry. Next we untied the rope from our harnesses, and I helped him to take the kinks out of it and coil it. When it was coiled I picked it up and tied it off as neatly as I could. Next my boots came off. With great relief I pulled off the heavy, constrictive, plastic outer shells and felt the circulation start to flow through my feet. Left on my feet were what looked like leather, lace-up slippers – the liners. They, too, came off and were placed on the verandah to dry. I slid my feet into the joggers Anton had given me.

I ripped off the sweat-soaked thermals and hung them out, but my head was still pounding and I knew I had to attend to it. I walked inside the hut while Anton was regaling the other guides with details of the climb, particularly his step-cutting exercise on the ramp. I didn't want to deny him his moment of glory; he certainly deserved it. As we were the first party up the ramp for over a fortnight, there was great interest in the conditions, particularly the amount and condition of the snow, as this would determine which route the guides would use for their clients in the morning.

I grabbed a shirt from my bunk, then walked out onto the verandah, down the steps and around the back of the hut to where a basin had been built underneath the rainwater tank. I filled the basin and plunged my head into the freezing water. It was magnificent and I began to recover almost immediately. I washed all the sunscreen off my face and splashed the cold water on the back of my neck and through my hair. As I washed, I reflected on a dream that was almost 40 years old.

Maurice, you lying French prick.

The water trickled over the back of my neck and ran down my cheeks.

Where is the sense of accomplishment, the sense of achievement, the comradeship of the rope? It's all bullshit. Mountaineering's all about humiliation. Either the mountain is humiliating you, or your climbing companions are, I thought. The dream of mountaineering excellence and comradeship that had sustained me for over 40 years was now in tatters. I'd seen mountaineering for real now – men frightened and making mistakes, men cursing at each other. I'd seen fear and felt the pressure that was never mentioned in my childhood adventure books.

I cupped my hands and drank and drank from the tap. Then I stripped off my shirt, stuck my head in the basin again and splashed cold water all over the top of my body. I could feel my body temperature dropping. I walked back onto the verandah in time to watch another mountaineering drama unfolding beneath us.

The two Western Australian doctors could be seen struggling back across the glacier, following the footsteps we had made earlier. They were a long way off, but clearly they were experiencing many of the same difficulties I had encountered. Both stopped frequently, and sometimes one would sit down. I watched their progress, willing them on.

Come on, fellas. Keep going, I said under my breath.

'They're tired. Been out there a long time – about 15 hours. Snow's really soft,' someone said. I went inside to make myself another cup of tea and put on a pair of dry socks. I was gone awhile. When I returned to the verandah, they had disappeared from sight and obviously were now climbing the last steep cliff up to the ridge where we stood. A small head finally came into view, then, slowly with great effort, both climbers appeared at the top of the cliff. They shed the rope from the second climber, who immediately sank to his knees and then onto all fours before his head slowly collapsed on the snow. I think he was being violently ill. His brother stood over him protectively. I looked around. There were three guides on the verandah, including Anton, but no one moved.

Shouldn't someone go and help? I wanted to ask, but didn't. I was unsure what the procedure was. Besides, I was incapable of helping him myself. I was completely stuffed. The two men finally got going again and were shortly climbing the steps to the verandah. More slaps on the back.

'Congratulations. Well done, fellas. You made it back.' I shook both their hands as they went past.

'Thanks, mate,' the elder one said.

They were done, too. Sweat poured off them, ran from under their sunglasses, and their faces glowed bright red from sunburn and exertion.

That must've been what I looked like when I came in, I thought to myself.

The rest of the afternoon passed in a blur. I drank endless cups of tea and several litres of water but remained resolutely thirsty. I tried to snatch some sleep, but it was impossible. The hut was now jammed full. Every bed held gear – sleeping bags, food, climbing jackets and pants lay everywhere. Drying socks and other gear festooned the rafters. I counted eight fuel stoves going at one stage, and everyone was tense. The crowding exaggerated the tensions, as did the babble of different languages spoken in the hut. The climbers' clashing preferences soon surfaced in the confined space.

Someone would get up and close the door to the hut to stop the wind blowing in. Another person would walk through and leave it open to get some fresh air. Then it would be closed again.

Anton cooked dinner – rehydrated stew. I had eaten this type of food many times in the desert and relished it. I wolfed it down, followed by some cake, but I wasn't hungry so much as ravenously bone dry. No matter how much I drank, I still felt thirsty. After I finished washing the dishes, Anton dumped our remaining food supplies on the table and we began sorting it into piles.

'We've got to decide about tomorrow. Got to make a decision about how we get out of here,' he said. The two doctors were sitting at the end of the table, listening intently. 'We can get a helicopter out from Bevan Col. Cost you about $750. Get us back to Strawberry Flat in less than 30 minutes.'

'Or?'

'Or, we can do it the Kiwi way, which is to walk out,' he replied.

I took this as a form of challenge, which I'm sure it was. There could only be one answer from an Australian.

'Well, that'll do me. Let's walk out,' I replied, with more confidence than I felt. 'What's involved? How long does it take?' I already had a fair idea of the answer, but I wanted to get Anton's view.

'Depends on how fit you are and how fast you travel, but it's rough either way – about two days' really hard travel, and we've got to carry all our gear out. We can go back across to Bevan Col, then down the Matukituki River to Aspiring Hut. Stay there tomorrow night, then walk to the car the following day. The other way's to follow the glacier up to Mount French then cross the Quarterdeck and head down French Ridge,' he said. The Quarterdeck's a pass, like Bevan Col, that allows climbers to climb out of the steep glacial bowl under Mount Aspiring.

'Whadda you recommend?'

'It's up to you. It's a long haul up the glacier. It's about five kilometres just to the Quarterdeck, all uphill.'

'What would the snow be like?' I asked.

'Umm, soft probably. More of what we had today.'

I thought about it for a while. One part of me wanted to take the tough option and haul up the glacier. I'd secretly hoped, when planning the trip, to summit Mount French as well. I'd then be able to tell myself that I'd climbed two mountains on my first mountaineering endeavour. If I was a good climber that would've been within my capability, but now I wasn't so sure.

'I'll let you know in the morning. My legs are pretty tired.' In reality, at that moment I couldn't have walked anywhere, certainly not five kilometres up the Bonar Glacier in knee-deep snow, and I was wary of making more mistakes. I was talking a little later with the Perth doctors, when suddenly a loud voice stopped me cold.

'Hey you, shut up!'

I looked around. It was a well-known Wanaka guide. Originally from North America, he had been guiding for over twenty years in New Zealand and had over 40 ascents of Mount Aspiring to his credit. He had arrived during the day with climbing clients and wandered into the hut from the verandah. I looked around to see who he was talking to.

'Yeah *you*,' he said to me. 'Keep your voice down. There are people trying to sleep in here.'

I felt absolutely stunned. It was broad daylight outside; the sun didn't set until about 9 pm. I looked around the hut. All the bunks were empty. I stared straight at the loud-mouthed American guide and something exploded inside. The red curtain that always appears when I lose my temper descended before my eyes, and the black dog of rage leapt on my back and sank his fangs into my neck. I crunched my fists into a tight ball.

I felt a rattle go down my spine. I'd had the same sensation on the several occasions in my life when I've exploded in a violent temper. I looked at Anton. He was staring at me, but made no comment. Only the thought of the humiliation a prosecution for assault would cause my family prevented me from launching myself at the guide and smashing my fist in his face.

I uncoiled my fists, crossed over to my bunk and, still seething, unrolled my sleeping bag. *Bloody loud-mouth Yanks, they're everywhere, even in New Zealand climbing huts. I wasn't talking loudly, and anyway there's no one in here trying to sleep*, I muttered to myself. Then, just as I was getting into my sleeping bag, someone on one of the top bunks stirred. In hindsight, I thank my lucky stars I'd not given in to my violent impulse on feeling wronged.

As I lay on my bunk I felt too wired from all the cups of tea and the stresses of the day to sleep. My thoughts turned to the weight of anger and shame, and the wish for revenge, that I'd carried around with me all my life. That night, in a tiny hut in the New Zealand alps, it finally became an unbearable burden. I was tired of it.

After my mother's death, all I had was a name – Kevin Moraghan. I had no idea how to find my real father, how old he was, or whether he was still alive. My mother's sisters wouldn't tell me anything. It would be years later that I finally got what I needed from one of Mum's sisters – an address. It was years old, but it was a start. I stored it away until, achieving success as a stockbroker, I could afford a lawyer. Other brokers when they get their first big bonus cheque, buy themselves a Zenga suit or a Ferrari. I bought a lawyer. The firm's brief was to find my father and get from him an admission of paternity.

'He'll never do it. It's our experience that, after all this time, he'll just deny everything. Otherwise, he would have contacted you long ago,' they advised me.

I insisted it was worth a try and opened my cheque book.

Within a couple of months, the firm had located my father. The hard part was getting him to admit paternity and that took much longer. He'd had no news of me for over 40 years. Initially, when the legal letters arrived, he squirmed and denied everything. Perversely, he simultaneously put pressure on my mother's surviving relatives to pull me off. I was bitterly disappointed that he seemed to lack the courage to meet me and face the situation.

This game went on for some time, but it became more urgent when Hilary, my middle daughter, was afflicted with severe allergies and her doctors wanted both my parents' medical records. My need for closure with my father now involved one of my children, and my lawyer demanded medical records. Moraghan refused and stalled for months, claiming to my aunt, Edna Emelhainz, who still lived in my hometown of Wellington, that he wasn't legally obliged to provide them. My lawyers confirmed this, but I was determined to get those records.

'Subpoena the bastard. Tell him we'll drag him through the courts. That'll scare the shit out of him, if all this comes out into the open and his wife finds out.' These were my blunt instructions to my lawyer following a final refusal.

'We can write to him and do that, but it won't have any legal effect. He doesn't have to give them to you if he doesn't want to. We can't force him.'

'I don't give a shit. He won't know that. Do it anyway. Tell him he's got seven days to produce them or we go to court. I want him to know how serious I am.'

'And failing that, what do you want me to do?'

'Failing that, let him know quietly that we're going to write to his wife and fill her in on all his activities several decades ago.' He had shown my mother no mercy so he couldn't expect any. One of my daughters now needed medical help. It was bare knuckles time.

Almost immediately, I received a phone call from my aunt in Wellington, who had borne the brunt of my father's attempts to pull me off.

'Kevin Moraghan's been on to me again, pleading with me to get you to stop your lawyer sending letters. His wife's dying, and she's suspicious about all the mail arriving from a legal firm. He's frightened she'll open one of them while he's not there.'

'Good. So, what does he want me to do?'

'Just wait until she goes, then you can sort it out between your-selves. He doesn't want to get his wife caught up in this. He feels she doesn't deserve it.'

'Nah, sorry. Cannot do. I've been waiting too long. He'll run for cover as soon as his wife dies. He's just stalling. When she goes, so does my leverage. I'm really sorry you've been caught up in this; that was never intended. But I want those records.'

'It's not her fault,' my aunt replied. 'Why do you want to upset her?'

My aunt had touched on a troubling point. Deep down, I wanted his wife to suffer, like my mother had suffered. I secretly hoped that Moraghan would stand his ground, which would've given me the chance to write to his wife and expose him. I would write that letter myself, rather than have my lawyers do it.

'If you must know, I want her to discover just before she dies what sort of man she's married to. My mother didn't know any peace before she died, and I can't see why this woman deserves to, either.'

'Oh, Kieran. That's a terrible thing to say. Your mother wouldn't have wanted that. She was such a kind and gentle person. She wouldn't have hurt anyone.'

'Well, Edna, I'm not my mother.'

'She'd be so upset about this,' she replied.

I started to seethe. 'Whose side are you on, anyway? I'm doing this for your sister, remember? This is about justice. Also I've got a sick daughter. She's entitled to those medical records, whether he likes it or not.' Despite her entreaties, I wouldn't budge.

Finally, without warning, my father crumbled and called my aunt, offering a deal: he would hand over all his medical records if I called off the lawyers and didn't contact his wife. The records arrived at my aunt's house along with a request to meet me. I refused, but I now had the admission of paternity I'd been denied my whole life. I'd won a small piece of revenge for myself and my mother.

Strangely, when I'd achieved this small victory over my father, I took my foot off his throat and let him up for awhile. On reflection, before I'd embarked on this campaign, my moral compass had been secure – my mother and I were the victims, of that I was sure. We were the virtuous ones. Moraghan had escaped unscathed, his family unaware of our existence. Anything I did in retaliation was justified, I believed. But I became troubled that I would consider upsetting a dying woman, someone I'd never met and who had done us no harm. I realised I didn't want revenge, I wanted mayhem. My mother and I had always held the moral high ground and, in my quest for revenge, I'd come very close to surrendering it.

Up until that time, the main driving passions of my life had been hate, rage and the desire for revenge. These emotions made me think and behave very differently from other people. As I watched my own young family start to grow, I began to ask myself whether love, compassion and forgiveness should have played a bigger part in my life. Then I answered my own question: *No. Fuck that. You're just being a sook and avoiding responsibility.* I had made a vow to my mother on the day she died and I couldn't walk away.

One day in 1998, I was sitting in my office staring out the window at the sun playing on the harbour. Suddenly, I came to a decision.

He's gotta pay. He hasn't suffered nearly enough. His time's come.

I put on my coat and walked out of the office, telling my secretary that I'd be gone for the rest of the day. I took the legal file on my father with me and drove to the beachside suburb of Maroubra.

The angel of retribution's coming to get you, shithead, I said to myself as I drove along. I was fearful of finally meeting my father, fearful of the emotional confrontation, but I desperately wanted to relieve myself of the burden of guilt and shame that my mother and I had carried around for so many years. It could stop on this day. I could leave it behind on his doorstep and, unencumbered, get on with the rest of my life.

When I pulled up outside an old house in a nondescript Maroubra street, I was shocked. *Jesus, the prick's as poor as we were.*

I had always hoped that my father was successful, so that I would at least have had good genes from him. Looking at where he lived, this was far from certain. I wouldn't find a role model in this house.

He must be a bum, I thought. Still, I felt relieved that it was finally about to end. My years of loneliness and shame, my time in the orphanage, my mother's grief had all been caused by the man who lived here. And he was about to pay, was about to have his life changed dramatically. I wasn't going to kill him, but he would be spending that evening in hospital and he would be taken there in an ambulance, of that I was certain. His wriggling days were over, and he was about to get the fright of his life. I pushed open the front gate and walked up the steps. The house was quiet. It seemed deserted.

I hope he's home. I don't want to come all the way out here again, I said to myself.

I knocked on the door. I curled my fist into a ball and drew it back ready to strike. When he opened the door, I wanted to whack him on the point of the chin – 40 years of rage and frustration were going to land on his jawbone. I also wanted to follow the principle I'd learned in the orphanage: 'Retaliate first.' I had never seen any pictures of him, so there was a chance he was bigger than me. I didn't want to come out on the wrong end of it. I had to get in first.

I knocked again, this time pounding on the door with the butt of my closed fist. I thought the door might come off the hinges I hit it so hard, but there was still no answer. I stood and waited. *Should I kick in the door?*

'There's nobody there.' A voice came out of nowhere.

'What?' I looked around.

'There's nobody there. Nobody lives there anymore.' I looked for the source of the voice. A woman was standing in the driveway of the next-door house leaning on a broom.

'Doesn't a bloke called Kevin Moraghan live here?' I checked the address in my file as I spoke.

'Yeah. Used to. He died about two years ago.'

'What! You're kidding?' I said.

'No, he's dead. What'd you want to see him about?'

My heart sank into the pit of my stomach. 'What about his wife?'

'No, she died last year.'

I couldn't believe it. 'You're sure?'

''Course I'm sure. What'd you want to see him about?'

'I'm a relative of his. What'd he die of?'

'Cancer. Melanoma, I think.'

I was shaking with disappointment and thought I would have to sit down on the verandah. My legs started to wobble. I'd been denied my revenge. With deadening shock, I realised my burden wouldn't be taken away and that I'd have to shoulder it through the rest of my life. My last chance to square up was gone. I'd had my chance, and I'd blown it. Worse, I would now never really know who I was and where I came from. Only a father could answer these questions for a son.

I stood on the verandah for some time, not knowing what to do. I looked around at the house. I learned from the neighbour that my father had had a son and daughters, and she gave me the son's name. I had just gained some additional relatives. I thanked the woman and walked down the path. She watched me go. I could tell she was suspicious and keen to know who I was. I thought of kicking the front gate off its hinges, just in spite, but what would that achieve? In the end he'd beaten me. Somewhere he was laughing at me.

No closure. The words clanged in my head like a foundry hammer.

I drove away with a heavy heart. Revenge is a dish best served cold, but I'd let the dish get far too cold. I'd planned and plotted with my lawyers for this day for so long that I couldn't believe it had been taken away from me. I heaped scorn on myself all the way back to the city for not acting sooner.

That day I joined the company of illegitimate boys who would never meet their fathers. He had deserted my mother and now he'd escaped me. To this day, I've not seen a photograph of him. I have no idea what he looked like or what sort of person he was, but it doesn't matter. It's too late now. I had missed my chance to look him in the eye and see his fear as he realised that justice had arrived.

No peace.

The hut was still. Hours had gone by since lights out. Only the breathing of climbers buried deep in their sleeping bags disturbed the quiet. A rustle and shuffle somewhere in the room would indicate someone rolling over on the hard benches. Then it would be still again. Through the hut window the stars blinked in the cold night air. Mount Aspiring was asleep. I seemed to be the only person still awake. Every sinew and muscle hurt, especially in my legs and feet.

As I thought about the past, and about the events of the day here in New Zealand, I wondered where all my anger came from. What part of me was broken? Deep inside me, in the place where love resides in most people, is a black pit of hate and barely suppressed rage that boils to the surface at the smallest slight or whenever I feel wronged. I realised, as I lay there and looked deep inside myself, that it had coloured my life. How had living with someone like me affected my children? I wondered. The time to reflect in the hut that night convinced me that I had some fences to mend with my children, and then probably some fences to mend with myself.

While I'd missed my chance at some form of personal closure with my real father, I had remained determined to square up for my mother. I'd continued to feel that she had been terribly wronged by life somehow. There was one last thing I could do for her. Kevin Moraghan was dead, but his family wasn't. In the late 1990s I'd set off to find them.

All I had was the name given to me by my father's former neighbour in Maroubra, and a profession – a teaching brother at a private boys' school. It didn't take me long; I didn't even need my lawyers for this project. Within a month I was driving through the grand sandstone gates of St Joseph's College at Hunters Hill, the learning citadel of the sons of the Catholic aristocracy. I smiled at the irony that my quest for my father would end here in a place as far removed from my life's experiences as it's possible to imagine.

'I'm an acquaintance of your father,' I said when I'd called him cold on the phone. 'There's some things I'd like to discuss with you, if you can spare me a minute.' He had readily agreed to meet me. He walked into the small office and we shook hands.

'Hello, Kieran. Everyone calls me "Paddy".' He was taller than me, a bit stouter and about five years older, at a guess. *This is what I'd look like in my mid-fifties*, I thought. He spoke about his father, confirming that he'd passed away from a melanoma in his jaw. He talked of how religious he'd been. He obviously held his father in high regard. I was wondering how I'd break the news, then he asked: 'So, how did you know my father?'

'He was *my* father, too.'

There was a stunned silence. I just let my words sink in. I have never felt silence and shock hang like a blanket as it did in that room. His face registered complete disbelief.

'*What?*'

'Your father was my father, too,' I repeated.

I told him the whole story and watched his face go white, then ashen. I don't know what shocked him most – the realisation that his father wasn't all that he'd purported to be, or that the complete stranger sitting opposite him was a half-brother he'd had for 46 years and never known existed.

There was another long silence. I had no more to say and made ready to leave. He began to collect himself. 'Well, I want some proof. How do I know this is true? If it is, I'll have to tell my sisters. They'll be very upset.'

I handed him a list of names of people to ring, including one of his father's sisters who had known the whole story all along. He seemed stunned.

'If this's about Dad's estate, well you can forget about it.'

I felt a ripple of anger, but let it pass. *Mate, you just don't get what this is about, if you think it's about money*, I thought.

I wouldn't take a cent from your family if I was dying of starvation in the gutter.

But I had no more to say. I was done. I just wanted to get out of there. We shook hands and I left. I walked through the leafy grounds, taking in the grandeur of the facilities and traditions of this historic old school.

That's it, Mumma. We're finished. I can't do anymore. His family knows all about us now. He tried to sweep us under the carpet, but he didn't get away with it. At least, right at the end, I stopped that. I hope that helps and that you can rest in peace now. It's the best I can do. His son seems like a decent bloke. I think you'd like him. Not as hard-edged as me.

I thought about that visit as I lay there on my bunk in the hut and, like the dying breeze on the roof, the flame of revenge that had burned so fiercely for so long flickered, guttered and then blew out. Only my anger still burned, and now it was time to deal with that. It was time for *all* this to be over, time for it to end. I couldn't carry the burden any longer. It was too heavy. Some wrongs will never be righted. Some wounds don't heal. But I had to leave this anger behind. It was killing me.

Sometime before midnight I finally drifted off into a deep sleep, wondering what tomorrow and the trip home would bring.

Chapter 11

The Walkout:
Birthplace of a River

I saw mountaineering as more than a will to climb, or as brief moments on virgin summits; it was a living and a sharing of the best and the worst that is in men.

PAUL POWELL, *MEN ASPIRING*

After I fell asleep I drifted in and out of consciousness, almost in a dream. Sometime during the night the light in the hut was switched on and small fuel stoves were lit. I smelt coffee brewing and heard nervous whispers. About a dozen climbers and guides jostled and dressed in the small hut, but I was only vaguely aware. Sometime later, a muffled *clank, clank, clank* of crampons on the metal steps of the hut signalled that the various parties were leaving for their assault on the mountain.

Must be 4 am. There they go. I felt wistful regret and a loss of innocence. Yesterday that was me; now I knew what a difficult challenge lay ahead for them. Silence rolled in and enveloped the hut. A gentle breeze beat against the windows. I slept on.

Anton was up at first light and soon had the water boiling. I rolled out of my sleeping bag, stretched and registered three different sensations. The hut, which had been the scene of so much chaos and pushing and shoving the previous night, was now almost deserted. It was back to Anton, the two Western Australian climbers and me, just as it had been on the first day we arrived.

Also, I expected to have sore, stiff legs, especially in my quads, from the lactic acid built up after yesterday's climb. Instead, they felt light, almost numb. I took this as a sign that I'd recovered and would be strong enough to walk out. I had a black and yellow bruise across my ribcage where I'd landed on the axe, but no ribs were broken. The spare pair of glasses that had been in my jacket during the climb were twisted and smashed beyond recognition by the axe handle. Other than that, I seemed to be in good shape.

'Morning, Anton,' I said.

'Morning.'

He was his usual brisk self, cooking breakfast, sorting food, divvying up loads for the day, checking weather forecasts. Our two companions in the hut were still comatose in their sleeping bags, so we had all the space in the hut to ourselves to get our final preparations sorted.

As I walked around I noticed a third sensation, and this one wasn't good. The instep of my left foot throbbed painfully. I touched it gingerly – discovering that it was bruised and swollen from the boots that I hadn't had time to wear in. I'd noticed a vague pain in my foot while crossing the glacier the previous evening, but had ignored it. Now it was back with a vengeance.

'So, what do you want to do?' Anton asked as I propped my leg on the long stool next to the table and massaged my foot. It was decision time.

'I've thought about it and I don't think I'd make it up to the Quarterdeck through that soft snow.' This was a very hard admission to make. I have always believed that the most difficult choice is always the most worthwhile one.

'Probably better we go up to Bevan Col, then down the Matukituki,' I said.

'Very good,' he replied. I couldn't tell what he thought of my decision, but I'd resigned myself to not climbing Mount French. I was disappointed, but deep down I knew that I'd made the right choice. The mad part of me desperately wanted to have a go, but another part of me was counselling caution. I felt satisfied that when presented with a really critical decision in mountaineering, I'd assessed the situation correctly and made the right choice.

I took my final cup of tea out onto the verandah. Mount Aspiring gleamed against a perfect blue sky. Somewhere up there were a dozen people. I scanned the slopes but couldn't see anything. I wanted to say goodbye to the two doctors, but they were still asleep. The Alpine Guide's handbook recommended a rest day following the Aspiring climb and before starting the walkout, but the weather-bound period in the hut before our climb meant that was a luxury we didn't have.

Inside, Anton was packing.

I washed the last of the dishes, including my tin cup, placing it in my pack with my share of the food before hauling the pack onto the verandah. I collected everything I'd need for the day from where I'd hung it in the vestibule. I placed my axe and hammer, trekking poles, crampons, boots and harness on the long benches on the verandah. I grabbed the neatly coiled rope and took it outside. I strapped my helmet onto the outside of my pack as Anton had done the previous day and lashed on the hammer, as it would no longer be needed. We'd be walking using the long ice axe and one ski pole. We then kitted up, putting on our boots and crampons. I was familiar with the routine now and was able to do it reasonably quickly. It remained only to rope up.

Anton shook out the rope into two piles at each end of the verandah, quickly whipping a coil around himself and tying off.

I ponderously wound the coil around myself with my 'cack' hand method, and he supervised the tie-off. The rope snaked along the verandah between us and I watched it with no less attention than I would have paid to a tiger snake slithering towards us. I checked that all my harness straps were cinched up tight and folded back on themselves, and heaved my pack on, buckling up the troublesome hip band that had to go under the rope and leave all the gear on the harness accessible.

'Right, let's go,' Anton said, after watching me patiently.

I noticed it was exactly 9 am. 'How long?'

'Eight hours, depending on how you go. We've got a long day ahead of us.'

I did the calculation. We would be walking till 5 pm. *Not bad. I can do that*, I thought. *We used to walk eight-hour days in the trip across the Tanami Desert and I did that for 35 days non-stop.*

Anton turned and walked off. Sucking one last gulp of water out of the Platypus, I followed. The *clank, clank, clank* of crampons on the hut steps was a parting serenade to my time at Colin Todd Hut.

We reached the top of the steep slope above the glacier bowl and Anton stopped. 'I want you to go down first, axe in your left hand, trekking pole in your right hand. Step into the holes. Be careful. Stay on your feet. You don't want to fall now.'

I looked down at the long line of foot holes punched into the slope that fell away onto the glacier glistening below. We set off.

It was a now familiar routine but still I found it unnerving when I plunged the long-handled axe into the snow and it sank to where my hand gripped the adze. We reached the floor of the glacier without incident and my confidence rose as I studied the broad ice plain stretching south to Mount Bevan. A well-cut series of bootprints from the previous day's inbound party stretched into the distance.

'Follow those tracks,' Anton said. 'Step exactly in the holes and watch for crevasses.' He lengthened the rope until there was about twenty metres between us. I took the lead and immediately got into my stride. The snow underfoot wasn't as firm as the day we walked in, but was much firmer than we'd experienced on the névé the previous day.

'This's better,' I said over my shoulder to Anton. I stretched out. Using the long, easy strides I'd perfected in the desert years ago – effortless and easy on the legs – I found I was often able to take the holes two at a time. It was a tremendous relief to be walking on flat country, with no pressure on my legs.

'Slow down, you're going too fast!' Anton shouted, after we'd been on the glacier for fifteen minutes. I ignored him and strode on, feeling pleased for once to be in the lead. *Your turn to try and keep up, mate*, I muttered. I kept up the rhythm. It was hot on the glacier despite the early hour; however, I'd expected this. I had no thermals on, just a shirt and my shell jacket. My thermal long johns and thick glove liners were also in my pack. I revelled in this part of the journey, liberated from the suffocating heat of the extreme-climate clothing. My pack was lighter than I'd trained in, and on all sides was the magnificence of the Mount Aspiring corrie. I forged along; Anton was forced to keep up by the rope between us.

We stopped for water after about an hour in roughly the same spot we'd paused at on the way in. Mount Aspiring dominated everything. I looked at it with a mixture of awe and wonder. I've probably read more mountaineering books than any Australian my age, yet the past few days had left me wondering whether I really knew anything at all about this sport. Was it even a sport?

The mountain towered over us, resolute and undefeated. Hundreds of people have tramped on her, beaten her with axes, kicked holes in her, wound ice screws into her, but like a battered boxer she refuses to bend and there she stands, bloodied but unbowed. I thought of Hillary's joyous exclamation about having scaled Everest, 'George, we knocked the bastard off.'

Bullshit, Ed, I thought. *You never knocked off anything. You did a wonderful, courageous thing, but these mountains aren't conquered. Everest, Aspiring or Annapurna, they're still there. We'll soon be gone. You and me, mate, we'll soon be just a memory. These mountains will be here forever.*

I thought of all the books I'd read and the same words echoed through them: *conquest, triumph, assault, attack, penetrate defences, victory, defeat* and *battle*. Words like *tactics, reconnaissance* and *siege* are the lyrics of the mountaineer's song. Hillary's sentiments reflected those found in the climbing literature written while I was growing up, when mountaineers saw climbing as being resident somewhere between sexual conquest and hand-to-hand combat. I no longer agreed with them. Yes, it *was* a battle, but it was a battle a mere human never wins, as the mountains outlive us all. A climber no more conquers a mountain by standing on its summit than he owns a woman by sleeping with her. No one owns or conquers mountains like Aspiring or Everest.

I meant no disrespect to Sir Edmund. He was a great climber and an even greater humanitarian. I would have liked to have asked Anton what he thought of Hillary's sentiments. However, given that Hillary was rightly a New Zealand treasure and I was with a New Zealand mountaineer, I thought better of it. In hindsight, I wish I *had* asked him. I'm sure he would've had an interesting and informed view.

Anton was staring up at the mountain almost in a trance and I broke his daydream with a topical question. 'You've been around these mountains for a long time – seen any changes on this glacier from global warming?'

He thought about it for awhile. 'No, not here. But on Mount Cook, definitely. The glacier's receded so much it's completely changed the way we climb the mountain. No safe or easy way to climb Mount Cook now. It's changed a lot just in the 25 years I've been guiding there.'

That gelled with reports I'd read that Mount Cook was ten metres higher until, in 1991, a large chunk of the northern peak fell off and billions of tonnes of shattered rock and ice plunged down its sides. The mountain is now smaller than when Freda Du Faur climbed it almost a century ago. And it's not just happening in New Zealand. The north face of the mighty Eiger is becoming unclimbable. A steady shower of ice and rock tumbles down the face virtually round the clock. The mountain appears to be melting from within, losing its grip on its stony skin. This shower of boulders increasingly threatens death to any climber who now ventures onto the famous face, especially in summer. In July 2006, a two million cubic metre piece of the Eiger fell from the east face. As it had been cleaving for several weeks beforehand, no climbers were injured.

In 50 years the majestic scene that lay before me may be no more. The glacier, the snow-covered ramp, the tightly packed névé may be but a memory. Snow and ice climbing as we had done it – its traditions and trials – would be experienced by my grand-children only vicariously through books.

We set off again, me striding out, Anton following. Half an hour more brought us to the steep slope up the southern wall of the glacier, the southern névé. Above us towered Mount Bevan. To the left of this was the col we'd have to climb up to. Further above that was the helicopter landing site. Anton began to re-arrange the coils. Because of the steep slope, he'd take over the lead.

'You were walking much too fast across there,' he said, matter-of-factly.

'I was only trying to make good time. We've got a long day. That's the pace I always walk.'

'This's different. You're not on flat country. You've got to take smaller steps. You're not walking *properly*, either. Your heels are striking first, then you're rolling over onto the ball of your foot. It's like you're walking in hiking boots. That's not how you walk in crampons,' he said.

I listened, but Anton was talking to my tin ear. I didn't want to admit to myself that I still *really* didn't understand how to walk in the metal spikes and take advantage of them fully.

In a fit of hubris, I mistakenly believed that Anton was having a whinge because he was tired and struggling to keep up. As is my habit when being criticised, I either lash out or shut down and stop listening. This time I stopped listening.

'It's important that you walk properly in crampons and that all the points hit the snow at the same time. It's part of mountain safety. You can only do it if you take small steps,' Anton repeated.

I ignored him and glanced up the slope to the col. Anton was trying to tell me something. I wasn't listening. Instead, I looked forward to the contest on the flat country once we'd crossed the col. Anton set off. I was in trouble as soon as we moved off the glacier on to the névé. The snow softened, my thighs began to burn, my axe disappeared into the slush, and I struggled to keep up with Anton's slow stride. Still, unlike yesterday, I didn't ask for a halt. Up and up we climbed. The reflected sun burned my face; sunscreen dribbled down with the sweat and ran into my mouth. It left a sour taste. I kept going. We finally reached the saddle, about two hours after leaving the hut.

It was only about 200 metres from the glacier up to the col, but I needed water at the top. We plodded on. I had expected to see trees and grass and birds on the other side of the col; instead, there was more snow. Dodging crevasses, Anton picked his way down into a small snow gully and up the other side. He stopped at the top, where I joined him.

Oh crap, I mumbled to myself. I didn't want to see this.

'That's where we're going, down there.' He pointed with his ice axe, down into a vast open space. We were standing on a sharp snow arête, something like the ridge cap on the roof of a very large tiled house. Below and to the left was a steep snow slope which gave way to sheer rock cliffs dropping down into a gorge filled with rotten snow, glacier debris, and rock that had rained down in avalanches from the cliffs above. We had reached the headwaters of the west Matukituki – the birthplace of one of the most famous rivers in New Zealand. The river bubbled out of the ground beneath the snow under our feet. From where we stood, perched like eagles on the thin arête, the river tumbled down the gorge. We could see where it emerged onto the flats of the valley about 900 metres below us.

'See that first clearing? That's Pearl Flat. We'll take our climbing boots off there and change into runners. Shovel Flat's the next clearing about a kilometre on from there. Aspiring Hut's on the other side of the far clearing. That's what we're aiming for.'

He was pointing to a bright patch of green about four kilometres beyond Shovel Flat. The river wound though the landscape like a thin silver ribbon. The distances didn't bother me. I estimated it was about five kilometres from where we stood on the arête to Shovel Flat. Nothing. I was more worried about the steep rock wall. I prayed we didn't have to climb down it.

'How're we going to get down there?' I regretted asking the question as soon as it was out of my mouth.

'Two choices. We could go straight down the gorge on the snow piled up in the bed of the river, but that would be tough. Snow's breaking up and you might fall through. Waterfall halfway down, too. We'll have to dodge around that.'

I dreaded the second alternative.

'Or we can climb down those cliffs; we follow an old chamois track, actually.' Both alternatives looked like crap to me.

'Why don't we just follow this spur we're standing on right down into the valley? It doesn't look so steep.'

'It isn't, but it ends up in cliffs. We can't get down that way.'

My heart sank as I recalled the words of Jim Josephson from the Climb Fit gym in Sydney: 'The climb's not too bad; the walk-out's a killer.'

'Anyway, we have to get down here first,' Anton said, pointing to the steep snow slope in front of us. 'Once we get down here, I'll decide which way we're going to go.'

I looked down the slope. A climber had come up the day before – the classic New Zealand approach, walk-in/walk-out and had cut neat steps all the way up the slope.

'I want you to step into those tracks. Use all your points, and use the axe like a walking stick. It's slippery, so be careful,' Anton instructed.

I looked down the slope, looked at the tracks; it seemed straightforward enough, so I'm not exactly sure what happened next.

'Face out and go straight down. Put your left leg into that first hole.' Anton pointed to a hole with his axe.

I looked at the hole and moved forward. I saw my boot descending towards the step. It missed, landing on the downhill side of the hole. The inner crampon points of my left boot bit into the snow, but my knee had rolled in slightly so the four points along the outside of the boot found only air. It felt like I was putting the crampons onto a pane of glass. I had a sensation of sliding, then a feeling as if someone had pulled the mountain out from under me like a giant icy Persian rug. I saw a flash of blue sky, then *thump*. I landed on my back on the slope and began to slide. A savage jerk on my harness pulled me up and I hung suspended by the rope, now bowstring tight. I looked up. Anton was sitting on the arête, his boots dug into the snow leaning back

213

on the rope, taking my weight – a classic arrest. I waited. I knew the drill now. I didn't have to wait long.

'*Right*. Fuck! You're going to down-climb the whole way. Now, get your crampons dug in and come back up here.' I rolled onto my stomach while my boots scrambled against the ice, desperately seeking some purchase. Anton hung on grimly.

'*Dig your points in!* Dig your front points in! Kick 'em in!' he shouted. I kicked each boot in separately, driving the sharp front points into the ice. By digging in my front points and levering up slightly, I was able to take some of the strain off the rope and give Anton relief from holding the entire mass of my pack and body weight on the rope. I tried to drive the spike of the axe handle into the slope to anchor myself, as I'd done on the mountain the previous day. To my surprise it just clattered off, making a tinkling sound as it bounced off the ice like a hammer lightly tapping a fine porcelain vase. Reversing the axe, I managed to drive in the pick far enough to get purchase. I then hauled myself on my stomach back to the arête where Anton now stood hauling in rope.

I was shaking from the shock of my second fall. However, I knew we wouldn't be hanging around for long salving my battered ego. Anton unceremoniously took my long trekking pole. I had dropped it during the fall, but it stayed leashed to my right wrist. He telescoped it short and after taking the ice hammer off my pack lashed the pole in its place. He handed me the hammer.

'Now, you're going to down-climb and I want you to put your boots right in the holes, *right in*, not next to 'em. Use the axe and hammer to dig in like this.' He demonstrated the dagger technique in the air. It was the one he'd used on Mount Aspiring yesterday. I turned to face the slope once more, feeling severely chastened. Obediently, I put my boot into the first hole. My face was only inches away from the slope and I could see the minute texture of the snow granules. I jammed the front points in and then the daggers on the tools and began to descend steadily, looking down between my legs for the next foothold.

I was concentrating hard and gradually recovered my composure. Halfway down, I wondered what Anton was doing. I looked up and was stunned. He was striding down the slope about two metres above me, facing out. The rope ran from his coils down to me – he was performing a sort of portable downhill belay. He carried his axe in his left hand, using it for support, coils of rope in his right hand, and stepped easily and confidently from foot hole to foot hole. No other image so graphically expressed the vast gulf between our mountaineering skills, fitness and athleticism. I was crawling backwards down the mountain; Anton was striding down it as unconcerned as if he was strolling the streets of Wanaka.

We reached the bottom of the steep snow slope without further incident. Anton lengthened the rope, as I would be taking the lead again. 'Right, I blow up sometimes,' he said, almost in passing. I'm still not sure what this meant. Was it an apology?

I set off in the tracks the intrepid climber had made the previous day, heading steadily down the southern slope of Mount Bevan. There were crevasses everywhere and the track wound between them. I saw in two places where the climber's leg had gone right into one. I shook my head in wonder. *Why would anyone climb on their own?* I thought. Ahead, the sheer rock cliffs on the other side of the gorge towered above us into a cloudless blue sky. Ominously, the sound of gurgling water could be heard beneath our feet as the spring snow melt began its long journey to the ocean. Often, we crashed through the snow as we walked over the birthplace of the Matukituki River. Eventually, Anton took over the lead when the crevasses had become so big that the route forged by the previous day's climber was no longer available to us. The smaller ones we could jump. It's one of the great heart-in-mouth mountaineering experiences to launch yourself across a metre-wide crevasse, not knowing if the snow will support you when you hit the other side. I leapt and landed on both feet, the way Anton had shown me. Sometimes I stayed upright, sometimes I didn't. He did it effortlessly. The snow was increasingly rotten, and sometimes I'd feel and hear my crampons scrape solid rock underneath.

Eventually, we reached the top of the gorge and Anton paused, sizing up the options. The gorge was full of snow and large boulders from the cliffs above. In places the stream broke through as a roaring torrent. It was a very steep cascade, known in New Zealand as a 'gut'. I couldn't see a track anywhere, and the gorge seemed very exposed to rock avalanches from the cliffs above.

'Normally, at this time of year, we'd go straight down there,' he said, pointing his axe down the gorge. 'But usually it'd be free from snow and we'd scramble over the boulders. There's been so much snow this year we would be taking crampons on and off and it would be slippery.'

I nodded.

'I don't think you'd make it down there. You'd be breaking through the snow all the time.'

I looked towards the cliffs. I didn't know if I would make it down them, either.

'Head off to that grassy knoll over there,' Anton said. He pointed to a patch of snowgrass and rock that jutted out of the snowfield, right at the top of the slopes that we would have to down-climb.

We walked side by side for 100 metres across a flat snow terrace to the snowgrass-knob. For the first time since the climb began, there was no danger of falling. It was a great relief to be able to walk normally, without fear of pitching head-first down the mountain. We also walked side by side for the first time, giving me a rare sense of equality with Anton. When we reached the snowgrass, I threw off my pack, sat and took a long drink from my Platypus. I took off my gloves and stashed them in my pack. It was good to feel the grass against the palms of my hands.

'We'll take our crampons off now; the rest of the climb is on rock,' Anton said. 'Might have to put them on again near the bottom, to cross the tongue of the glacier. See when we get down there.'

I unbuckled the bails, shook off the snow and tied the medieval-looking implements together with the straps. Anton lashed them on my pack, which now held crampons, hammer and one of my ski poles fixed to the outside webbing. It at least looked like a mountaineering pack, even if its owner couldn't really lay claim to being a mountaineer.

'Do we stay roped?' I asked.

'Yep, we stay roped right to the bottom. It's steep and slippery.'

After I'd taken my crampons off and caught my breath, I became fully aware of the pain in my left foot. The instep felt almost as if it were broken. I would love to have pulled off the heavy boot and massaged my foot, but it was likely so swollen I wouldn't have been able to get the boot back on.

The grass on which we sat was dry and warm from the sun. I could smell the earth. It held the promise of living things. We were almost home. I would have liked to sit awhile and take it all in – the sheer cliffs on the other side of the stream, the song of the water crashing down in a series of cascades, the melting snow, majestic nature getting down to its early-summer business – but the pressure was always there to move on.

In what seemed only a minute, we were heading for the black cliffs. At the top, we paused. 'We're going to follow that old deer track down across these ledges. Go down using the ice axe and pole for support,' Anton said.

I looked down the slope. It was very steep, but the ledges looked safe enough. Also, *it would be easier climbing without*

217

crampons, I thought. My first step down the cliff, however, showed me it wasn't.

I stepped onto the first ledge and, to my horror, the hard plastic sole of my climbing boot slid about half a metre and I nearly overbalanced. I paused. Standing stock-still, I looked closely at the cliff and made a startling discovery. The cliff face was black because it was covered in snow-melt water. Underfoot was a thin cover of moss and lichen that clung to the rock but slid away as soon as I put my boot on it. I tried again, and again my boot slid almost from under me.

'Gee, this is slippery,' I called out.

'Careful,' Anton replied. 'Use your pole to stay upright.'

I dug the ice axe in my left hand into the cliff face, but it clattered off the rock. I tried to balance myself with the long trekking pole in my downhill hand. Anton was on the ledge above and slightly behind. He had a fierce grip on the rope. We slowly began to descend, me slipping and sliding; Anton hanging on to me and trying to stay upright as every time I slipped, the sudden jerk on the rope threatened to rip him off his stance. Travelling along the ledges wasn't too bad, but eventually they would peter out and I would have to climb down to the one below. This was usually only about a metre, but it was a metre of slippery rock covered in moss and water. When I grabbed a rock for support, it often came away in my hand. Below was the abyss of the gut in which the river boomed and roared over the boulders. Being roped up, but climbing over rocks instead of snow and ice, was another new experience which I found unnerving.

About halfway down, Anton pointed to a series of ledges that I managed to slide down in a seated position in the steep sections. He stayed above me, securing the rope. Then I ran out of ledge; there was nothing below me but sheer rock.

'We've come the wrong way,' Anton called out. 'We can't get

down that way. I think the track's up here. You'll have to come back up here.' He was about ten metres above me on a small ledge. Between us was a wall of rock covered in lichen and small thorny bushes. I started to traverse back up the way I'd climbed down.

'No, come straight up. Use the cracks in the rocks for footholds,' he shouted. I looked up the wall to where he stood. This wasn't going to be easy. I reached up as high as I could and got the fingers of both hands into a crack. Heaving myself up, I tried to push the welts, or protruding ridges on the base of my climbing boots, into the cracks and drive from underneath. My legs felt very tired, making it hard to keep pressure on the wall. I used my knees for extra leverage. The weight of my pack threatened to topple me backwards. Anton hauled savagely on the rope.

'Use your boots. Don't use your knees, they're too slippery. Use your boots!' I wished he wouldn't shout at me. I felt I would have done better if he'd just left me alone and let me work it out for myself. *Ah, go fuck yourself, Anton*, I swore at the wall under my breath, but it didn't make me feel much better.

'Get your left hand in that crack. Jam your fingers in.' My left hand was useless. I tried, but the fingers just wouldn't work. I couldn't ram them into the cracks, so I started grabbing the stubby bushes which were covered in thorns. Try as I might, I couldn't get purchase with my boots and they started to scrabble up and down like I was riding a bicycle. Stones loosened by my boots went bouncing down into the gorge. I rammed my knees into the wall and started to climb using my kneecaps as feet. It was painful but it worked, and I forced my way upwards.

'Don't use your *knees*; use your *feet*. You're on all fours like an animal. Stand up and walk like a human being. Haven't you done any rock climbing?' His shouts came down from the ledge above. I didn't answer him, but thought, *As a matter of fact no, I haven't done any real rock climbing*. Part of the problem was my boots. A modern plastic climbing boot is like a ski boot with a hinge at the cuff to – theoretically – make them easy to walk or climb in. They have what's known as a hard chine – a sharp angle created by the wall of the boot and its sole – which good climbers can use to exert tremendous pressure on a rock wall, enabling them to climb it. My boots had a smooth sole, which kept slipping on the wet lichen. My inexperience really showed on those cliffs.

I ignored Anton and somehow, driving with my knees and grabbing any handy protuberance, eventually flopped over the lip of the ledge on which he was standing. I sat for a moment catching my breath, then slowly got to my feet. Anton wound in the last of the rope. He was calm now, but began to lecture me.

'Australians come over here and fly into Bevan Col and scoot up Aspiring then back to the hut and think the climb's finished. But you're still up on the mountain – you've still got to get down.'

I nodded.

'New Zealand's mountains are really steep and rough, and not just near the top. Australians always underestimate these mountains. This is all part of it.' Anton pointed down the cliffs towards the valley. 'Ed Hillary got up Everest because he was so fit. He trained by climbing in places like this. You've got to be really fit to climb here.'

Clatter, clatter, rattle.

A noise from across the other side of the gorge interrupted him. 'Chamois!' he cried out. An animal that looked a lot like an African antelope – a fully-grown, horned deer – was galloping up the opposing cliff face, which was even steeper than the one on which we stood. His iron-hard hooves clattered on the rock.

'Look at him go!' Anton said excitedly. The sight of the chamois made him more animated than I'd seen at any time during the climb. 'He'll get caught if he keeps going up that way. He's heading for a cliff. He won't be able to go higher.' But he did. Driving with his hind legs he went straight up, bounding from ledge to ledge;

50 kilograms of wild flying muscle, tireless and majestic. Stones rained down from his wildly flailing hooves. He was now above us but still going strong when he came to the last steep section. We watched in silence. I held my breath. A slip and he would fall several hundred metres through the air before smashing into the gut. A final drive and he was up and over, his black winter coat reflecting the sun and his face a white splash against the dark wall. He was gone. Silence returned.

'Gee, he made that look easy. The speed was unbelievable,' I said. The animal's great athleticism and poise, and the speed and assurance with which he'd moved over the rocks, humbled my clumsy efforts.

'Find 'em all through the South Island. They can run up anything,' Anton said. Chamois are native to the central European Alps. Eight chamois, two males and six females, were set loose in the Mount Cook area in 1907. Since then, they have adapted well to the harsh, rugged South Island ranges and their numbers have boomed, reaching plague proportions. They are well known in New Zealand for their ability to move over steep, precipitous country at speed, and it's not often they encounter cliffs that they can't traverse.

We quickly returned to business, as Anton was getting ready to send me down the next series of ledges. He appeared to have forgotten his lecture. It occurred to me again that he might be over the job of being a mountain guide. He was only two years younger than me, and maybe the strain was starting to tell. Like me, he had a bit of a problem with his temper when under pressure, but it would soon pass and then be forgotten. I brooded and never forgot.

'This next section's really steep. You might find it easier just to sit and slide. We do it a lot, tramping in New Zealand. Use your feet to break your speed.'

I sat and began to slide on my rear, with Anton following me down. While I've never been a good athlete, I've managed to overcome it by being determined and physically fit, something I've worked hard at since my teens. Combined with my ability to handle a lot of physical pain, I've managed to get by. Not now. I was just about spent. I slid down, stood up and walked when I could, then sat down and slid again, across and down for over an hour. Anton stayed on his feet the whole time, keeping the rope tight and stepping lightly from ledge to ledge, never losing his footing.

Jeepers pal, you might have a sharp tongue but you really are nimble, I thought. The grace he displayed coming down the cliffs reminded me of the chamois we'd seen effortlessly eating up the cliff face.

We were now below the gut – the cliff walls on both sides of the gorge towered above us. I willed myself to keep going. The river grew closer and closer.

Boom, boom, crash. The noise above us broke my focus. 'Avalanche!' Anton shouted, pointing high up on the opposite face. Down a chute in the cliff poured tonnes of rock, mud and rotten snow. It made a thunderous racket in the confined space of the gorge as rock shattered and exploded, bouncing down in long arcs before landing in the river. The gorge filled with the cordite smell of pulverised rock. A great hunk was torn out of the side of the mountain and dumped in a rubble pile in the bed of the rushing stream. If we'd been down on the lower stream-bed track we'd have been buried. We kept on. Finally, after what seemed an eternity, we reached a point about 50 metres above the river.

'Right, one last difficult bit. To get down to the river, we have to get around a pinch like a little alcove in the track. You have to hang on and step down and around. But we don't need the rope from here.' I untied from my harness and Anton took the rope and wrapped the last of the coils around himself, then tied off. We were now free to walk at our own pace. We walked about 50 metres along one of the ledges and came to the edge of a set of cliffs – 300 metres down was the floor of the Matukituki River valley. The trail disappeared.

I looked back up the mountain. The sharp arête where I had fallen hours before was visible high above us near Mount Bevan. It became a spur and ran down to the edge of the cliff and stopped where a thin waterfall plunged like a thread of silver into the valley. If I'd been on my own up on Bevan Col, I would have instinctively walked down the spur. In a blizzard or a fog, I would've walked right off the end of the spur and fallen about 500 metres down into the valley. The way we had retreated broke one of the rules of Australian bushmanship, particularly when walking with camels or horses: always come down the spurs, not down the cliffs. Those rules seem to mean nothing in New Zealand. So little of my experience counted here. I was sure that, without Anton's help, I would have been killed somewhere on this mountain.

'OK, we go down here. Follow me.' He stepped down onto a rock perched precariously on the edge of the cliffs, then out onto another before placing his hand lightly on the rock wall and swinging down into a small alcove, whose ceiling projected out into the valley. He looked up at me. The ledge on which he stood was only about half a metre wide; behind him was the void. I began to step out. If I missed the ledge, it would be a shocking drop to the bottom. I hesitated. I now missed that rope.

As I stood trying to collect myself, I realised that while I was still acutely conscious of the danger and the risk of falling if I missed my footing, the sheer terror that I would normally have felt in this situation had abated. Slowly a sense of self-esteem was starting to grow in me; only small, but a real glow.

'Put one boot on here and the other there.' Anton pointed up to two rocks with his trekking pole. I squatted and stretched one leg down to the first rock, slid, and used the second leg to reach the next rock. I began to slide and grabbed frantically for a small bush. The thorns tore my hands. Half falling, half sliding, I finally made it down to Anton's stance in the alcove. It hadn't been pretty, but I'd made it. I felt a flush of pride that I'd managed to confront the drop and not panic.

We wound around a well-defined track to the riverbank, where the water gushed over stones and tore around boulders. Still wearing his climbing boots Anton plunged into the river, which rose above his knees. I followed, splashing across, from rock to rock, thinking that my heavy boots would give no purchase on the smooth water-worn river stones and that I would topple over at any moment. But the rocks were completely free of moss and algae, probably due to the frigid, glacial meltwater, and to my great surprise I made it across the river without incident. I looked up the riverbed to the base of the waterfall. Anton had been right; I never would have made it down there.

A wall of ice now blocked our descent to the valley. This was the tongue of the glacier Anton had mentioned earlier. He began to climb it by using his axe and kicking steps into the soft snow and ice. I followed. At the top of the wall, the view of the valley floor beckoned, tantalisingly close now. About 100 metres of glacier and 50 metres of rock scree was all that separated us from the valley floor. To our left, the river gurgled and roared. Anton tested the snow with his axe, walking several metres onto the glacier.

'Pretty slippery. We'll put crampons back on,' he said, dumping his pack. I followed suit and was soon tramping along behind him as he gingerly picked his way down the sloping glacier.

'Follow my tracks,' he said in a now-familiar refrain. The snow was wet, soft and slippery, just as he'd said. Every so often, he would stop and poke the surface with the point of his axe handle. We had gone a short distance when a miraculous thing happened. The god of mountaineering, who'd previously been out to lunch, arrived back in the office and began to answer my many emails calling for help.

The glacial tongue on which we walked sloped down towards the valley, but it also inclined slightly to the left as it fell towards the river. Without having a rope to worry about, I began to imitate Anton's slow, methodical plod. Then, all of a sudden, I got it. My legs were too tired and the slope too steep to stretch out the way I'd done in the morning. Instead, I simply lifted one boot, then let it drop slightly ahead of the other. I let the weight of the boot and my leg generate enough momentum to drive the crampon points into the snow. I used my leg muscles to lift the boots, but not to drive them downwards. I began to take very small steps with my knees bent. I was crabbing along, just as Dave Lucas had done at the gym in Sydney months before, and just as Anton had been doing methodically over the last few days. I wanted to sing out 'Hey, Anton, ya big Kiwi wanker. I *get* crampons! Mate, look at this. Let's go back and do the climb again.' I was overjoyed.

Because of the slight sideways slope of the glacier, my left boot pointed downhill and to the side as I let it drop. The gentle slope also allowed me to angle the right boot up the glacier without stretching and straining my ankle ligaments. The ten points bit solidly every time I let each boot drop and I felt very secure, almost as if the points were bolting me on to the mountain. For the first time on the entire climb I knew I was doing something properly, felt secure, and knew that I wasn't going to tumble down the slope or slide sideways into the river.

My elation was shortlived. The last 50 metres was noticeably steeper, and Anton paused. 'Last bit of slope. You should be able to walk straight down, facing out. A good climber could run down this slope, even in crampons. But just in case, why don't you glissade down, like I showed you?'

I sat on top of the slope and, holding the adze of my axe in my right hand, I drove the spike of the handle into the snow at my left hip. My left hand held the handle in front of my chest.

'Lift your boots up; keep your crampons off the snow.' I lifted my boots, laid back and began to slide. It was fantastic. Rocking slightly from side to side, I leaned on the axe and any time my speed picked up I pushed hard on the point, which acted as a brake. I felt like a big kid. When my crampons touched a small grass ledge at the top of the rocky scree at the bottom of the slope, I wanted to climb back up and do it again.

I turned around, expecting to see Anton right behind me as he had been for the whole climb. Surprisingly, he was still at the top of the slope. Then the show began. Seeing I'd arrived safely at the bottom, he launched himself down the slope. With one great stride after another, he bounded down – he was running, downhill, *in crampons*. I held my breath. The slightest miscalculation or stumble, and he would have taken off, sailing head-first into the scree slope where I stood. As neither of us now wore a helmet, this would have had very unfortunate consequences. He made it most of the way down the slope, never breaking stride. Then, with only five metres to go, he stumbled and nearly lost his footing, but with a slight lurch he recovered and ended up next to me at the top of the scree.

'Well done,' I said. 'I thought you were gunna fall arse over head.'

'No worries. Let's get these crampons off and get down this scree,' he said, sounding pretty pleased with himself.

My climbing education continued apace. Crampons safely stowed in our packs, we turned to tackle the scree slope. Anton turned sideways, took a big step down and immediately slid half a metre. The whole area of broken rock around him started to slide, but he didn't stop; he just took another big step and kept going.

Step and slide, step and slide. It looked precarious, but he seemed to be doing it easily. I had a good look at the slope. It was composed of shattered rock fragments, some no bigger than a marble, deposited there by glacial action over millions of years. In reality, it was just a huge shifting rubble pile.

'Jeepers, this country never gives up. I now know why New Zealand produces such great mountaineers. It's no bloody wonder the first guy to climb Everest came from New Zealand.'

I drew a deep breath and followed Anton, putting one boot down on the slope and sliding half a metre before stopping. I was then stuck with one leg on the grass ledge and one boot in the scree. I thought that if I put more weight on my left downhill leg I'd start an avalanche and slide straight to the bottom. Anton was halfway down the slope, looking back up at me.

'C'mon. Just get a big pile of rock under your boot and push it. Let it slide.' I took a tentative step, slid and stopped. Then another and found that it worked, although the sliding sensation was unnerving. I soon learned that if enough scree was collected under my boot, it soon stopped the downward motion and gave me something of a ledge to stand on to begin the next stride down the slope, where the process was repeated. Eventually, I made it down that last steep incline which supposedly marks the end of the difficult part of a Mount Aspiring climb. We reached the flats of the Matukituki River at around 2 pm, re-crossed it at a rocky bar and dumped our packs against a big boulder. I breathed a huge sigh of relief. It was over. Or was it?

Chapter 12

Garden of a Savage God

I have given my whole life to the mountains. Born at the foot of the Alps, I have been a ski champion, a professional guide, an amateur of the greatest climbs in the Alps, and a member of eight expeditions to the Andes and the Himalayas. If the word has any meaning at all, I am a mountaineer.

LIONEL TERRAY, CONQUISTADORS OF THE USELESS

Peter Jackson could have made the *Lord of the Rings* movies anywhere in the world. He chose New Zealand's South Island as the filming location for his three cinematic blockbusters. Many of the scenes were shot around Wanaka, not far from where we sat. Our lunchtime halt that day definitely had an 'other worldliness' to it. I'd never seen anything to match it, even in the high Himalaya.

I stripped off my climbing harness and put it in my pack. Next, my reliable Macpac jacket came off, was folded up and stashed away. The heavy climbing overpants were last into my pack. I was down to shirtsleeves and long trekking pants. My shirt was sopping wet with sweat, but this had a marvellous cooling effect when exposed to the light breeze.

'We'll stop here and have some lunch.' Anton rummaged in his pack and pulled out sandwiches. We both gulped water – the Platypus bladders providing ample flow in the warmer lowland clime. We ate in silence. I sat on my pack relishing the feel of warm rock against my back and the smell and feel of the grass. It felt alive, unlike the cold malevolent mountains. Around us was a vast amphitheatre of soaring cliffs. The river wandered off down the valley through verdant grasslands and dark forest. Above the rims of the cliffs, snowy peaks dominated the skyline. We couldn't see Mount Aspiring, but the sharp arête where I fell on Mount Bevan was clearly visible. What gave the place its particular enchanted quality were the waterfalls. Down the many cracks and fissures in the black cliffs fell long, silver ribbons of water. We couldn't hear a thing. Despite the heights from which the waterfalls fell, they made no sound. They were too far away for the sound to travel across the vastness to the rock bowl in which we sat.

From my spot against the rock I could see up the scree slope into the gut and the big waterfall that tumbled down it. Both the alcove and our route down the cliffs were clearly visible.

'Doesn't look too bad from here,' I commented aloud. 'Doesn't look as steep as it really is. I'm a bit disappointed. My fitness really let me down, coming down there. I don't think I'd have had as much trouble getting down there, except my legs gave out.'

'Maybe you didn't do enough training,' Anton replied.

'Nah, I did heaps. Swam every day, did lots of walking.'

'Swimming's no good. Got to build up your legs. Where'd you walk? I bet it was on flat country.'

'Yeah, it was. Mainly around Mosman and Manly.'

'Any hills there?'

'A few . . . not really big ones. I did spend a week in Tassie training every day with a pack on, but the mountains there are nothing like New Zealand's, I s'pose.'

'You should'a been up in the Blue Mountains, walking all day with a big pack on. Get your legs used to it. Got to train on really rough ground. It strengthens your ankles. And you're going to be walking on really rough country, so you need to get into the mountains to train. No use walking on footpaths if you're going to be climbing in this sort of terrain.' He pointed his sandwich up at the gorge we'd climbed down.

I thought about this for a while.

'I don't know about the swimming. I think my aerobic fitness is pretty good. I haven't had any trouble with my breathing.'

Anton continued to stare into the distance. 'The only real training for mountaineering is climbing mountains,' he said with an air of finality. We resumed our silent eating.

I pondered over why Anton reminded me so much of my stepfather. He'd been one of the most capable men I've ever met. A born engineer; with tools in his hand, he could fix or build anything. As a child I'd helped him build the house in which we eventually lived. We even made the bricks. A crack shot with a rifle, a good horseman and a former representative cricketer, he was everything that a child could idealise in a father and want to emulate. But that's the problem; he was a six handicap golfer who never once showed me how to hold a club. Not once did he send a cricket ball down the wicket to me or my brothers, even though we continually pestered him. I even had to teach myself to ride horses. I found his rejection of me especially hard to understand; eventually he broke my heart. The flipside to his practical talents was his bad temper and the sullen silences when he was angry. They frightened me and cast a pall over our home for years. Anton was a very capable bloke with the same sort of reserve about passing on his vast knowledge and helping those less able. He also had a short fuse, but unlike my stepfather he didn't brood. I wondered what sort of father he might have been.

My gaze drifted to a waterfall plummeting off the cliffs that marked the end of the spur we had crossed earlier in the day. A slight movement caught my eye. 'Chamois. A whole family of 'em.'

Anton looked where I was pointing. 'Where?' His eyes followed my outstretched finger, but he couldn't seem to see the grazing deer.

'There, near the base of that waterfall.' It took him a moment to get them. 'Mmm, I see 'em. Good pickup. There's four of them.'

I looked again. I counted five: four adults and a weanling drinking in a stream just ahead of the main group. They had perfect camouflage, black coats against the black cliffs. I wouldn't have seen them except they'd moved.

I don't have exceptional eyesight, but years of hunting as a child made me sensitive to the movement of animals at a long distance. Spotting rabbits over the iron sights of a rifle had been a great childhood pastime and pleasure. I wondered about Anton's eyesight, but didn't contradict him. I munched on my sandwich and thought about the competiveness that exists between many blokes – people like Anton and me, who hardly knew each other. The climb had revealed a deep insecurity within me that saw almost every encounter with other blokes as a competition. I had always found it hard to form emotional bonds with people, and often the only way I could relate was to compete with them. I had spent my life trying to prove myself the equal of other men, and it just made me angrier when sometimes I wasn't. I decided, then and there, that this had to change. Anton's demonstration of his superior prowess, by running in crampons down the snow slope, had shown me I wasn't the only one in our shared adventure who was competitive. Blokes have to find a better way to relate to each other, I realised. Constantly measuring oneself against others is a barrier to empathy and real friendship.

Sandwiches done and resolution made, I turned my attention to my left foot, which was on fire. I could stand it no longer. I undid the laces on the plastic outer boot, unlaced the inner foam boot and pulled both off. Under the socks a livid welt extended across the top of my instep. The foot, encased in climbing boots for the last two days, had gone soft and pink. It looked and felt like a bony baby's bum.

Anton provided strapping from the small first-aid kit in his pack. He seemed to have come prepared for every eventuality. Grimacing, I pulled both inner and outer boots back on and laced them as tight as the pain would allow. I vowed never to wear rental boots again. Anton began to pack, and although nothing had been said I knew it was time to go.

We had stayed at the rock only long enough to eat our sandwiches and reorganise our gear. In all my days in the bush, I've never seen a bloke in such a hurry. I like to linger and dawdle in the countryside and drink it in. Anton seemed to want to get out of it as quickly as possible. My dawdling must have driven him nuts.

'Mate, I was enjoying that. Would've liked to sit here for awhile. Sure is pretty country,' I said, as I stood up.

'Mmm,' he said, noncommittally.

I heaved on my pack, which was noticeably heavier with the harness and extra clothing. The two ice tools, the snow stake, my crampons and helmet were now strapped to the outside. I wondered how much Anton's pack weighed. He had everything in his pack that I had, but also the rope and all the climbing gear such as karabiners and pitons. I wouldn't mind betting that he also had an emergency bivvy sack or tent in there, in case we got stuck in the western end of the valley in a storm. Plus he had most of the food. He had a much tougher walk in front of him than I did.

'Right, we'll follow the track down the riverbed until we get to Pearl Flat. That's the first clearing. We'll take our boots off and change into runners there. It's an easy walk from there to Aspiring Hut.'

From my memory of the map it was about nine kilometres from where we sat at the top of the valley to Aspiring Hut. *Two hours, tops. We'll be there by about 4 pm*, I thought, but I couldn't resist asking Anton what *he* thought. I regretted the words as soon as they were out of my mouth. Only sooks ask guides how far there is to go.

'About four hours. Quicker when we get to the flats. We'll make time there,' he said. I started doing the numbers. I couldn't match the distance with Anton's time. Four hours to do nine kilometres – I didn't think I could possibly walk that slowly. We stood looking at each other. He strode off.

I had one last look around. It was a magnificent setting on a magnificent day. There wasn't a cloud in the perfect blue sky. It was warm, like early summer. I've often wondered where I'd choose to live if ever I had to leave Australia and concluded that New Zealand would be a candidate. Its mountains and scenery are superb. I have no interest in ordered, sculptured landscapes; they give me a feeling of claustrophobia and of nature being tamed. The wild, untouched places in Australia steeped in antiquity, really captivate me. I was beginning to think the same about New Zealand.

'At least it's easy walking now,' I said lightly to Anton's retreating back. And it was, for about 50 metres! The well-beaten path led south, before stopping abruptly at the riverbank. Anton rolled up the trouser legs of his trekking pants and plunged in. I followed suit. We climbed up the western bank, clambered over rocks, climbed down into the riverbed, climbed back up the eastern bank, walked along for a while, then descended into the river again. Within an hour I realised how tired I was. It was a strange feeling to be clomping along in the middle of the stream with water over my knees, my big climbing boots completely submerged. It didn't seem to bother Anton, though, so I plunged on.

Often he would step up onto the top of one of the large boulders in the stream bed and jump lightly from one to the next. I'd sometimes get marooned on top of one, taking time to figure out how to progress. 'C'mon, just jump,' he'd say, with a touch of irritation in his voice. But I couldn't. My heavy pack threatened to unbalance me, particularly as my legs were so tired. I was very reluctant to jump from one rock to another, risking a sprained ankle or a broken leg. Sometimes I slid off a rock down into the river and climbed up or around the boulders until I caught up with him, inevitably waiting for me to arrive. I sensed his frustration. I was clumsy and slow, but kept going.

After what seemed an eternity, we reached the first landmark, the Scotts Rock bivouac. The stone shelter – not really a hut, more like a cave – was built many years ago as a refuge for climbers in bad weather. It was cold and wet and uninviting.

'I'd rather take my chances and sleep out on the track,' I said to Anton.

'Yes, when it rains the creek runs right through the middle of it. It's not much of a shelter,' he said.

About 200 metres further south was the first of a number of footbridges that cross the deep gorges through which the Matuki-tuki River descends on its way to the sea. 'Only one at a time,' Anton said. 'I'll cross, then you come after me.' He set off across the narrow suspension bridge, bouncing confidently up and down, crossing the 30-metre span without any problem. *He must have made this crossing numerous times*, I thought. I stepped out onto the bridge and looked down at the river, roaring and thundering below. It would have bothered me once; it didn't now. I was too tired to allow myself the luxury of a fear of heights. I swayed across, looking resolutely at the pylons on the far bank and not at where my boots were landing. Anton watched me closely all the way across.

We continued down the western side of the river and I sensed the afternoon drifting away. Soon two hours had gone by and we had yet to reach Pearl Flat. South of the bridge the riverbanks became steeper and rougher, but at least we were on a well-defined track. We wound along through dense, dark, old growth forests, then down into the riverbed again before climbing back up into the dark woods. The gnarled trees with their fantastic twisted roots threatened to trip me up every step. It was a childhood fantasy place where I imagined the twisted silver beech talking to each other, plotting our demise, deciding which one would reach down with their ancient limbs to throttle us. It became a living, breathing, *Lord of the Rings* forest, and if we'd bumped into Bilbo Baggins out for a stroll with Frodo I wouldn't have been surprised. It was that kind of place.

The ups and downs were a killer on my legs. I managed on the flat sections, but when I stood on the riverbank and saw the trail ahead disappear up the mountain and into the forest, my legs cried out in agony.

Anton kept about 25 metres ahead and I'd often be swallowed up in the gloom. To my surprise, I found myself walking alone on occasion. I enjoyed the solitude but didn't want to lag too much. I'd often come up to him standing in the middle of the track, looking ahead. When he heard me coming, he'd start walking again. We didn't exchange any small talk.

Finally, after some time, Anton didn't walk off as I approached. 'We're just about at Pearl Flat. When we get there we'll stop and put on our runners. I warn you that the grass is full of sandflies. When you sit down, they'll swarm all over you and bite you. They don't bother me, but Aussies have got no resistance to them and you'll come up in big welts. Some Aussies are allergic to 'em and still have the bites months later.'

'Righto.'

He turned and walked on. After all I'd been through, insect bites were of no concern to me.

Five minutes later, we burst out of the timber onto a flat grassy plain bathed in sunlight where the Matukituki River briefly spread out – Pearl Flat. I practically staggered as I reached Anton and shed my pack. He was already unlacing his boots.

I was too tired to do anything and for a moment just sat on my pack and looked across the river to the cliffs on the other side. It was an unbelievably peaceful spot. As Anton had warned, from out of the long grass, massed squadrons of sandflies descended on me and found a home up my nose, in my eyes and all over my arms. They crawled under my shirt and down my back. I felt myriad bites, but I didn't care. *ALL-I-WANTED-TO-DO-WAS-TO-PULL-THESE-BOOTS-OFF. AAGH.*

It was the sweetest feeling to pull off my boots and socks and let my toes wriggle in the fresh air. My feet were immediately attacked by the sandflies. They bored into me – a living, breathing corporeal Australian banquet. I swished them away from my eyes as I sat in a stupor and rejoiced in being able to wriggle my toes. The bites from these busy residents of Pearl Flat would leave me with welts that were still visible months later. Sitting there on my pack, in the warmth of the late afternoon sun with the air drying my feet and my toes in motion, I couldn't have cared less.

I didn't rest for long. Anton had his runners on and was strapping his climbing boots onto his pack. He grabbed my boots from the grass and began to lash them onto my pack. I quickly pulled on socks and joggers – they felt light, almost surreal.

'Alright, let's get going. We'll make good time from here. We cross Shovel Flat and then pick up a graded walking track to Aspiring Hut. About two hours.' I looked at my watch and was stunned. It was 5 pm. We had already been on our retreat for eight hours. This was the time I'd predicted for the whole trip. This was why Anton kept the pressure on, I suppose. I was slowing him down and he didn't want to get stuck out here in the dark with a tired client.

I slowly got to my feet. A wave of weariness came over me. I would have to summon my last reserves of willpower to start walking again. I had no energy left. Everything hurt. I grabbed my pack. It now looked like a clearance sale at Paddy Pallin with my heavy boots lashed on the outside with the other climbing paraphernalia. My knees buckled under the weight, and the straps of my pack bit into my shoulders. It felt really heavy now and my collarbones were beginning to bruise. The climbing boots felt like they weighed a tonne, not a couple of kilograms each.

We headed south out of Pearl Flat. It should have been the nicest part of the journey. Walking was easy across a flat meadow covered in short tussock grass. We no longer had to walk down into the river or scramble up the steep hillsides into the forest. To walk in flexible running shoes was a delight after the rigid climbing boots. My toes wriggled freely. The lengthening shadows of the late afternoon bathed the meadow and the surrounding hills in varying shades and colours; deep gloom was creeping up the side valleys. The peaks of the far-off snow-capped mountains soared impossibly high into the sky, appearing to inhabit a land of eternal daylight. It was New Zealand at its most majestic.

Less than half an hour after leaving Pearl Flat, I saw one of the most memorable sights of the entire retreat. We were skirting the lower slopes of Mount Barff, which rose sheer on the western side of the valley. To my surprise, we suddenly got a full view of the mountain from the valley floor to the summit. It was dense forest on the lower slopes, rock in the middle and snow on top. Down the mountain was carved a broad swathe. No trees, no grass, just bare dirt and rock. It looked as if a giant bulldozer had been driven from the top of the mountain straight down into the valley, cutting a rough gully 300 metres wide. Scattered stumps were the only remnants of the forest that had once flourished there. I stopped and stared.

'Did a bushfire do that?' I had noticed that fire had scorched right across the river and demolished trees on the lower slopes on the opposite side. Anton looked to where I was pointing.

'No. An avalanche came down there about ten years ago. Whole side of the mountain came down. Took everything with it.'

I was awestruck. 'Look at the way it's flattened the trees on the other side of the valley. How did it do that?'

'It's all the air that gets pushed down in an avalanche. It starts up high as a snow slip, then it picks up momentum and pushes a huge wall of air in front of it that knocks over all the trees. By the time it hit the bottom, the air was travelling so fast it blew right across the river and knocked over trees on the other side.'

'Jeepers, imagine climbing up there when *that* came down,' I said. I could trace the avalanche chute right up to a point near the summit. It must have been nearly a kilometre high. 'So, even if you were standing down here in the valley the force of that would've killed you?'

'It would. Definitely.' I was shocked. Up among the ice and rock towers, where you expect danger, where death is at your elbow, avalanche risk is just part of the equation. It comes with the territory. Here, we were standing in a grassy meadow with a river gurgling nearby and butterflies drifting on the breeze. I felt completely safe, sure that all the dangers were behind us. It now seemed that an avalanche could come off the cliffs above us that was so large it could pulverise us to atoms – and it could do so without warning, especially in the early part of summer.

The differences between Australia and New Zealand were rammed home to me by that avalanche gully south of Pearl Flat. Many times I've been beguiled and caressed by the somnolent antiquity of central Australia. To stand on a sand ridge watching the moon set, or the sunrise turn the endless horizon into a solid line, is to know the quiet and stillness of a timeless land. It feels to me like the landscape's been there forever. New Zealand is different. I felt I was watching the noisy, wrenching, birth pangs of a landscape with avalanches and blizzards, crevasses opening and closing, rivers tumbling through deep gorges, and glaciers grinding away huge mountains. This was New Zealand. Everywhere, there was action and violent movement. The whole landscape was on the move.

I had no time to share my thoughts with Anton. He was already 50 metres away, striding across Pearl Flat. We settled into our familiar routine: Anton walked just quickly enough to stay 25 metres in front of me. When he got further ahead he would stop, wait patiently and then move on just as I arrived. We exchanged few words.

I had expected that this part of the trip would be more relaxed – that we'd just walk along and talk, but I was to be disappointed.

I watched him striding out ahead of me, bending slightly under the weight of his pack, his long, springy strides eating up the ground. He seemed tireless. I wondered about this enigmatic character. Did he have kids? What had his climbing career been like? Were all mountain guides like him? Was Lionel Terray like him?

Anton *was* mountaineering. He was a superb athlete, and a brilliant climber and guide, steeped in experience of the mountains. But I had somehow expected more of the relationship between guide and client than these past five days with Anton had produced.

It had taken me until almost the end of the trek to realise that the climbing fee bought a mountain guide who could increase your chance of survival; it didn't buy you a friend.

We crossed the footbridge onto Shovel Flat and continued walking south, two men lost in their own thoughts. We walked through another forest, this time on a well-made track, before bursting out into yet another tussock-covered plain. A kilometre away, tucked under a steep mountain on the other side of the Matukituki River, Aspiring Hut was already deep in shadow, preparing for night.

Anton waited for me to catch up. I was getting increasingly exasperated that he continued to walk slightly ahead of me. Without realising it, he was again opening ancient wounds left by my step-father, one being an aversion to people walking off in front of me.

'The track curves back into the forest here, then crosses the river over a bridge, but it's a long way round. So, we're going straight across this flat to a spot just opposite the hut. There's cliffs above the river, but you can get down hanging on to trees. We'll wade across the river and then walk straight up to the hut.'

And that's what we did. The riverbank was steep, but nothing more than we'd already experienced, and I managed to make it down without falling over or resorting to sliding on my backside. I went from one tree to the next, hanging on grimly. If I'd fallen, I would have been pitched head-first into the river.

Across the river was one final obstacle – a bank about five metres high, covered in gnarly old tree roots. Anton stepped up to the first one and leapt nimbly from root to root, taking just seconds to get to the top. I stepped up to the first tree root, about waist high, and willed my leg to shove me upwards. It wouldn't budge. My energy was completely spent. Anton was at the top, looking down. I reached up as high as I could, grasped a root and began to haul myself up using only my arms and upper body strength, locking my knees into the roots below to stop myself sliding back. My pack seemed to double in weight. I was using my knees again as surrogate feet, back on all fours, but it worked and eventually, panting and covered in mud, I flopped over the top of the bank. To my great relief, Anton had already set off towards the hut and hadn't witnessed my strange quadrupedal locomotion and my less than elegant exhibition of bushmanship.

We dumped our packs on the verandah of Aspiring Hut among the detritus of hiking gear deposited there by two girls' schools who were using the hut for their holiday camp. I couldn't move and I noticed that Anton sat a while longer than normal. I wondered if he was finally starting to tire. I noted the time. It was 7 pm. A walk that Anton, in the past, had done in as little as six hours, and I'd expected to take eight hours, had ended up taking ten hours. My body and brain had reached their limits. If the hut had been one kilometre further on, I may not have made it.

The night was a blur. The hut, which was much larger than Colin Todd, was full, with the two school groups and backpackers from all over the world jamming the bunks. There were a lot of people moving around and talking. The girls were typical shrill school-kids. Just like my daughters had been. I felt a pang of regret that I would never again accompany my daughters on school excursions. My sense of bewilderment about what the future might hold returned briefly despite my exhaustion.

Anton cooked dinner. I washed up. I was so sore I could hardly move and within seconds of finishing drying the dishes I had crawled into my sleeping bag.

The boisterous noise of the schoolgirls eating dinner, the laughter at the long dinner tables, the chatter and excitement, all lulled me to sleep. It was still light outside, but I didn't care.

It seemed that I'd barely closed my eyes when I was awake again, stirred to action by the sound of Anton organising his gear on a nearby bunk. We were the first up that morning. After a quick breakfast, we swung our heavy packs on our backs and set off. It was about 8 am.

Another magnificent day greeted us. We stopped just outside the hut for a last look up the valley and to take photographs. It was a view that might have graced a box of Swiss chocolates or a New Zealand travel poster. Across the tussock flats the meandering river was boxed in by the gorge-like walls of the west Matukituki River valley. Far away, marking the top of the valley, was Mount Bevan. Below it, visible even from this distance, was the sharp arête that had brought me undone the day before. Towering above them all was the peak of Mount Aspiring. The glistening one really did glisten that morning. The summit and southern face were dark against the blue sky – proud, immovable and rampant.

Anton took a photo of me against this backdrop, then asked me to take a photo of him. I sensed that he loved this landscape as much as I loved the landscape of Central Australia, and felt equally at home and comfortable here.

We set off, Anton maintaining his 25-metre lead. I thought he might relax a little and we could have a yarn, but it wasn't to be. He didn't quite leave me behind, but I couldn't keep up with him.

The nine-kilometre walk from Aspiring Hut to the road-head at Raspberry Flat must be one of the prettiest walking trails anywhere in the world. It goes through green tussock meadows next to the western branch of the Matukituki River, with mountains all around. It was like yesterday's hike, but with the hard bits left out. We had a halt after an hour. I noticed from the direction of the sun that the river had swung from the south to the southeast and would soon be heading due east. 'Why's the water that colour?' I asked, as we stood eating muesli bars. It was a sparkling clear aquamarine – a most unusual colour, almost the colour of the sky.

'It's the minerals. The rivers bring down all the crushed rock and minerals coming off the snow-melt from the glaciers, and they're absorbed in the water.'

'It's amazing. I've never seen a river that colour at home. Ours are all big muddies.'

I hadn't had a wash for six days and the big, clean pools looked very inviting, even though the water temperature was probably no more than 5°C. 'I'd love to have a swim,' I said.

Anton looked at me strangely, but said nothing. I couldn't imagine him hanging around while I had a dip, so I put the idea out of my head.

We heaved our packs on and started walking, with me again plodding along behind. I was enthralled by the scenery. It was like walking through a vast alpine garden. I spent this part of the trip deep in thought about the lessons my life's journey had presented to me, going back to my childhood. I thought about Marc Freedman who never got to do the walkout. And I thought about Sue Fear. Why had they been cut down in their prime, while I – a novice – had survived? We walked in the garden of a savage God, a God that for no reason took the lives of two young people and spared the life of a man who was already in his autumn years. Was it the spring-heeled guide who was slowly drawing away from me – and not God – who had kept me from the abyss?

I thought about my children, and about what I was going to do with myself now that the girls no longer needed me in their lives on a daily basis. This trip didn't seem to have clarified for me what I was going to do with the rest of my life. However, as my thoughts over the recent days had returned again and again to the past, I had seen clearly that somehow I had to leave my anger behind, if I was to live out my last years in relative peace.

I was very tired, and so absorbed in my thoughts and the surrounding scenery, that I didn't notice that I'd begun to fall further and further behind. Anton was now about 60 metres ahead of me, and was picking up the pace, if anything. I looked at the rapidly retreating back of this tireless guide.

You're a better man than me, old son. I thought. *I'm outta the fight, mate.* Anton steamed further and further ahead.

As I watched his diminishing form, my thoughts again turned to my stepfather. Like many young boys who suddenly acquire a stepfather, I'd spent many years trying to please him, to gain his affection and to have him notice me, even though he had sent me away and then subsequently ignored me. He never once acknowledged all the work I did on the farm. Every year at shearing time, I would often stay back late at night in the shed as the old man classed and I ran the press rolling out 150-kilogram bales of wool. Armed with wharfies' hooks, we would strain and groan and sling the heavy bales, as big as refrigerators, into a stack that grew and grew as the weeks of shearing flew by.

As we walked the two kilometres to the homestead each evening through the brilliant Australian night, I longed to walk beside the man I'd worked beside all day, to have a chat, and for him to say, 'Well done.' Like all teenage boys I needed to sense that an older male – my stepfather – was proud of me. It never happened. Every year through my teenage years, I worked until my back ached and my fingers bled, but he never once said, 'Thank you.' On our evening walk home, he always stayed fifteen or so metres ahead. If I walked faster to catch up, so did he. It's not just bashing and abuse of one kind or another that can strip away a young person's self-esteem. Just ignoring them will do the trick.

Maybe Amelia had been right about my mountain climbing; maybe all I wanted was some recognition and acknowledgement. I sensed that I was being cast back to my teens when I had to see the back of someone else that I admired. I hated it then, and I hated it now. It was too close to something I thought I'd left behind.

Suddenly, a terrifying inner voice spoke. *This is bullshit. You're not a teenager anymore. You don't have to put up with this. That peak up ahead's the Shark's Tooth. It's above Raspberry Flat, where the cars are parked. We're nearly there. You're not going to trudge in there with Anton up ahead and you shuffling along behind like you used to with the old man, just like a dog on a chain. You're gunna lengthen your stride and walk this Kiwi bastard down.*

This was the side of me that perpetually got me in trouble. One part of me is shy, not very confident, and happiest sitting in a quiet place reading a book. This is the part of me that as a child became frightened of heights, and who has remained so ever since. This is the side of me that worries constantly about my children.

My other side is angry, hyper-competitive, hard, demanding and ruthless on any internal weaknesses. This side thinks my more thoughtful side is a sook.

I can't, my thoughtful side said. *I'm too tired. I just want to sit down for a while. My legs are killing me. Anyway, I'm tired of all the competition. It's gotta stop. It's not gunna change anything.*

Shut up and start walking, you bludger, my tougher inner voice shouted. I looked up at the Shark's Tooth, gritted my teeth and somehow flogged my legs into gear. Although the pain was excruciating, I lengthened my stride and picked up my pace. Slowly, Anton started to grow larger. The distance between us shrank from 60 metres, to 40 metres, to 30 metres.

C'mon! Walk faster! the voice shouted. It felt like claws ripping down my back.

Twenty metres. I was taking huge strides now, and was staggered that Anton could walk such long distances at this speed. Ten metres. It had taken me almost 600 metres to catch him. As I drew level he seemed to snap out of a stupor. When he suddenly realised I was walking beside him, he quickly lengthened his stride and I was soon ten metres behind again.

Come on! Walk faster!

I can't, I pleaded to myself. *If I walk any faster I'll have to run and I'll sprain an ankle, or tear a muscle or something.* My injured Achilles tendon started to throb. The pack straps bit into my shoulders. The gear on the outside of the pack rattled and banged.

I caught him again, just as we came to the edge of a deep gully with a stream running through the bottom. To my horror, he bounded down the slope. He was running!

Fuck you! I'll run too.

Anton splashed through the knee-deep water of the creek. I was right on his tail. He then jogged up the far bank. This mad competition along the river was yet another form of anger that was burning me up and making me hollow. Nevertheless, I felt powerless to resist the voice that urged me on, and I started jogging, too.

We set off across the flat. The Shark's Tooth was dead ahead. Fifty metres away was a stile, the old Scottish ladder used in sheep country to allow shepherds and their dogs to cross fences. Anton stepped lightly up the steps to the top and then jumped off. Fully laden with his pack, he landed about three metres into the next paddock and hit the ground striding out.

Shit! The bastard jumped off the top with his pack on. How'd he do that?

Shut up, the voice said in my head. *Run up the steps.* I half-ran and half-stumbled up to the top and then down the other side. My legs were on fire as I tried to walk even faster under the weight of my pack. But I was beyond pain, in a place where my damaged psyche was trying to salvage some pride and self-respect from the trip, so that I wouldn't have to go home with my tail between my legs.

Anton and I splashed across Downes Creek together. To our left was a spectacular sight – the mighty hanging ice cliffs of Rob

Roy Glacier. It was clearly visible, less than five kilometres up a narrow valley to the north. We barely paused to acknowledge its presence, the competition between us having now supplanted everything else.

'People go walking up there and sit and watch the glacier calve. Those big cliffs break off and come crashing down all the time,' Anton said. I nodded.

Anton took off, but I was hot on his heels. I knew from comments he'd made that he had completed a few triathlons and was a good runner, and I knew that he could put a sudden break on me, a break I couldn't close. I was desperate to reach the carpark. I couldn't keep this up forever.

At a footbridge that crossed the Matukituki River and gave trampers access to Rob Roy Glacier, Anton was greeted by friends from Wanaka. They asked him how the climb of Mount Aspiring had gone, and he stopped briefly and chatted amiably. I waited, hopping from one leg to the other and staring towards the carpark. They looked at me like I was demented.

When we resumed walking, it was as fast as it is possible to walk without jogging. Everything hurt. I felt sure I'd sprain something. The cars were just 500 metres away. We flew across the tussock flat and reached the carpark gate together – walking quickly side by side. With only 100 metres to go, I felt Anton start to slow slightly.

Come on! We can walk this Kiwi prick into the ground, the voice said.

I briefly strode ahead of Anton, but then the fight went out of me.

Get stuffed. No more. It's over. I'm not doing this anymore, I responded.

There was stunned silence from my worst self.

We reached Anton's truck on the far side of the carpark, and two simultaneous thuds – the sounds of our packs hitting the ground – signalled that it was over. Yes, it really *was* over this time. I realised that I would never gain Anton's respect or friendship by competing with him or beating him in a walking contest. The climb and walkout had given me another remarkable insight.

Anton retrieved his keys and rummaged around in his truck. I stood there, numb with pain. My legs shook and I was desperate to sit down, but as a mark of respect for Anton's efforts in keeping me alive and to acknowledge his capabilities as a mountaineer, it was important to let him sit down first. My self-respect also wouldn't let me sprawl supine and exhausted on the grass while he was busy organising gear. *Please Anton, sit down*, I thought. As Anton pulled his tramping boots out of the truck and put them near his pack, pulled out a clean shirt and put it on, took the axes and stake off his pack and stowed them away, I was going demented.

'For Christ's sake Anton, *sit down*,' I mumbled. Finally, as he finished what he was doing, he took a brief look at the far-off mountains and sat down. I collapsed onto the warm grass. I couldn't have stood there a minute longer.

The one-hour drive back to Wanaka would be the closest I came to having a long conversation with Anton. I slumped in the passenger seat while he drove. Landmarks familiar from the drive-in sped by. There were a couple of questions I had to have answered, things I had to know before I went home. I broke the silence. 'So, did you ever have a go at Everest?'

Surprisingly, he answered straight away. 'Yes. In 1990 I went up with the last fully sponsored New Zealand expedition.'

For the first time I sensed that he was almost wistful. I suddenly came awake. 'You make it?'

'No. I ended up in a crevasse.'

Wow, I thought, and stared at the windscreen. For the first time on the journey, Anton had opened the door into his private world.

'We came in from the northern side.'

'That's the Tibetan side,' I said.

'Yes. We went that side to avoid the Khumbu (ice fall). I was skiing down from Camp 2 to Camp 1 and heard a crack, and the next thing I knew the snow opened up underneath me and down I went.'

'Weren't you roped up?' I asked.

'No. Funny that. Here in New Zealand we usually don't rope up when we're ski touring on glaciers. Don't need to. But the snow's different over there, crystal structure's different, so in I went. Bit of inexperience of local conditions, I suppose.'

I was mesmerised. I knew that it's sometimes safer to ski on glaciers in New Zealand, where the snow is constantly thawing and freezing, than it is in a place like Antarctica or the high reaches of the Himalayas, where the snow is constantly frozen. In New Zealand, the thawing and freezing action turns the snow bridges in the crevasses to ice and makes them concrete hard. In Nepal and Antarctica, the snow often never thaws and it's sometimes not as strong across the top of crevasses as it is in a place like the Bonar Glacier.

'So, what happened then?' I asked.

'I hit a ledge about eight metres down. Landed on my head and right shoulder, and knocked myself out. I must have been out for twenty minutes. When I came to, I realised I'd dislocated my right shoulder.'

Anton's predicament would have been a death sentence for most: alone in a crevasse with a useless right arm and without a rope or climbing companion. Even a fit climber has only a very limited time to extract himself or herself from a crevasse. The temperature is always freezing, whatever it is on the surface, so hypothermia is a real threat.

Amazingly, despite the fall, his skis stayed on. Extracting a climber from a crevasse is a dreadfully tricky business. He must first shed his pack and secure it to his harness with a sling. Next, he sets up a complicated series of prusik knots and slings, or mechanical ascenders such as tiblocs, that allow him to climb up the rope that's tethering him to the climbers on the surface who have held his fall. Getting over the lip of the crevasse is another dangerous manoeuvre. All this is hard even with a fully functioning climber. For an unroped and injured climber in pain and going into shock, the chances of survival are minuscule. But survive he did, managing somehow to crawl out of the crevasse unaided with only one good arm.

He staggered down to Camp 1 where attempts to reset his arm were unsuccessful. Alone he then climbed down to Advance Base Camp, where the doctor examined the injury before sending him even further down the mountain to Base Camp. This was a remarkable journey: over 30 kilometres in length with a vertical descent of 2,000 metres undertaken over several days. The shoulder was set at Base Camp, but the damage had already been done. For Anton, the Everest attempt was over.

'So, did anyone make it up to the summit on your trip?'

'No. After I pulled out it unravelled a bit, as I was the senior climber.'

'Why didn't you go back another time and have another go?'

'Couldn't afford it. As I said, that was the last big sponsored New Zealand expedition to Everest. I haven't got the money to fund my own attempt.'

A guided trip up Mount Everest costs about US$60,000. Then add the airfares, gear, accommodation and food in Kathmandu, and three months at least off work. It's readily undertaken these days by cashed-up people with a climbing CV that wouldn't fill the back of a postage stamp. Yet, here was one of New Zealand's best climbers who wouldn't get another shot because he didn't have the funds. Sandy Hill Pittman, the New York socialite got to the top of Everest in 1996 because she was rich; Anton Wopereis didn't because he wasn't. It seemed terribly unfair.

'Probably getting a bit old for it, anyway,' he said.

I finally sensed something that Anton and I had in common – our best days were probably behind us. The realisation was dawning on me since we'd left Colin Todd that my legs had let me down – not only because I wasn't fit enough, but also because I was starting to show the effects of time. My years of embarking on expeditions were probably drawing to a close, just when I wanted to start cranking them up.

The shoulder on which Anton had landed in the crevasse was the one he had just had reconstructed. I shook my head in wonder as I remembered the pounding it had taken step-cutting up the ramp. We drove along in silence for a while, and passed a lake dotted incongruously with Australian black swans who floated serenely with a snow-capped alpine backdrop. They were a long way from the Swan River in Perth. I was emboldened to ask Anton more questions.

'Those mountains are so rugged, they must be great for training people. Does the New Zealand Army train its soldiers up there? Do you ever get involved in that sort of thing?'

'We don't take the military up climbing, but I do a lot of ski touring instruction for the Special Forces – survival training, really.' Anton then told a wonderful story about taking New Zealand, Australian and Canadian SAS soldiers up on the glaciers for training exercises.

'They have to carry everything with 'em to survive – so they end up with these really heavy packs. Some of them are really good skiers, but then sink into the snow when they put their packs on and can hardly move. Some can't ski much at all, and we have to step-turn them to get 'em down a mountain. And eat? Boy, can they eat! They'd eat steak five times a day if you'd let 'em. Don't mind a drink, either. But they're young, fit blokes. Understandable, I suppose. I don't try and keep up with 'em.'

I realised while listening to Anton that there is a part of me that is still a child and has never grown up. I loved listening to his stories of Mount Everest and of training soldiers. It was like having a talking book. I felt again like the small boy who had run across the room to pump up the lantern so that he could read tales of derring-do late into the night. I wondered why I found the memory so comforting.

We arrived back in Wanaka, where I collected the gear I'd stashed at Anton's house. He then dropped me at Brookvale Manor, saying he'd come around later to say goodbye. I emptied my pack on a bed and the room was soon strewn with gear. I picked up Mum's copy of *Annapurna*.

'Bullshit.' The book bounced off the shade of the bedside lamp, as I hurled it across the room, before it hit the wall and landed on a sofa. I immediately felt remorse. Mum would be horrified that anyone would treat a book in that way. I picked up the book and retrieved the dust cover, which had flown off and now lay on the floor. Thankfully, the spine wasn't broken. I sat on the bed looking at the photographs and the jacket with new eyes.

The fellowship of the rope – as Herzog had described the relationship between himself and his fellow climbers Lachenal, Terray and Rébuffat – was, I now knew, a myth. I understood now that mountaineers are like everyone else, and make mistakes, swear at each other and get frightened. They are not superhuman. The book had sucked me in as a child, but had any harm been done? Probably not. I laid it aside and continued unpacking.

I'd torn the bottom of my pack in two places. It had two big rips from the scramble down the cliffs. My Macpac jacket and trekking pants were muddy; the harness looked scuffed. While the climb was already fading into memory, the gear was proof that I'd finally turned a dream into reality. I'd finally confronted my worst fear. I'd felt the cold embrace of the mountain under my knuckles as her hands grasped mine.

But I'd had enough of mountains for a while. I headed for a hot shower, my first in six days.

My favourite photo of mountain climbing isn't of someone on a summit. It's not of someone doing something heroic. It's not even of a vast snow-covered panorama or glistening glacier. It's of Edmund Hillary and Tenzing Norgay having a cup of tea on returning to Advance Base Camp after their successful climb. Both blackened by the sun, unshaven, hands filthy, they sit drinking from white enamel mugs. Hillary, his head turned slightly, is saying something to Tenzing. The Sherpa listens intently, looking into the distance. Tenzing sits on a coil of rope to keep his arse out of the snow. There's a big rip in his pants. Hillary sits on a folded blanket on top of a Royal Agricultural Society provision box. Unadorned, simple, easily understood – a bee keeper and his reliable mate. It's egalitarian to its core. Edmund Hillary would have spent his life in New Zealand making honey if it hadn't been for the help of this uneducated, peasant Sherpa, and the look on Hillary's face shows that he knows it. From two different cultures, a Buddhist and a Christian, these men were united in their love of mountains and adventure. As a child, this photo defined mountaineering for me; these were the men that as a boy I wanted to become. This photo still defines for me the essence of the sport. It's about trust and respect between men.

Anton arrived at about 5 pm, having showered and cleaned up. With all the mountaineering gear packed away, and dressed in ordinary clothes, we should have been more like two ordinary blokes of around the same age. We weren't. He was still the guide and I was still the client. We could never speak to each other as equals. 'D'ya wanna cup of tea?' I asked.

'Yes, thanks. I brought another map to show you. It's the Rees Dart map. It's got Mount Aspiring in the middle – not on the edge, like the one the company gave you. I don't know why they recommend that. I'll have to speak to them.'

We chatted for a while and the conversation turned to our climb. I'd been dreading this. I expected that, in the nicest possible way, I'd be told either that I was too old, too clumsy or not athletic enough to be a mountain climber. I also expected to be told that, at my age, it would be too difficult to learn the technical aspects of the sport. But I wasn't told any of this.

'I don't think the training you did was correct. You should've come over here earlier and practised on some of the lower peaks. You just weren't . . .'

He trailed off while opening the map. He was going to say, 'You just weren't fit enough', but I suppose he didn't want to hurt my feelings. Surprisingly, when he opened the map, he recommended a climb I should do if I wanted to come to New Zealand again.

'You could get a guide and walk up the Fox Glacier, or possibly fly in and stay at Pioneer Hut. There's peaks all around there within easy reach. You could do five peaks in a week if the weather was right. And it's not as demanding as Mount Aspiring. There's only two pitches of climbing off the glacier on most of these,' he said, pointing at the names on the map.

I looked at the ring of peaks circling the hut. There was Chancellor Dome, Douglas Peak and Mount Haast. There seemed to be mountains everywhere.

'If you'd spent a week or ten days climbing there, you would've been better able to tackle Mount Aspiring,' he said.

I thought of the Hillary–Tenzing photo as we sat there over our cups of tea. It had been naive of me to think I could come to New Zealand and experience that same 'fellowship of the rope' bonding. The way of the rope is about trust; it's a relationship among equals. The reality is that each climber must trust the other to save his life in a fall. It can never work if one climber is an expert and the other a passenger. Bryan Carter and Dave Lucas had tried to warn me about this when they'd said a client would never be allowed to belay a guide. The guides don't trust the clients – and rightly so, I now had to admit. With my level of climbing skills I would never know the comradeship that Hillary, Tenzing and Anton had known – a fellowship of trust among equals. I thanked Anton for getting me up and back safely. I offered to wash his legionnaire's cap, which was covered in sweat and sunscreen.

'No, thanks. I've had lots of clients take gear home to wash, and I never see it again.' Strangely, his response hurt. He didn't even trust me enough to wash and return his hat.

I saw Anton out and we shook hands. There is no higher reward for a climber than to be considered a brave and dependable member of the team. I hadn't earned this honour, still as we said our goodbyes I felt a twinge of regret that he hadn't found some positive contribution I'd made to our climb. If he'd said, 'Well done, you didn't quit and didn't bug out up high. You might've been a climber if you'd started younger,' I would have gone home feeling ten feet tall. I'd even have settled for, 'You made some mistakes, but overall it wasn't a bad effort for a 54-year-old on his first climb. I've had a lot worse clients than you.' But he didn't say any of this, and I realised how much positive affirmation I wanted from others when I take on difficult challenges.

I leaned over the balcony and watched Anton walk to his truck parked below. So be it. If Amelia was right and I'd come to New Zealand looking for praise, I wouldn't get it from the tall Kiwi with the spring in his step; I'd have to get it from within myself. But that's *my* problem, not his. Mount Aspiring had shown me the wisdom of Amelia's observation and the depth of this crevasse in my personality. With a final wave, I watched Anton drive away.

Goodbye, old son. God speed. I hope your days on the mountains are all bright and sunny, and that you step over all the crevasses, not in 'em. I hope the clients aren't all dickheads. I also silently prayed that I wasn't the worst client he'd ever had.

The following morning I boarded a flight to Christchurch and was asleep before the plane reached the end of the Queenstown runway.

Chapter 13

Coming Clean:
The Tenth Box

Man must evolve for all human conflict a method which rejects revenge, aggression and retaliation. The foundation of such a method is love.

MARTIN LUTHER KING, JR

There is a famous black-and-white photo that you may see if your wanderings take you to the tiny French alpine village of Argentière. I first saw it there in 1978 on the wall of a café. It's a photo of a group of men standing around a statue, in the middle of the village square in nearby Chamonix, the climbing and skiing centre just down the valley, in the shadow of Mont Blanc. They're men of all ages, shapes and sizes. They are standing in orderly ranks, with some perched on the statue's plinth to secure a vantage point. There is something arresting about the photograph. The men, some with Second World War campaign medals proudly displayed on their chests, are impeccably dressed, many in coat and tie, some in traditional alpine knickerbockers and long woollen socks. In an incongruous juxtaposition, some have climbing ropes coiled over the shoulders of their carefully pressed

257

suit jackets. What struck me was their obvious pride. They look at the camera with a confidence that is hard to define. Something about the men tells you that this isn't a convention of French bankers on a jaunt to Chamonix or members of a French rugby club. They display the pride of belonging.

I wondered who they were, but I already had a hunch. The statue in the photograph is a dramatic depiction of two men. One is roughly dressed, with a climbing rope coiled around his shoulder. He is pointing upwards, bringing something to his companion's attention. The other man, taller and better dressed, gazes intently at where the first is pointing. This was a guide and his client, immortalised in bronze.

In my halting schoolboy French, I asked the café proprietor, *'Excusez-moi, monsieur, qui sont ces hommes?'*

'C'est la Compagnie des guides de Chamonix,' he replied. He pointed to various famous people in the photograph, running on in French, none of which I understood, until I heard the word 'Terray'.

I interrupted him and asked, 'Terray? Lionel Terray? *Est-il le héros de la montagne d'Annapurna?'*

'Oui, monsieur. Le héros de l'Annapurna et de l'Eiger.'

The famous guide was in the front row in white knickerbockers and a jumper, head turned slightly from the camera. His colleagues and fellow guides Rébuffat and Lachenal were not in the photograph, presumably already dead. That must have placed the photograph sometime in the early 1960s. It was probably taken about the time I sat in a country farmhouse in Australia and read the book.

He pointed to the statue in the photograph. *'Balmat . . . de Saussure . . . Mont Blanc.'* He pointed out the door of the café. He was referring to Jacques Balmat, the Chamonix guide who, in 1786, climbed Mont Blanc for the first time. His companion was

Horace-Bénédict de Saussure, a Swiss aristocrat, who also climbed the peak and helped to develop mountain climbing as a sport.

So, this is what they looked like. I came face to face with the elite club that had so inspired me as a child. To join the famous Compagnie, you must be a mountaineer, born not just in France, but in the Chamonix Valley, and you must be invited to join. Terray was the first climber not born in the valley to enter this brotherhood. For most of my life I could think of no greater honour than being a member of that illustrious clan. That is, until in my mid-fifties I went mountain climbing in New Zealand.

I came back from New Zealand a changed man. While I had spent my life denying it, and trying to hide it, I realised during my long walk down the Matukituki River with Anton that I belong to an even more illustrious club than the distinguished Company of Guides – the Esteemed Company of Bastard Boys. Our company has very strict entry qualifications: you have to be born into it. No amount of family money or influence will gain you entry; no amount of political prestige or pressure will open that door unless you have that one defining qualification – no father. It is the ultimate form of hereditary peerage – a type of bastard nobility.

Not for us the ordered world of a settled family, of a loving father keen to see us grow up in his image. We inhabit a world of shunned or abandoned women, and we are often close to our grandmothers as it is they who often protect and guide us through those formative years while our mothers are at work. That is, if like me, you are a lucky member of the Company who scored a loving mother and grandmother and didn't end up permanently institutionalised. For those unfortunates, their young life would be spent alone.

What would the photograph look like if the boys of the Esteemed Company were piled up on the wrought-iron-clad verandah at Croagh Patrick Orphanage in Orange? There, at the top of that sweeping drive, I see it still after a passage of 50 years. The boys would be all shapes and sizes, just like the guides, but there would be no suits or ties, no proud badges of office, such as coiled climbing ropes. They would have jumpers, but some might be old and patched; hands might be in pockets. Some would look frightened, some angry, and some, like me, might look ashamed. No one would look proud. Many would appear to be bewildered by the fate that had marked them out for a life so different from that enjoyed by other boys their age. The one grim feature that would shine from the photograph would be determination; all would be determined to carve out a place for themselves in the great brawl of life, for if athleticism and skill defines the Compagnie, then it is a determination to survive that defines the Bastard Boys. They have to fight to make a place for themselves in a world that doesn't want them.

Not for them a father's loving embrace, the bedside story, or the figure standing on the sidelines in all sorts of weather at sporting matches. We can only imagine what that's like. We've never felt calm, rough hands picking us up after we're knocked out of the ring, whispering, 'You can do it' and encouraging us back into the great contest of life.

No, the Company of Bastard Boys has none of this. The photograph would show a group whose defining trait is an angry passion to succeed, a knowledge they will have to do it without help, and in some, a need to have their own family, so that they can savour all that they've missed. The mighty Company of Chamonix Guides may be more skilled and glamorous, but the Bastard Boys is a tougher club to join and its members are possessed of strength and steel that would flatten the mountain men.

*

I could tell my family none of this. This was deep and personal and incomprehensible to anyone who hadn't walked down the same path. I had instead to try and explain to them the strange endeavour that is mountain climbing. I wanted to talk about the good stuff: what it's like to walk across a glacier in the dead of night, moonlight on snowy peaks, the vast spaces below, the blackness of the crevasse and the feel of crampons on snow.

They didn't want to hear about climbing. They wanted to hear about Anton – what sort of person he was – and to offer their thoughts on why they felt he'd given me such a hard time.

'Is he married? Does he have any children? Does he take them climbing? What does his wife think of him climbing for a living?' These where the first questions Prue asked on the way home from the airport. I couldn't answer any of these questions, because I didn't know.

'I can't ask a bloke I don't know that sort of stuff, especially when he didn't ask me.'

Later that night we were sitting around the dinner table with Catherine and again I tried to talk about how frightening the ramp was, how steep some of the faces on Mount Aspiring were, and about my two falls, but my wife covered her ears with her hands.

'Stop! We don't want to hear any of this. We don't need to know how steep it was.'

Again, the talk drifted back to Anton. Strangely, now I found myself defending him, even though I had earlier told them how difficult I had found him as a climbing companion.

'*Omigod*, Dad. He was so mean to you, some of the things he said to you,' Catherine exclaimed, a comment typical of someone who has never climbed.

'He reminded me a lot of the old man, that's for sure – a hard bastard, a cranky bastard – but he'd never ask you to do something that he wouldn't do himself. My old man was like that. I really admire people like that. My old man treated me like shit, but I still admire him in a funny sort of way. Anyway, this guy could really climb. I've only read about it in books, but he could really do it.'

'Well, you'd never go up there with *him* again,' Prue said with conviction.

'Sure, I would. If I went climbing again, he's the first guide I'd ask for. He was really capable and he kept me alive. That's all you can ask for. That's what you pay a guide for, at the end of the day. I'd recommend him to *anyone* going climbing in New Zealand.'

'*Whatever*, Dad. You're a crazy man, and he sounds crazier,' Catherine said as she got up to leave the table.

'Caps, mountaineering's crazy. But if it wasn't for him, I'd be dead. Nothing else matters.'

'*Whatever*,' she said again, shook her head in exasperation and walked out of the dining room.

'Yes, I don't understand any of this,' Prue said, as she also rose and left the table. 'It's beyond me, too. At least you've got it out of your system and you don't have to do it again.'

As often happens in our family life when issues like this are discussed, I was left sitting at the table alone with my thoughts.

Well, maybe not right now, anyway. Not tomorrow, I thought.

My family didn't want to know what happened on the mountain, and it's impossible to make them realise how hard it was for Anton. I came back from New Zealand convinced that amateurs like me shouldn't be allowed on Mount Aspiring – not because it's too dangerous for us, but because it's too dangerous for the guides.

My family also couldn't know what motivates us Bastard Boys – our life-long search for legitimacy and acceptance, although Amelia had stumbled across it. I had never explained any of this to them. That's why I decided to write this book. It was time to come clean. I hope they understand why I'm not like other fathers. There will be other mountains.

The hardest conversation I had on arriving home was with my muse, my eldest daughter Amelia, who was living on the Gold Coast. She didn't want to hear about the climb, either, having already spoken with her mother.

'So, Dad, are you pleased with yourself? Do you feel better about yourself now?' she asked, when we caught up on the phone.

'Dunno. I guess so. I learned that even when I'm really frightened I don't panic and I can still keep functioning, so I suppose that's good. I didn't choke near the summit, even though I was frightened of the height, or on the ramp. But I did get very tired. I found out that I'm not a coward, which was really important to me.'

'But it won't be enough for you, Dad. I bet you're already planning what you're going to do next.'

'Umm, not really. I'm buggered at the moment. I've had enough for awhile.' That wasn't completely true, as I was already considering an exploring kayak trip down the Ord and Negri rivers in the Kimberley region of Western Australia for the 2007 dry season.

'I don't believe you, Dad. I bet there's already something stewing away in your little brain that you're going to try and do. You'll never be satisfied. Anyway, we can't stop you doing these things, but you're eventually going to get hurt. You gotta learn to love *yourself*. That comes from inside. I told you that no one in Australia cares about mountain climbing.'

'Yeah, I guess so. I thought a lot about what you said while I was in New Zealand. But all of this is a big journey for me, and sometimes I don't exactly know why I do things.'

'Well, no matter what you do, you've got to realise that you can't bring back your parents so that they can tell you that they love you, or so that your father can tell you how proud he is of you. That's not going to happen, so you'd better get used to it.'

Not only was this true, but it was also so insightful that I could think of nothing to say in reply.

'Anyway, I've been talking to Mum and we're really proud that you didn't lose your temper with those men or hit anyone. We can't believe you let an American shout at you and you didn't do anything.'

'Amelia, that makes two of us.' I found this very strange, too. Maybe I was finally coming to terms with myself.

My climb on Mount Aspiring shows that you are never too old to learn or to change. I noticed the first, subtle changes in my behaviour stemming from the climb, on Australia Day, 2007, at Palm Beach on Sydney's northern peninsula. I'd been back from Aspiring for about a month, but I was still fatigued and mentally drained. I stood on the sand at the starting line for the annual swimming race to Whale Beach – a two-kilometre, mid-summer trawl down the coast. Normally my guts would be churning at the start, winding myself up, determined to push myself inside out, hammer people aside at the buoys, swim over the top of them if necessary – all to be competitive and to prove something to myself. This time it seemed different.

The mad competitiveness with Anton convinced me that this behaviour had to end. There would always be someone bigger, faster or fitter. I would ultimately wear myself out looking for people to compete with and always failing to. It was just a way of guaranteeing perpetual low self-esteem, another form of anger. I was done with it.

I was aware of the sand between my toes, the sound of the waves, the warmth of the sun. The hubbub of voices receded and the quiet flowed in. Even there on a crowded public beach, where everyone else was amped up prior to the start, I was happy to be alone with my thoughts. For the first time in my life I was happy just to be there and happy to be alive. The starter's gun cracked and I waded out through the surf and without haste, began swimming. I noticed the fish darting past, the shells on the bottom and the ripple of the sand. Other blokes went pounding by in a furious maelstrom of arms and legs. I let them go. I was cracked on the back of the head a few times and kicked in the face once and didn't react. At the turning buoy I went wide so as not to impede anyone.

I thought about Anton and Marc Freedman and the mountains. I felt the joy of warm water lapping over the back of my head and how good it was to be alive. I was done with competition.

However, I also returned from Mount Aspiring profoundly troubled, as if confronting my long-held fear of heights had made me think about other things I didn't want to see. One was the livid red stab of anger that tore out of me under pressure. Somehow, on the sheer slopes of Mount Aspiring, I realised that this flame may have burnt those closest to me. I had always assumed that I had been a good father to my three daughters. Somehow, the mountain's ability to produce clarity of thought forced me to acknowledge that maybe I hadn't been. Now I had to summon the courage to go and talk to them, acknowledge my responsibility and apologise. It had turned out to be much more than a mountain climb.

Facing your own failings and having to accept responsibility is a difficult thing, especially for a father. I looked for the right opportunity, aimed up and tackled each of my children one by one. Each handled it differently.

Amelia, as was her habit, burst into tears as she acknowledged how much the bushfires of rage that had swept through our family had hurt her. This wounded me to the core. The pretence, which I had long enjoyed, that I had provided my girls with safety and security was stripped away. We had a cuddle and she agreed to let bygones be bygones. We are now probably better friends because I acknowledged a wrong and then tried to right it.

Catherine was easier – younger, and so less affected.

'*Whatever*, Dad. I just think you're a cranky old man. But at least you seem to be getting less cranky. I never saw all the really bad bits, the way the other girls did. But it's nice that you came and talked to me about it.'

Hilary, my middle daughter, would be the toughest. I knew that. I'd left her until last and had to go to Turkey for my mea culpa. She was on the last leg of a year-long trip around the world. Over a cold beer in an Istanbul café, I explained to her in detail what had happened to me as a child. I talked about the orphanage, the rejection by my stepfather, the boarding school beatings, the fruitless search for revenge against a father I never knew. I tried to explain why I was such an angry, bitter person. I offered justification and hoped there would be vindication.

'I brought you three girls up on the negative principle of parenthood. When I was growing up we had no money, so I made sure you all had plenty. We never had a proper house, so I gave you guys one with water views up on top of a hill. I never had a holiday anywhere with my parents, so I made sure we had plenty of holidays overseas. I would've been happy just to go to Terrigal when I was a kid.'

Hilary listened impassively, and I wondered if I was making any impression. I explained my nine box principle of parenthood.

'There were nine boxes I tried to tick. You know all the stuff we've talked about; good house, clothes, financial security, good education, lots of cuddles and affection.' We had also talked about the other four obligations that I saw in parenting – lots of holidays together, opportunities for children to discover their talents, no shame in making mistakes and encouragement that a woman can do anything she wants too just like a bloke. I didn't need to go into all these again.

'I think I probably ticked all nine of 'em, Hilla, but after talking to Amelia, I think there was another box, and I didn't quite get the last one. That's the safety and predictability box. I tried, but I missed it. I'm sorry.'

I looked at her for a response.

'If it's any consolation, I don't think my brothers and sister and I got that box from the old man, either.'

Then she said something telling. 'Daddy, most of the things you talk about are material things. They're the easy things. The tenth box was the most important – it was triple points. You never *got* that.' She seemed a bit exasperated at my confusion and my inability to grasp the importance of this tenth box. She had summed up a female's perspective on parenthood in a sentence.

'Yeah, but I missed a lot of the boxes one to ten, so you can't blame me for not knowing how important each one of 'em was.'

'That's seeing it through *your* eyes,' she said. 'Don't talk about what it was like for *you*. I'm talking about what it was like for *us*, and I am telling you that the tenth box was the most important.'

'I know that now. How was I supposed to know that? How can you know that when you're having kids, when you're just 30 years old? No one gives you a book of instructions; no one tells you the tenth box is the most important. I had no role models to base my parenting experience on. I just tried to give you guys a life as different from mine as possible. That's the only guideline I had.'

We sat in silence for a while watching the tumult of Istanbul life on the footpath of the Divan Yolu thoroughfare. Tourists mixed with home-bound commuters, carpet sellers and knick-knack vendors, under the shadow of Hagia Sophia mosque. It was a strange place for an Australian farm boy to seek absolution from a daughter.

'Part of my problem was I didn't think it was that bad. I never whacked any of you girls or your mother, and none of you have ever seen me even a little bit tipsy. I listened while my stepfather belted my mother one night. It sounded like a butcher hitting a side of beef. Now, that's frightening. I just blew up from time to time and wrecked some things. I never hit any of you. I just never thought it was that bad.'

The muezzin wailed down from Sophia's minarets and we stopped talking to listen. We were getting used to the strange cadence of the mosque singers.

'I know that, but it's the unpredictability that was scary. We never knew how you were going to react to things, or when you were going to blow up. Sometimes really little things would set you off. It made us feel powerless. I would just go in my room and close the door and cry. I didn't want to come out.'

I had no answers to this. I was shopping in the brutal honesty bin at the supermarket. No bargains here. I apologised again and said I hoped there was no lasting hurt for her. I stressed how important it was that she never got involved in a serious relationship with anyone who had a violent nature or bad temper. But if I was hoping for absolution, there wasn't a lot on offer.

'I can't say it didn't hurt, because it did; a *lot*. You were very scary when you lost it. It made us all very frightened – Mum, too. But it's a long time ago and you've tried to get on top of it, and now we've got to look forward. There's no point looking back.'

There it was: parenthood in a snapshot; such wisdom from a 21-year-old.

We sat and watched the life on the street. I tried to explain that for modern fathers the bar is set very high. The things that my stepfather's generation viewed as goals – food on the table, a roof over the family's head, some clothing and a basic education – are all taken as given nowadays. 'Fathers only seem to get judged on the extra stuff now. I think fathers have very high standards to meet, and a lot of it's to do with emotional nurturing of children and building their self-esteem. It's subtle stuff, Hilla, and you've still got to go out and work.'

'No one said being a parent was easy, Dadda.'

I had one last go at self-justification, running with the line that boys from a working class background like mine are going to find it so much harder when they enter the professions to carve out a place for themselves and provide a decent standard of living for their families. With no family role models in commerce, no mentors or social networks, and few people skills, business can be a tough place to hack out a living.

'I think I was entitled to be cut a bit of slack, because I was under so much extra pressure and I had no family role model.'

'No excuses for bad behaviour around your wife and children, Dadda. Sorry.'

I thought about it for awhile, had another beer, and realised with a sigh of resignation that it was time to throw in the towel. I understood for the first time that while childhood experiences can determine adult actions, nothing that I'd experienced as a child would be accepted as an excuse for shortcomings in my own performance as a parent.

'Yeah, you're right, Hilla. No more excuses.'

I was relieved that it was over; another mountain climbed, with some bits of skin off, but I guess I survived this one, too.

A rewarding two-week tour of Turkey followed – just the two of us, with time for healing.

Finally, we said goodbye. Hilary headed off on the last leg of her trip and I boarded the plane home from Istanbul, exhausted from the experience of getting my parental scorecard marked. I'd always presumed that I'd scored AAA+. In reality, it was probably a B–. Not great, not terrible either – somewhere in-between. Having to accept responsibility for my own failings was tough. Like many fathers, I wanted to blame someone else.

At least there's nothing else I have to confront. No other scary shit in the closet; it's all done. It's finished, I said to myself, looking out the window as the blue stretch of the Dardanelles slid by and the plane turned for home. But then, somewhere over India, a sudden thought popped into my head. I don't know where it came from.

No, it's not over. I realised there was one more mountain I had to climb. One last big hairy, scary demon I should go and look in the eye. I had been avoiding it for nearly 50 years. I pondered this for awhile. *Fuck that. I'm not going there. That's way too hard.*

I hunkered down in my seat, turned the sound on the head-phones up loud and became absorbed in a very bad *Spiderman* movie.

My hands were wet on the steering wheel. My sweat-soaked shirt was stuck to the leather of the bucket seat. I sat in the car, not moving. I was parked outside the gates.

I can't do this. This is way too confronting. Let's turn around and go home. The quiet, tremulous voice that had coaxed me on the walkout from Mount Aspiring was back. Unfortunately, so was its partner.

No, come on. We've done so much other scary shit this year.

Let's aim up one last time, then it's all over. It was my other voice; the loud, authoritative one. It now seemed less violent, even resigned. It seemed to have realised that a journey was coming to an end. An aria from Jacques Offenbach's *Tales of Hoffmann* played softly through the car's CD speakers. A gentle rain had begun to fall. The windscreen wipers came on automatically. I waited, listening to the music.

Friday, 7 December 2007 was a grey, almost winter's day as I drove west from Sydney. A year earlier I had finally summoned the courage to confront a major mountain climb. Now, after months of procrastination and a three-hour drive from Sydney, I sat outside the gates of Croagh Patrick Orphanage, looking up the driveway and trying to summon the courage to repeat a journey I'd made as a very small child. I waited and sweated and listened to the voices in my head, arguing back and forth. I noticed that the sign over the driveway was gone. Finally, I had to take control and make a decision.

Stuff it, let's do this. I turned up the volume on the car stereo and pressed my foot gently on the accelerator. To the haunting lilt of Joan Sutherland singing Offenbach's *Barcarolle*, the car rolled forward with a purring sound of fine German engineering. The two journeys were a contrast. Last time, I'd made this journey in a green, battered Holden farm ute that smelt of dogs and hay and stale sump oil. Now I was surrounded by opera and the smell of leather. Then I'd been sandwiched between a distraught woman and a grim-faced stepfather, and I'd clutched an old stuffed koala bear and a brown paper bag on my lap. Now, I was alone; even the voices were quiet. One constant remained: I'd been filled with dread then, and I was filled with dread now.

Up the circular drive I went, creeping through the pines and around past the fountain and the Virgin Mary grotto, still there after all those years. Whether it was Sutherland's soaring voice, the

grey, rainy day, or the looming Victorian building that held so
many memories for me, I was overwhelmed with old feelings of
abandonment and loneliness. I was catapulted backwards in time,
couldn't hold on and cracked open. A huge sob of grief came up
from somewhere behind my belt buckle and burst out in a river of
tears that ran down my face, just as they had the last time I was
here. I have seldom cried as an adult, but now I felt like a small
child again – felt the loneliness and separation as if I was living it
again. I parked where the old green ute had parked, rested my
head on the steering wheel and tried to compose myself. I wiped
my face on my shirt sleeve.

Waiting at the top of the stairs was Stephen Nugent, the
Deputy General Manager of OCTEC, the educational training
institute that now ran Croagh Patrick and which was supervising
its restoration. The small boys who had lived at the orphanage,
and the Daughters of Charity who had looked after them, were
long gone. OCTEC seemed very keen to have a former resident
returning. I was the first to come back from its days as an orphanage. I climbed the stairs that I had once climbed with my mother.

'Welcome back. Has it changed much?'

I looked around. The brass plaque bearing the words 'Croagh
Patrick Orphanage' was still there, as was the old white bell
button. I noticed that the stained glass in the heavy, panelled front
door was gone.

'Nah, not a bit. Not on the outside, anyway.'

As I crossed the top step, I strode over the spot where my
mother had hugged me goodbye five decades before. I looked
down. Here was a sacred site in my life. My stomach was heaving,
and I tried to keep smiling and to hold back the leaden weight of
dread inside me. We went through the front door. Immediately, the
quiet and the smell hit me. It's interesting how smells can evoke
so much of our childhood. It was the smell of polished wood floors,

of old plaster ceilings and marble; an institutional smell. The broad timber stairs still led up from the foyer. The magnificent stained-glass window on the second floor was just as I remembered it, as were the black-and-white tiled floors. My knees sagged.

'This is one of the rooms that we've completely renovated. We're not sure what it was used for.' Stephen Nugent fiddled with a bunch of keys.

'It was the Mother Superior's parlour.'

He stopped and looked at me. 'Really?' He seemed genuinely surprised.

'At one end there's a deep bay window and at the other end's a fireplace. The Mother Superior sat behind a big desk with her back to the window.'

He opened the door and we went into the room. It was just how I'd described it.

'This was the first room I was brought into when I came here. I think all the boys came here first. Her desk was here.' I stood in the bay window. The dappled light shone through the blinds, just as it had in my memory of the day I first saw that room all those years before.

'I sat just over there, facing the window. When I looked at the Mother Superior, all I could see was her silhouette.' Her stiffened, starched-linen cornette, with its sweeping wings, was backlit by the sunlight filtering in through the window and had a suffused golden glow. I learned later that the cornette of the Daughters of Charity had been modelled on the bonnets of French peasant women.

'That must've been pretty frightening.'

'Yeah, it was pretty scary. I couldn't really see her face because of the sun shining in through the windows. She sat here and told me how the place worked. She wasn't unkind – but yeah, it was pretty scary.'

We did the tour. I showed Stephen where the old refectory had been and we crossed the tiny three-sided quadrangle where we'd played after school. I showed him where the upstairs boys' dormitory had been and where the dairy had been out the back. Everything stirred a memory. This breathlessly quiet building, now deserted, had once echoed with the shouts of boys and the sounds of their pounding feet and the softer voices of the nuns trying to keep order. There was something sad about the quietness of the place now. Even though our lives here had been circumscribed, I was touched somehow by the efforts those women must have made to be surrogate mothers to a bunch of bastard boys and orphans like us.

At the end of our tour, Stephen handed me a booklet. It was a history of Croagh Patrick. In it were photographs of boys taken in the early 1960s when I'd been a resident.

'Jeepers, look how little they are. They're just babies,' I said. This came as a great shock to me. Together we peered at the young faces looking out from the old photographs. 'One of 'em might be me. Look at the nuns trying to look after all those little boys. They certainly had a big family.'

'What were the nuns like when you were here?'

'I remember them as being pretty kind. I only had one bad incident here and it wasn't their fault. I just remember it was tough because I was pretty young and I'd never been away from my mother or grandmother before. I didn't know how long I'd be here, either.'

I could tell that Stephen found my situation curious, but he was too polite to pry any further and I didn't feel like discussing it.

We said our goodbyes. I was welcome to stay as long as I liked and to wander about, he said. As I walked down the hall to the now open front door, I saw, across the verandah and the top of the stairs, the fountain framed against the garden and a backdrop of

274

sky. The last time I had seen this view was in 1960 when I ran to greet my mother climbing the stairs. I stopped and stared. I felt seven years old again.

I sat on the steps of the deserted building, lost in thought, looking at the photos of the babies who had lived here. I'd once been one of them. The voices in my head were silenced; for the first time in decades, there was no arguing. I felt sadness and some grief, but no anger. There was sadness for never having known a father's love, and grief for the whole man I might have become but never did. I thought of the guiding themes of my life: the mother I should have forgiven and hadn't; the stepfather who could have been my life's shining light but wasn't; and my real father, who got away untouched. There was regret, but no anger now. Misty rain bent the tops of the tall trees and crossed the lawn, raising splashes in the fountain. I should have felt lonely but didn't. The forces unleashed on Mount Aspiring had ultimately brought me to the top step of this old orphanage, but they were extinguished now.

I'd had an epiphany sitting watching the rain and achieved a sort of reconciliation. For the second time since Mount Aspiring I thought not just about myself, but about all the boys who had passed over these steps. In some ways they were all my brothers. I was just one of many young boys who had come here. Not only members of the Esteemed Company had lived here, but also boys whose parents had died, whose parents had suffered financial loss and couldn't afford to keep them, or whose families had been ruptured by illness, unemployment or drink. None of us should feel the shame that I'd felt for almost 50 years. I felt, finally, that I was part of a brotherhood.

I hadn't noticed that sharing the top step with me, and also looking out into the rain, was a small boy. He couldn't have been more than seven years old. He looked a lot like the boys in the photographs. Someone must have loved him. He had brightly shined black shoes, neatly pressed grey school shorts, and a well-worn but neatly ironed blue shirt. His short-cropped hair was plastered with Brylcreem and had a razor-sharp part on one side. In his lap sat a stuffed koala bear. He clutched a brown paper bag in one hand. He was sobbing uncontrollably. I put my arm around his shoulders and gave him a hug.

'I know it's tough coming to a place like this when you're little. You can't work out why your mother left you here, can you?' He shook his head and looked forlorn as he wiped his nose on his shirt sleeve.

'Mate, while it seems hard now, you'll survive this. It'll make you tough. You'll be different when you come out of here; a bit more alone and a bit sadder than other blokes. You'll be like that for the rest of your life – there's nothing you can do about that.'

He looked at his feet and his tears fell in big drops on the step.

'But you'll survive stuff in your life that'd knock other blokes flat. That's what you'll take away from this, mate – the ability to survive.' I gave him a squeeze and he leaned his head against my shoulder.

'One thing you gotta realise is that none of this is your fault. It wasn't your fault you didn't have a father, and it wasn't your decision to come here; you can't be ashamed of things you never controlled. Look at me and promise me you won't be ashamed.'

He looked at me and nodded. Through the tears I saw he had the same colour eyes as mine.

'I'd give anything in the world if we could just go out on the lawn and kick a footy. I bet you'd enjoy that, wouldn't you?'

He nodded and gulped. We sat in silence for a while and I held him tight.

'Why did my mum leave me here?' His voice broke through the patter of the rain.

'I dunno, mate. I can't answer that for you. I guess we'll *never* know. But she must've had her reasons, and I bet it nearly killed her.'

A nun wearing a white cornette opened the stained-glass door behind us and stood waiting. 'I have to go in now.' The boy wiped his eyes on his sleeve and stood. I gave him a final embrace. Clutching his koala and the brown paper bag, he turned to walk inside.

'One day you'll have a daughter who'll tell you that the most important thing is to learn to love yourself. Promise me you'll do that?'

At the sound of my voice he hesitated and looked back at me one last time. It was a haunted look.

'Don't ever forget what a good person you are, and don't grow up bitter and angry. Promise me?'

He nodded and turned away to begin his new life. He walked past the nun, who closed the door gently behind him. He was gone. Only the gentle sound of the rain on the iron roof of the verandah broke the perfect silence.

I hoped that the young boy who had gone inside, and all the other boys who had walked through that big panelled door, would make compassion, love and forgiveness the cornerstones of their life. My driving forces – anger, hate and revenge – had been a powerful fuel. They had helped me achieve a lot in life, but ultimately they had burnt me up and left me empty. I realised that now. Forgiveness heals you and gives you release; it allows you to become unstuck and to start to love and feel affection again. Forgiveness doesn't burn you up, but it's the hardest to talk yourself into. I had never managed it.

I walked down the stairs for the last time and turned to look back at the old building, so full of stories. I hoped that all the boys who had lived in this house had learned about forgiveness before it was too late.

I took a deep breath and walked to the car. It's over. I swung the car down the driveway. It's over. And out through the gate. It's over. A new life beckoned. All my demons, all the voices that had plagued me over the years, were now stilled. Finally, there was quiet. I had now confronted all my fears; there were none left. I had made peace with my children and borne the responsibility. I'd come back here. A journey prompted by a man who had reminded me of my stepfather, and that began on the icy slopes of Mount Aspiring a year before, was complete.

My daughter was right: you have to learn to love yourself. This was the start of my new journey.

Croagh Patrick Orphanage disappeared into the gloom of rain behind me. It was gone.

Epilogue

He shall grow
not old . . .

On Anzac Day 2007, I visited Barbara Easson, mother of Marc
Freedman, to pay my respects and seek permission to publish
the photograph of Marc and Giovanni Trambaiolo taken on the
summit of Mount Aspiring shortly before Marc's death.

It was a difficult meeting for both of us. I was confronted with
a single mother torn with grief and still coming to grips with the
death of her only son. It was especially distressing as the photographs of Marc around the walls of the family home reminded me
that Amelia is now the same age as Marc was when he died. While
I could describe the conditions on the ramp for Barbara, and tell her
of its peculiar terrors, I couldn't bring any consolation for her loss.

On display was the heartbreak caused by a climbing accident,
showing that no sport approaches mountaineering in its ability to
leave a trail of misery behind it. Mountaineering, like war, is a
killer of young people. Young men will always go and test themselves and chance their arm. Like Marc, they will push themselves

just that little bit beyond where they should, and fate will often intervene with tragic consequences. It is a brutal and unforgiving sport, and it is always women like Barbara who have to pick up the pieces and suffer the carnage. No parent should outlive their children; it is an impossible burden to bear.

For Barbara, it must have seemed unfair that I should have survived a climb on the mountain that had claimed her son. Marc, an accomplished climber with a full life in front of him, deserved to live. I wish I could offer some answers, but I can't. I don't understand it, either.

For me, Marc has achieved some degree of immortality, as he will forever be associated with the mountain he came to climb. Unlike me, age shall not rob him of his powers, nor will the years condemn him to regrets for the things he might have done. His was a short, full life and he died doing something he passionately enjoyed. I never had the pleasure of a loving relationship with a father, nor have I known the challenges and joys of raising a son. I have only experienced it vicariously through watching other parents. I'm sure his father is very proud of him, and if I'd had a son it would be wonderful to think he may have grown up to be like Marc Freedman. He will forever remain the bright-eyed youth smiling in the Mount Aspiring summit photo.

Vale

Anton Wopereis
A Craftsman of the
Mountains
1954–2008

Anton sent me an email on 29 December 2007, a little over a year since our climb on Mount Aspiring. I had sent him a list of questions seeking clarification of some technical points for this book.

'*Received the questionnaire. It may take awhile to get all the questions complete. Very busy with guiding at the moment. Three ascents of Aspiring so far this season and I'm off to Mount Cook tomorrow.*'

Anton never returned from Mount Cook.

He fell to his death on 1 January 2008, guiding the experienced Scottish climber Vicky Jack. The accident occurred on mixed snow and ice terrain close to the summit in the area known as the Summit Rocks.

Anton had secured his client using an anchor, just as he had done for me on the ramp at Mount Aspiring. He then climbed on, running the rope out to set the next anchor higher up the mountain. When placing his ice tools, the ice slab bearing his weight came away from the mountain and he fell 60 metres.

Despite wearing a helmet, Anton sustained head and facial injuries from smashing into rocks but was alive when his fellow guides reached him, still dangling from the rope attached to the same anchor as his client. They quickly organised a stretchered helicopter lift; however, the rescue team's quick work was to no avail and Anton died from head injuries and blood loss in the helicopter on the way to hospital.

As a testament to his craft, the anchor he built for his client held, and she escaped unharmed. His last words to her were, 'I can't stop', said in a very calm manner, before he disappeared over the rock bluff. It is thought he struck his head on a ledge as he fell, or smashed against the rock face.

I learned all this not from a phone call but from the modern way that news travels, by the internet. When I hadn't heard from him by mid-January, I Googled his name to get his home phone number. Instead, up came notice of his death. It was a devastating shock and remains so. Despite the difficult time we had together, I respected him enormously and appreciated all the efforts he made to keep me alive.

Anton first summited Aoraki/Mount Cook in 1976 as a 22-year-old, and this was to be his 31st ascent of New Zealand's highest mountain. He had also climbed, skied or guided in Australia, on Everest, in Canada, Alaska, Peru, Ecuador, Antarctica and Europe. He was very active in the Wanaka community, and a member of both the Search and Rescue and Wanaka Mountain Safety Council (avalanche and alpine safety coordinator).

He had been climbing for more than 35 years.

As I read the tributes that flowed in, I learned that Anton was the eldest of four brothers and had a long-term partner, Barbara, in Wanaka who described their time together as very happy.

Anton was 'a gem, a real gentleman and a wonderful stepfather to my four children,' she said.

It was a tragedy that I got to know the climber, but I never got to know the man.

Tributes to Anton flowed onto the internet. All spoke of a thoughtful and considerate, almost shy man away from the mountains, who transformed into a strong, energetic leader in the mountains.

The photograph of him taken just moments before his death at the Summit Rocks shows a smiling man, content with life and at ease with the great responsibilities of his job. You can tell that there is nowhere else he would rather be. He was a craftsman of the mountains and turned his hobby into his job, and in that he was most fortunate.

That's how I wish to remember him – the sure-footed, spring-heeled, tireless mountain guide with his Kiwi coils and a big smile.

Goodbye, mate. We'll miss you.

Kieran Kelly
Sydney
January 2008

Acknowledgements

To Barbara Easson, for agreeing to meet me and describing something of Marc's life and death, and for granting permission to publish the photograph, many thanks. To our mutual acquaintance Belinda Grant for arranging the meeting, thank you, also.

To Stephen Nugent and the staff of OCTEC in Orange, thank you for permission to visit Croagh Patrick and for organising the tour.

To Sister Julia Denton, custodian of the archives of the Sisters of Charity at Marsfield in Sydney, thank you for allowing me to view the order's photographs and for permission to reproduce some of them in this book. Jane Emelhainz, my cousin, did an excellent piece of detective work in locating my orphanage records in the archives of the Sisters of Mercy. These records were officially classed as lost. I learned while writing this book that Sister Bernard Byrne, the nun who welcomed me to Croagh Patrick nearly fifty years ago is still alive, however she is now too ill to see me or provide any insight into those events of long ago. I wish her well.

My friend Monica Masero helped me to understand the linkages between childhood experience and adult behaviour, and encouraged me to shine a light into the dark places.

My family have been very patient through the enormously time-consuming and emotionally taxing process of writing this book. My wife Prue never tried to stop me climbing or writing the book, even though she didn't see the need for either. She deserves much credit and my eternal thanks. My daughters provided a constant source of support and wisdom. I hope the girls' insights shine through these pages as they deserve to. This is really their book.

The original draft of the manuscript was typed by Catherine Hunter with great efficiency and cheerfulness, allowing me to complete the project despite the savage time constraints of running a business and managing a family.

My sister Fiona Kelly read the draft manuscript, a particularly gruelling task as she experienced first hand some of the incidents portrayed therein.

My literary mentor, Bert Hingley, also read the manuscript and provided his usual wise and considered counsel. He also provided some unexpected insights, both as a native New Zealander and as the publisher of many of the late Sir Edmund Hillary's books.

To the staff at Alpine Guides (Aoraki) Ltd – Bryan Carter, Arthur McBride and the late Anton Wopereis – thanks for your professional approach to handling novice clients and for introducing me to real mountaineering. Without your expertise, I would never have made it back from New Zealand to write this book.

Vicki Thurlow proofread the printed manuscript with her usual diligence and skill. This is the third time she has done this for me and it's greatly appreciated.

Finally, to the staff at Pan Macmillan, particularly Tom Gilliatt and Brianne Tunnicliffe, many thanks for again supporting my literary endeavours.